Blues Guitar
FOR
DUMMIES®

by Jon Chappell

BICENTENNIAL
1807
WILEY
2007
BICENTENNIAL

Wiley Publishing, Inc.

Blues Guitar For Dummies®

Published by
Wiley Publishing, Inc.
111 River St.
Hoboken, NJ 07030-5774
www.wiley.com

For general information on our other products and services, please contact our Customer Care Department within the U.S. at 877-762-2974, outside the U.S. at 317-572-3993, or fax 317-572-4002.

For technical support, please visit www.wiley.com/techsupport.

Wiley also publishes its books in a variety of electronic formats. Some content that appears in print may not be available in electronic books.

Library of Congress Control Number: 2006934805

ISBN: 978-0-470-04920-4

Manufactured in the United States of America

10 9 8 7 6

1O/RU/RR/QW/IN

WILEY

About the Author

Jon Chappell is a multistyle guitarist, arranger, and author. He grew up in Chicago, attended Carnegie-Mellon University, and earned his master's degree in composition from DePaul University. He was Editor-in-Chief of *Guitar* magazine and played and recorded with artists such as Big Walter Horton, Billy Branch, Pat Benatar, Judy Collins, Graham Nash, and Gunther Schuller. Jon has also contributed numerous musical pieces to TV and film.

Jon served as Associate Music Director of Cherry Lane Music, where he transcribed, edited, and arranged the music of Joe Satriani, Steve Vai, Steve Morse, Bonnie Raitt, and Eddie Van Halen, among others. He has more than a dozen method books to his name and is the author of *Guitar For Dummies,* 2nd Edition, and *Rock Guitar For Dummies* (both published by Wiley), *Blues Rock Riffs for Guitar* (Cherry Lane), as well as the textbook *The Recording Guitarist — A Guide for Home and Studio* (Hal Leonard). Please visit Jon's Web site at www.jonchappell.com for more info.

Dedication

For my wife, Mary, and my children, Jen, Katie, Lauren, and Ryan. May you have only enough blues in your lives to play it well.

Author's Acknowledgments

I gratefully acknowledge the folks at Wiley Publishing, Inc., for their support in making *Blues Guitar For Dummies* a reality: Tracy Boggier, Kristin DeMint, Carrie Burchfield, and Tim Gallan. Thanks also to Morgan Ringwald and Robyn Orsini of Fender Musical Instruments Corporation; Leslie Buttonow of Korg USA, Marshall Amplification USA, and Vox Amplification USA; Kellie Wilkie and Tara Callahan of Roland Corporation U.S.; Brian McConnon of MTECH Marketing Communications and Steinberg Media Technologies; Tim Godwin of Line 6; Todd Stevenson and David Rohrer of DigiTech/DOD and the Harman Music Group; Andrea Arredondo and Evan Skopp of Seymour Duncan; Ari Surdoval of Gibson USA; Eero Kilpi; Jen Chappell.

I want to say a special thanks to blues scholar and writer Dave Rubin, the technical editor for this book, for his keen eye, insightful suggestions, and deep wisdom on all things blues; Pete Prown for his blues-rock expertise; and Woytek and Krystyna Rynczak of WR Music Service for their artful music engraving.

Publisher's Acknowledgments

We're proud of this book; please send us your comments through our Dummies online registration form located at www.dummies.com/register/.

Some of the people who helped bring this book to market include the following:

Acquisitions, Editorial, and Media Development

Project Editors: Kristin DeMint, Tim Gallan

Acquisitions Editor: Tracy Boggier

Copy Editor: Carrie A. Burchfield

Editorial Program Coordinator: Hanna K. Scott

Technical Editor: Dave Rubin

Media Development Specialist: Kit Malone

Senior Editorial Manager: Jennifer Ehrlich

Media Project Supervisor: Laura Moss

Editorial Assistants: Erin Calligan, Joe Niesen, David Lutton, Leeann Harney

Cover Photos: Jon Chappell

Cartoons: Rich Tennant, www.the5thwave.com

Composition Services

Project Coordinators: Michael Kruzil, Jennifer Theriot

Layout and Graphics: Carl Byers, Denny Hager, Barry Offringa, Heather Ryan, Alicia South, Erin Zeltner

Special Art: Woytek and Krystyna Rynczak, WR Music Service

Anniversary Logo Design: Richard Pacifico

Proofreaders: Christine Pingleton, Shannon Ramsey, Brian H. Walls

Indexer: Steve Rath

Special Help: Pam Ruble

Publishing and Editorial for Consumer Dummies

> **Diane Graves Steele,** Vice President and Publisher, Consumer Dummies
>
> **Joyce Pepple,** Acquisitions Director, Consumer Dummies
>
> **Kristin A. Cocks,** Product Development Director, Consumer Dummies
>
> **Michael Spring,** Vice President and Publisher, Travel
>
> **Kelly Regan,** Editorial Director, Travel

Publishing for Technology Dummies

> **Andy Cummings,** Vice President and Publisher, Dummies Technology/General User

Composition Services

> **Gerry Fahey,** Vice President of Production Services
>
> **Debbie Stailey,** Director of Composition Services

Contents at a Glance

Table of Contents

Introduction

As B.B. King might say, "You've got a right to play the blues!" And you've taken the first step in exercising your blues rights by getting a copy of *Blues Guitar For Dummies*. Your blues rights are inalienable — like life, liberty, and the pursuit of mojo. The blues is a form of music and a proclamation on the human condition, delivered proudly and loudly in song. The great thing about the blues is that it's universal because everyone at one time or another gets the blues.

To help you sort out the many aspects of playing blues guitar, I organized this book to help you in your blues pursuits. The following sections give you an idea of what you're getting into as you delve into the pages of this book and into the world of the blues!

About This Book

Blues Guitar For Dummies covers all aspects of blues guitar, from playing the instrument to understanding the legends and lore associated with it. This book is for the beginning to intermediate blues guitarist. If you don't know much about the guitar as an instrument, just hang out with me as I take you through the world of blues guitar. And even if you already own or know something about guitars, you can use the info in this book before you go out and make your *next* guitar purchase.

To get a meaningful experience from this book, you don't have to play or own a guitar. You don't even have to know what kind of guitar you want or what style of playing you want to pursue. This book is designed to help you figure that out. But this book is a guitar book, after all, so I focus on just guitars, guitar playing, and guitarists themselves.

Blues Guitar For Dummies also shows you how to play without requiring that you know how to read music first. Sure, I give you shortcuts in the form of written notation, diagrams, and symbols, but use these written figures as a reference as your specific needs demand.

You should find your own way to absorb the music in this book so you can play it back as your own. Do that through a combination of the elements below:

- **Chord diagrams:** You form the left-hand chords you need by looking at the diagrams and matching your fingers to the symbols on the guitar's neck.

- **Guitar tablature:** *Tablature* is a type of notation that tells you to finger certain frets on specific strings. No "notes" are involved, just locations on which frets and strings to play. The tab staff appears just below the standard music notation staff. If you can already read music — even just a little — you can always see what note you're fingering by looking at the staff immediately above the tab.

- **The CD:** Playing by ear is important because after you get a good idea of where to place your fingers, you want to let your ears take over. Listening to the CD is important because it shows you how the music sounds, so you can figure out the rhythm of the song and how long to hold notes by listening, not reading. The CD also has some cool features:

  - Provides accompaniment, so you can hear how the examples sound in a band setting — with drums, bass, and rhythm guitar.

  - Enables you to always find the track that corresponds to the printed music example in the chapters

  - Gives you a count-off so that you can play along in time

- **The tab staff and music staff:** To those of you who do like to read music (you two know who you are), this book delivers in that department, too. The music for many exercises and songs appears in standard music notation, just above the tab staff. You get the best of both worlds: tab showing you where to put your fingers and the corresponding music notation to satisfy all those schooled musicians out there.

Grab a copy of *Blues For Dummies* (no, I didn't write it; it was written by Lonnie Brooks, Cub Koda, and Wayne Baker Brooks) for general blues info. *Blues Guitar For Dummies* is about *playing* blues guitar, and I devote more pages to playing than I do historical stuff.

Conventions Used in This Book

This book has a number of conventions that I use to make things consistent and easy to understand. Here's a list of those conventions:

- ✔ **Right hand and left hand:** If you play the guitar as a right-handed person, the right hand strums and picks and the left hand frets. If you're left-handed, you can either play as a right-handed person, or you can reverse the process. If you choose the second method, remember to convert the terms and that I refer to the right hand and right-hand fingers as the strumming and picking hand and the left hand as the fretting hand. Nothing against lefties, mind you, but it's easier and shorter to say "right hand" instead of "strumming or picking hand."

- ✔ **High and low, up and down:** When I say "higher on the neck" or "up the neck," I refer to the higher-numbered frets, or the region closer to the body of the guitar than the headstock. "Going up" always refers to going up in pitch, which means toward the higher frets or skinnier strings — which happen to be closer to the floor than the ceiling.

- ✔ **One staff at a time, please:** Many of the exercises contain both music notation and tablature. The tab tells you what frets and strings to play; the music tells you the pitches and the rhythms. These ways present the same information in different ways, so you need to look at only one at a time. Pick the one that works best for you.

What You're Not to Read

Occasionally, you will come across some boxes of text that are shaded gray (also called sidebars). You have my permission to skip over this info. Don't get me wrong; the info is fun and interesting, but it's not the most crucial points of blues guitar.

Foolish Assumptions

In this book I make the following assumptions about you:

- ✔ You're an average reader who knows a little something about the guitar or the blues.

- ✔ You want to sound like a blues player and take the path that allows you to discover many things about the guitar and music.

- ✔ You want to play quickly without a lot of messing around with music theory and all that stuff. You want exactly what you need to know at that moment in time without all the lectures and teacherly instincts.

How This Book Is Organized

I've organized the book into seven sections that deal with holding, setting up, and playing the guitar, and then I tackle how to buy a guitar, what to look for in an amp, how effects work, and the major contributors to the blues.

Part 1: You Got a Right to Play the Blues

Part I devotes three chapters to the guitar basics that you need to know before you can start playing the blues. Chapter 1 helps you understand blues guitar, the kinds of guitars available, the gear you may need, and the parts of the guitar. In Chapter 2, you discover how the guitar works and the art of fretting. Chapter 3 explains how to hold your guitar, position your right and left hands, how to tune up (which is oh, so important), and how to interpret the written notation throughout the book.

Part 11: Setting Up to Play the Blues

The chapters in Part II all deal with playing the guitar (hooray!) and creating music. Chapter 4 presents chords — the easiest way to start playing real music. In Chapter 5, you strike the strings through different strumming patterns, rhythms, and fingerpicking techniques. The overview in Chapter 6 shows how blues songs are structured, and Chapter 7 has you playing real blues music!

Part 111: Beyond the Basics: Playing Like a Pro

Part III takes you into the world of the committed guitar student. In Chapter 8, you explore lead guitar, and Chapter 9 takes you into the expressive world of melodic playing. Chapter 10 puts the finishing touches on your lead playing with certain expressive guitar techniques.

Part 1V: Sounding Like the Masters: Blues Styles through the Ages

In Part IV of this book, you find the style chapters, where you get to play blues in all the different styles throughout the blues' colorful history. You discover the acoustic-based blues from the Mississippi Delta (Chapter 11), history of traditional electric blues (Chapter 12), and the electric blues' rowdy alter ego, blues rock (Chapter 13).

Part V: Gearing Up: Outfitting Your Arsenal

In Part V, you scope out the gear you need to complete your blues rig. Chapter 14 is a handy guitar buyer's guide that covers everything from evaluating a guitar to shopping strategies to dealing with the music store salespeople. Chapter 15, on amps and their effects, gives you a primer on guitar amps and those little magic boxes (effects) that give your guitar some superhip sounds. In Chapter 16, you find out how to change strings on both acoustic and electric guitars.

Part VI: The Part of Tens

The Part of Tens provides fun and interesting information in a top-ten-style format that rivals those late night talk show hosts'. The chapters in this part prioritize important information by the many blues guitarists and recordings.

Part VII: Appendixes

The appendixes cover important info not contained in the chapters. Appendix A explains reading music, and Appendix B provides a guide to the CD that comes with this book.

Icons Used in This Book

In the margins of this book, you find several helpful little icons that make your journey a little easier:

The remember icon signifies a piece or pieces of information worth remembering. Sounds simple, huh? Some of the info comes up repeatedly.

In the instances that I get all techy on you, I use this icon to mark the explanations that you can skip and come back to later if you want.

This icon highlights info for die-hard blues guitarists (and those in the making). To step up your blues abilities, take the advice in these icons.

This icon is a hands-on, explicit directive that can change your playing from merely extraordinary to *really* extraordinary.

Pay heed to this one, or you could do damage to something — your ears, your guitar, your audience's ears, and so on.

Where to Go from Here

Blues Guitar For Dummies can be read straight through like a novel or by individual chapter. Even though each chapter is self-contained, music instruction dictates that certain steps be mastered before others, so Parts II and III are best experienced in order.

If you're a beginner, a musical klutz, or someone who really wants to follow the steps, start with Chapter 1 and read the book in sequence. If you already play a little bit, skip to Chapter 3, where I decipher the notation used in the music figures in the book. Then you're ready for the playing chapters — Chapters 4 through 13. You don't need to master the E chord in Chapter 3 to appreciate the advice on buying a guitar in Chapter 14. But at some point, I hope you read all the material in this book, even the most obscure trivia.

Part I
You Got a Right to Play the Blues

The 5th Wave   By Rich Tennant

"Very nice audition, Vince. Let's talk a minute about that little thing you do at the end with the microphone."

In this part . . .

"Woke up this mornin' and I feel like playin' the blues." Well, you don't have to just sing about it; you can dig right in and start doing something about it! The information in this part gets you thinking like a blues guitar player. Chapter 1 outlines what's contained in the book and spells out what you need to do from buying a guitar to playing it to maintaining it. In Chapter 2, you jump into the mechanics of what makes guitars tick — their method of sound production and how the various gizmos and other hardware operate. Get ready to assume the position in Chapter 3 — the playing position, that is. You hold the guitar in a sitting and standing position, place your hands correctly, and figure out how to tune up. You see how the notation for the music figures works, and hey, you even get to strum a chord!

Chapter 1

Every Day I Have the Blues . . . Hallelujah!

*P*laying the blues is a healthy way of expressing emotion — therapeutic even. The great irony about the blues is that it's *fun* — don't let those gloomy lyrics fool you for one second. Experiencing the blues is entertainment for both the listener and the player. Because the blues is fun and healthy, it draws people into jam sessions, crowded clubs, and grand concert halls.

To listen to the blues is to be healed. To play the blues is to be a healer. Want to help people? Forget about being a doctor; you're only allowed to see one patient at a time. And there's no pill you can prescribe for an ailing mojo. Be a blues player instead and help thousands at a time just by playing a smokin' blues riff on overdrive. Now, that's what I call medicinal!

The blues has a wide range of sounds, feels, emotions, and passions, and people have many different associations when you say the word *blues*. To some, the blues is the sparse-sounding acoustic fingerpicking of Robert Johnson. To others, it's the gritty sound of Muddy Waters in a crowded club on Chicago's South Side or the hard-rock wall of sound coming from a stadium playing host to Led Zeppelin, Jimi Hendrix, or Johnny Winter. It doesn't matter which particular image is conjured, because it's *all* the blues. After reading this book, playing through the examples, and listening to the CD, you may have a more complete and expanded picture of all that the blues can be.

Capturing the Blues Train from Its Departure Then to Its Arrival Now

As perfect as the blues is for the guitar, it didn't come from the guitar. The blues sprang from the unaccompanied human voice. There have been sad songs since the dawn of music, but the blues is a special kind of sadness that was born out of the African American experience at the end of the 19th century and the beginning of the 20th. When the African-influenced field hollers and work songs met European folk songs, spirituals, and ballads (supported by harmonicas, banjos, guitars, washtub basses, fiddles, drums, spoons, and other instruments of the time) a unique form of music emerged that was neither wholly African nor European, but totally American.

Today, the blues can be anything from a solo acoustic guitarist strumming simple chords to a big band with a horn section, a lead singer, and background vocalists. Artists as diverse as blues diva Bonnie Raitt, rockabilly giant Brian Setzer (and his band), rock god Eric Clapton, and the great traditionalists B.B. King and Buddy Guy all play the blues. That sort of diversity proves how flexible, adaptable, and universal the blues is. It doesn't matter if you feel like crying in your beverage, listening thoughtfully, singing along, or dancing the jitterbug, you can find a blues format for any mood and occasion.

When Muddy Waters famously said, "The blues had a baby and they called it rock 'n' roll," he was both chronologically as well as metaphorically correct: Of all the popular forms of American music, blues was the first.

The pieces of blues that made the genre

The music that draws on the subjects of misfortune, infidelity, and bad karma for its inspiration pretty much sums up the blues. The great W.C. Handy, known as the father of the blues, once said that the blues were conceived in an aching heart, but it's pretty hard to tell what kind of guitar playing is appropriate for an ailing ventricle. However, you can identify certain common characteristics that help define blues guitar — including song structure, harmony, scales, and phrasing techniques. You can study and master these elements to create this special form of music that expresses a special kind of sorrow in song — special because it's not completely without hope, humor, irony, useful life philosophies, and, dare I say it, some joy. That's the blues for you.

I get into forms and progressions in Chapter 6, but you should know the song structure that makes the blues the blues. Besides the subject matter, blues uses a simple form that people can immediately understand. Classic blues consists of two lines that are the same in length and verbiage, followed by a third line that's different. Here's a quick example of the blues scheme:

Woke up this mornin' and I'm feelin' so blue.

Woke up this mornin' and I'm feelin' so blue.

My baby left me and I don't know what to do.

Believe it or not, that's the format that started it all. If you can think of a blues song — such as "Kansas City" or "Hound Dog" or "Whole Lotta Shakin' Goin' On" — you see that the formula applies.

The place of the blues' conception

The blues was born in the southern United States out of the African American experience in the fields and work camps that sprung up in the late 19th and early 20th century. Though many parallel developments took place, the most important growth occurred in a very specific part of the southern United States — the region in the state of Mississippi known as the Delta.

The "Delta" in Delta blues describes not the Mississippi River Delta, which is in southern Louisiana, but a vast alluvial plain a couple hundred miles to the north in northwest Mississippi. Many of the great early blues players were born and lived in this cotton-growing region, loosely outlined by the Mississippi River to the west, the Yazoo River to the east, Memphis to the north, and Vicksburg to the south.

The Delta isn't really a delta in the geological sense, nor is it limited to the state of Mississippi, because there were important developments and contributions from artists that came from Arkansas, Texas, and Louisiana, too. In most uses, *Delta blues* denotes more of a style instead of a narrow geographic perimeter.

Rejoicing over 100 years of blues: The shifting shape of the genre

Now roughly 100 years old, American blues has become timeless music, and its success over the past half century can be attributed in part to those blues-rock musicians who've kept the blues' torch burning and brought successive generations into clubs, concert halls, and record stores.

The blues remains so relevant and compelling because its songs are about honest, human feelings. Or maybe it's because the blues captures the human condition in a way that slick pop music or digital electronica can't. Blues is the music of real people, real lives, and real life lessons.

As to why the blues-rock age saw the worshipping of so many rock gods, it seems that the blues was custom-made for six strings, so any development in guitar technology, guitar styles, and creative guitarists themselves naturally include the blues. While bawdy singers front many a blues band, you'd be hard pressed to find a blues group without a guitar player to lend the sense of credibility, history, and heart that the blues demands. The guitar captures the nuances of blues soul in a way no other instrument can. Blues is simply the *perfect* guitar music.

The newer generation (born after 1970) is out there and coming into its own, too. I cover many of the most recognizable names in Chapters 12 and 13. To see such young players working so hard at mastering the craft, studying the history, and paying homage and respect to their blues elders encourages me that the blues is flourishing safely in the hands of the next generation.

The qualities that made blues cats hit the big-time

In addition to all the great chords, riffs, and solos you get in *Blues Guitar For Dummies*, you can also read about many of the most important blues guitarists who helped shaped the history of the blues and why you should care about them. A blues guitarist can be significant for many reasons, but the criteria I use for including the artists that I do in this book is that he or she must meet at least one of the following requirements:

✔ **He or she had great influence and a historical impact.** Muddy Waters, for example, merits inclusion not because of superior technique (although his playing was certainly formidable), but because he transplanted the blues from its acoustic, rural Mississippi roots to post-War Chicago, where it exploded into an entire movement that would define "Chicago blues" and influence everyone who played electric blues after that, including Eric Clapton and Stevie Ray Vaughan. No Muddy, no Stevie.

✔ **The guitarist has technique that is innovative or unsurpassed in virtuosity.**

  • Robert Johnson, for example, was at the tail end of the Delta blues movement and learned many of his licks from other players. But he was an extraordinary player and provided the best examples we have on record for Delta blues playing.

  • A lot of people tried to meld electric blues with the emerging heavy rock sound in the mid-1960s, but none quite as masterfully as Eric Clapton did. He was the best of a generation.

  • In the 1980s, Stevie Ray Vaughan was so good that you'd be hard pressed to find anyone who even got close to him in terms of raw talent.

✔ **The guitarist's style is unique or so highly evolved that it's responsible for his or her widespread success.** Sometimes you don't have to be the greatest player to achieve greatness. With many blues guitarists, it's not all about the technique, but the artistic work created with modest technique. Bonnie Raitt may not have the blistering chops of a Duane Allman or Stevie Ray Vaughan, but her beautiful tone, impeccable taste, and unmatched lyricism in world-class songs have advanced the blues into the mainstream like no other blues player has before.

Often a guitarist featured in this book has more than one of the three qualities in the preceding list. Take a couple of examples:

✔ T-Bone Walker, the great early pioneer of electric blues, was not only technically dazzling and innovative, but also historically significant as the first electric blues player to establish the guitar as a lead instrument, thereby influencing every great player in the succeeding generation.

✔ Jimi Hendrix is the best at everything as far as the guitar, the blues being no exception. He scores top marks in all three categories, so that's why he's in the book. Also, if you leave Jimi Hendrix out of any discussion about guitars and guitarists, people get really, really mad at you and make your life miserable.

You may or may not see your particular favorite blues guitarist in the pages of this book, which is understandable, as there are too many great blues guitarists for any book to list them all. But every guitarist you do read about here in some way changed the world of blues for the better — for listeners as well as other blues guitarists who heard them.

It's Not All Pain and Suffering — The Lighter Side of Blues

Built into the blues is its own sense of irony and even humor. How else could you sing of such misfortune if you didn't retain a sense of humor about the whole thing? It's not uncommon to see performers smiling while singing about loss and heartache, yet they're still totally sincere and convincing. It's maintaining that objective perspective — along with the hope of retribution and revenge — that keeps the blues performer going while airing his life's disappointments.

The blues isn't above parody, either, and this often includes the blues' strict sense of who's "allowed to have the blues" and who isn't. For example, you do not have a "right to sing the blues" if you live in Beverly Hills, make a killing in the futures market, or think that "my baby done me wrong" means losing your villa in Tuscany to your spouse in negotiation.

Among the early African American blues artists, the word *baby* was sometimes used as code for the *boss man*. This way the performer could complain or take a shot at the overseer on the farm or plantation without him being any the wiser. Of course, the African American audience understood.

Surveying the Means to Make the Music: The Guitar in All Its Glory

Just as soon as people could utter the primitive strains of proto-blues music, they sought to reinforce their vocal efforts through instruments. Unfortunately, the Fender Stratocaster and the Marshall stack weren't invented yet, so people did what blues players always did in the early part of the blues' history: They made do with what was available. And in the rural South at the turn of the 20th century, that wasn't much.

Some of the first blues instruments included a one-string *diddley bow* (a wire stretched between two points and plucked with one hand while the other changed pitches with a bottleneck or knife dragged up and down the string) and a banjo, descendant of the African *banjar* that was constructed from a hide-covered gourd and a stick. The harmonica followed close behind. Guitars didn't arrive on the scene until after the Civil War when they were left behind in the South by Union soldiers.

All guitars have six strings (except for 12-string guitars, of course) and frets, whether they're electric or acoustic. You can play chords, riffs, and single-note melodies on virtually any guitar. When the first mass-produced electric guitars were publicly available, in the mid- to late '30s, blues and jazz players similarly flocked to them, and not too much attention was given to what kind of guitar was best for what style of music.

The low-fi acoustic guitar

Early blues musicians weren't professional musicians. They were ordinary working people who created their instruments out of household items: washboards, spoons, pails, and so on. If you were a little more industrious, you could fashion a homemade guitar out of bailing wire, a broom handle, and a cigar box. Those fortunate enough to acquire an actual guitar would probably have an inexpensive acoustic guitar, perhaps picked up secondhand. As the blues became more popular, many musicians could make a living by traveling around to work camps and *juke joints* (which were roadside places without electricity that offered liquor, dancing, gambling, and sometimes prostitution) playing acoustic guitars and singing the blues for the weary working folk.

The semi-hollowbody electric guitar

Gradually, the different preferences of electric jazz and blues players started to diverge, with jazz players preferring the deeper hollowbody guitars and blues players choosing the thinner-bodied hollow guitars and the semi-hollowbody guitars. (The all-solid-wood guitar, or solidbody, hadn't been invented yet.) Many people consider the semi-hollowbody guitar, such as the Gibson ES-335, to be the ideal type of blues guitar. Driving this choice was the fact that the thinner guitars didn't *feed back* (produce unwanted, ringing tones through the amp) as much as the deeper-bodied guitars, and because blues players generally like to play louder than jazz players, feedback was more of a concern.

The Gibson ES-335 makes my list of one of the greatest guitars for playing the blues. See Chapter 18 for more of the best guitars on the market.

Solidbody electric guitars

Though pioneering rock guitarists like Scotty Moore with Elvis and Danny Cedrone with Bill Haley and the Comets were still playing hollowbody guitars, when rock 'n' roll hit town in the mid-1950s, some people were playing solidbody guitars, blues players included. Two of the most popular solidbody models, the Fender Stratocaster (Figure 1-1a) and the Gibson Les Paul (Figure 1-1b), were both released in the mid-'50s and are still as popular as ever and represent two different approaches to the solidbody guitar. Figure 1-1 shows these two guitars side by side.

In the early 1950s, B.B. King tried his hand with a Fender Esquire (similar to a Telecaster) and a Strat, but after he grabbed the thin hollow and semi-hollow Gibson that he named "Lucille," he never switched back. And Muddy Waters, who played an older, more traditional form of blues, was right in fashion with an early model goldtop Les Paul in the mid-1950s. He eventually settled on his iconic red Telecaster.

Figure 1-1:
The Fender
Stratocaster
and the
Gibson Les
Paul.

a   b

The Collision of Two Worlds: Acoustic versus Electric

Electric guitars came on the scene only in the late 1930s, and then only to those who could afford them. Thus, the acoustic guitar in blues had a long run, and the style continued even after the advent of the more-popular electric guitar. The acoustic guitar remained popular for other types of music (mainly folk and country), but for blues, the electric was the instrument of choice from about 1940 on.

Today, both acoustic and electric guitar blues exist. In fact, there are several sub-genres in each. Acoustic guitar includes

- *Bottleneck* or slide guitar
- Instrumental blues
- Singer-songwriter blues

Electric blues has two huge offshoots:

- ✔ *Traditional electric blues,* as practiced today by Robert Cray, Buddy Guy, and B.B. King
- ✔ *Blues rock,* which was started in the 1960s by British electric guitarists and continues on through Eric Clapton and John Mayer

Acoustics and electrics both produce great blues music, as will virtually any other type of guitar, whether it's an acoustic nylon-string classical or a purple metallic-flake solidbody with green lightning bolts. The blues is unrestricted when it comes to instruments.

Today, acoustic and electric blues each offer a guitarist a world of history, repertoire, styles, instruments, techniques, and heroes to study and emulate. It's no longer a conflict of "go electric or be a front-porch picker," as it may have seemed in the late 1930s. Many players, Eric Clapton being a notable example, are excellent acoustic-blues players and have paid tribute in concert and in recordings to their acoustic blues roots.

Though you should always strive for the best guitar you can afford, be aware that blues guitarists from Robert Johnson on often played cheap instruments like Stellas, Kalamazoos, and Nationals. Hound Dog Taylor performed timeless slide classics on 1960s Japanese solidbody guitars. Sometimes the funkier the guitar, the funkier the blues can be.

Getting a Grip on How Guitars Work

To understand why the guitar works so well for the blues, you must first understand how guitars work in the first place. In the next sections, take a look at how guitars produce their tone and how your approach to them makes them so expressive.

You've gotta use your hands — both of them

Of course, you play any instrument with your hands, but in the guitar, the two hands perform different tasks — unlike the piano or saxophone where both hands engage in the same kind of action. In a guitar, one hand strikes the strings (usually the right hand), and one hand decides what pitch to sound through fretting. The left hand's job doesn't end with just fretting, either. It has additional functions, too, when it comes to connecting notes together through slurs (covered in Chapter 10), which it can do without the right hand. The left hand is also responsible for two very important blues guitar techniques: vibrato and string bending (also discussed in Chapter 10).

The right hand is the engine that drives the sound. All the rhythm and dynamics (loud and soft sound) rests with the right hand, and you can't play even moderately fast and clean unless you've developed your right-hand technique (check out Chapter 5 for more info). But the training for the right hand is different than from the left. In the end, though, the two must coordinate to create music. (Chapter 4 gives you more info on training the left hand.)

Producing the tones: String vibration and pitch

A guitar is a string instrument, related to the violin and cello in that it generates tones by means of a vibrating string. You set the string in motion by striking or plucking it, which causes it to vibrate, which produces a musical pitch. For the sound to be heard by human ears, the vibrating string must be amplified in some way. In acoustic instruments, the body acts as the sound chamber, or acoustic amplifier. In electric instruments, the body contributes no amplification to the sound at all. Instead, the amplification is produced by the amplifier, which attaches to the guitar by a removable cable.

Some factors influence the string's pitch:

- **Fretting:** You can also change the pitch by shortening the string or, more practically, shortening its effective vibrating length. That's what you do when you *fret* (press a string to the fretboard at a certain location on the neck). You're playing shorter versions of the same string. Fretting allows you to play any pitch — flat, sharp, or natural — in the guitar's entire range. Check out Chapter 4 for more information about fretting.

- **Mass:** A string's mass, or thickness, influences its pitch. The thicker the string, the lower the pitch. That's why the low-pitched strings are thicker than the high-pitched ones.

- **Tension:** You can change a string's pitch by varying the tension of the string. Higher tension produces higher pitched notes. On a guitar, you tighten and loosen a string with the *tuning key* — a geared mechanism located on the headstock. Turning the tuning key is also how you tune the guitar, which is covered in Chapter 3.

Electric guitars only: Pickups and amplification

Getting your sound out of your electric guitar and to your adoring masses requires you to have command over not only your touch and technique but also the features and functions provided by your particular guitar. Two important features of electric guitars (or plugged-in acoustic guitars) are the pickups and the amplification.

Pickups are the little metal bars that "read" the sound coming off the vibrating string and are important because they transfer the sound down the line. The *amplification* part of the system is what makes the almost inaudible signal loud enough to be heard.

An acoustic guitar (or unplugged guitar) is pretty much a what-you-see-is-what-you-get kind of instrument. But when you bring the power of electricity into the picture, now that's a whole other story. Although you strike the strings on an acoustic and a sound occurs by coming out of the body of the guitar and through the sound hole (or F-holes on an archtop guitar), when you play an electric guitar your sound filters through an amp and takes your sound to the screaming masses at Madison Square Garden. What the multitudes hear is the pickups underneath the strings "sensing" (they don't "hear" because they're not using acoustics) the motion of the string through disturbances in their magnetic field. That disturbance generates electrical current that gets sent through a wire out of the guitar to your amp (see Chapter 15 for more info on amps).

Performing and Looking Like a Blues Player

Never forget that playing the blues is supposed to be entertaining — even if only to yourself. And after you engage in the business of entertaining, you are, by definition, an entertainer and a performer. So start thinking like a star! The following sections help you to get into the groove of being a blues performer.

Expanding and filling your brain with know-how

Besides having a guitar and a copy of *Blues Guitar For Dummies,* you can take several other key actions to help you become a better blues player.

- ✔ **Groove to some tunes.** Listening to the blues is about the best thing you can do with your time when you're not practicing the guitar, so start expanding your blues library with CDs and mp3s of classic blues recordings.

Listen to the blues not only as a casual observer but also as a musician. Listen to the chord changes and how the guitarist strums. Take note of licks or lead passages that are memorable. You may be able to use them in your own playing. (This is perfectly legal in blues.)

✔ **Get your nose in a book.** Read as much as you can in books and articles about the blues so you can sort out the history and discover the great artists who practiced this noble art. Knowing the different periods of the blues and the influences help in your appreciation. You can also check out Chapters 11, 12, 13, and 19 in this book. I cover a bit of history and the people who influenced blues guitar.

✔ **Rock out in your garage.** No matter how many records you listen to and books you read, you can't replace human interaction as a vital component in your blues education. Invite some guitar-playing friends over for a few jam sessions in your garage or basement (or wherever the noise may be the least annoying to those around you). Pairing yourself with one or two strong players can help make you a better guitarist because you're going to try to keep up with your friends.

✔ **Seek help.** Having a teacher is important because he (or she) can focus in on your particular weaknesses and bad habits and help bring those aspects of your musicianship up to snuff with your strengths. A teacher also guides you in your particular chosen style, recommending appropriate exercises and listening examples and providing an organized lesson plan on how to bring you closer to your goal. An experienced teacher or player can often help you pick out your first guitar and other gear purchases, too. Check out Chapter 14 for more info on buying guitars.

Looking the part

Many people decide they want to play the blues because they want to perform. Of course, performing can mean simply playing with a garage band on evenings or weekends or playing in public to perform. But either way, you definitely want to put on your stage face even when you're with a group of friends versus when you're shedding a tricky rhythm alongside your metronome in your bedroom.

First things first, acoustics and electrics satisfy different objectives, and you really need to have both types of guitars to be a complete blues player. Although that advice may signal financial pressure, you'll find that having any excuse to acquire and buy more guitars is worth its weight in gold. So you can say to your spouse or significant other, "But dear, I *have* to have this other guitar. It's in the book. Look it up!"

Aside from getting a good axe, the best way to look like a blues player is to play like one. But you can take some external steps to help the illusion along:

1. **Move your body in time to the music.**

   Getting down not only makes you look cool, but also it reinforces the rhythms of the music and your instrument with the parts of your body. That's essential for internalizing the music and making it your own, instead of a mechanical execution of technique. If you feel self-conscious about writhing around like a contortionist in public, try at first just moving your head along in time to the playing.

2. **Close your eyes, open them, and squint occasionally.**

3. **Make little facial expressions when you play a soulful bend.**

   Watch the greats when they play, especially B.B. King. One of B.B. King's wives once described the look he sometimes gets on his face when playing as if he was eating a lemon.

 As far as wardrobe goes, what you wear onstage should be different than what you wear normally. You can dress up or dress down to play the blues, but it's a good idea to find your stage garb and keep it unique from the clothes you go to work in or grocery shopping. You might just don an extra ring, but you should make yourself look — and feel — a little special when stepping onto a stage. Even a flannel shirt, torn jeans, and cowboy boots can be a stage uniform — especially if you're a stockbroker in your day job!

Blues Trivia For Dummies

How much do you know about blues guitar? Take this simple test to find out. The following 5 questions test your knowledge of the genre. If you don't know the right answers, don't worry — read this book and you'll end up a soulful, jiving, blues-playing machine (not that you aren't in some way already).

The questions

1. **By what name does B.B. King refer to his six-string soul mate (that is, his guitar)?**

   A. Bessie

   B. Maybelline

   C. Lucille

   D. Lola

2. **The famed Mississippi Delta, birthplace of the blues, is where, exactly?**

   A. At the mouth of the Mississippi River, in southern Louisiana

   B. In northwest Mississippi and southwest Arkansas

   C. In central Mississippi, in and around the capital, Jackson

   D. In southern Mississippi and western Louisiana, along the Gulf Coast

3. **The legend of the "Crossroads" in blues lore describes what?**

    A. The place where the blues was born

    B. A decision blues performers make when they decide to play the blues

    C. Where Robert Johnson met the devil and traded his soul for talent

    D. An intersection in Memphis, famous in blues history because many performers crossed paths there

4. **What are "blue" notes?**

    A. Notes that singers intone that are in between "real" notes

    B. Sad notes that make major sounds into minor ones

    C. The interval of the flatted 3rd, the flatted 7th, and the flatted 5th

    D. All of the above

5. **What is "mojo"?**

    A. A skill that enables you to make lucrative investments in the stock market

    B. A quality that the opposite sex finds irresistible in you

    C. A play on the French phrase "mot juste" for "apt word choice"

    D. A type of illicit liquor or "moonshine"

The answers

    1. C
    2. B
    3. C
    4. D
    5. B

Chapter 2

Blues Meets Guitar: A Match Made in Musical Heaven

. . . .

In This Chapter

▶ The roots of blues guitar

▶ What defines blues guitar music

▶ How acoustic and electric guitars each make the blues in their own way

▶ The essential gear you need to play the blues

. . . .

*T*he guitar and blues go together like apple and pie — as if they were made for each other. And you could argue that they were. The guitar allows you to sing along with yourself (try that with a flute), and singing was the way the blues started. And it's much easier to bring out on the front porch than a piano. It's cheaper to own (or make yourself) than many other instruments, and that helped bring the blues to many poor folks — the people who really *had* the blues.

As the blues developed, guitar makers adopted features that helped bring out the qualities of the blues to even better effect. An electric guitar is played with two hands and leaves your mouth free to sing (as an acoustic does), but electrics, with their skinnier strings, are easier to *bend* (a way of stretching the string while it's ringing, producing a gradual, continuous rise in pitch), and electronic amplification helps project the guitar's sound out into the audience of (often raucous and noisy) blues-loving listeners. In this chapter, I show you in detail why the blues and the guitar — both acoustic and electric — make great music together.

Because the blues was concentrated in the rural South, in the time before musical instruments adopted electricity, the earliest blues guitar music was played on acoustics. The "Delta blues" style was the first recognized style of the blues and consisted of strummed and plucked acoustic guitars with chords formed the same way as in other forms of folk music.

Beyond the Delta: Defining the Blues Guitar Sound

Blues guitar can take many forms, and has grown dramatically since its humble beginnings in the south-central United States. Blues players of this time were largely self taught (and many of them illiterate), and one of the easiest ways to create different chords was to tune the guitar to an open chord, such as G major or E major, and then use a metal or glass slide (a pocket knife or bottle neck) to change chords. In both slide and fretted guitar styles, guitarists would emphasize the driving rhythm of the blues by thumping out steady bass notes on the low strings with their thumb while in turn, or simultaneously, fingerpicking upper strings to sound out chords, melodic riffs, and fills.

Playing simple chords to back up a blues singer is still a form of blues guitar — as is playing chords with a slide. You can't help but sound bluesy when you move a slide from one position to another to play the different chords in a song — especially if you do it expressively. But beyond this, you can ascribe certain musical hallmarks to the blues that don't make you play any more soulfully but provide you with a deeper understanding when you hear the blues.

In the following sections, I've broken down the elements of the blues into four musical concepts. Keep in mind that these concepts are the main ones and there are certainly more, but thinking of and listening to the blues while considering these criteria helps in your understanding of this sometimes elusive music form. You may not be able to define the blues, but you'll know it when you hear it. Or as Sonny Terry says:

> *Sometimes I want to holler,*
>
> *Sometimes I want to shout,*
>
> *Sometimes I want to cry,*
>
> *But I wonder what about.*
>
> *I think I got the blues.*

The method to the music: Chord progressions

What defines a blues song is the way chords are put together, or the *chord progression*. Although there's such a thing as a jazz chord, there's not really a blues chord (but don't worry, there's no such thing as a classical chord, either). But if you put certain chords together in a certain way, you can definitely have a blues chord progression. The most common blues progression is the 12-bar blues, which I cover in Chapter 6.

Chords used in blues include major and minor *triads* (simple, three-note chords), dominant-7th chords — triads with the *flatted* (lowered by a half step) 7th added, and sometimes even jazz chords (with complex-sounding names like G13♭9/♭5).

The guitarist's language of melody

The blues definitely has a harmonic and melodic language, and even a scale named after it: the 6-note blues scale. If music is described as "bluesy," it usually means that the melody borrows or enlists notes from the blues scale (nicknamed "blue notes") rather than the standard major and minor scales that make up other, non-blues styles. *Blue notes* are the minor third, minor seventh, and flatted fifth (in shorthand, those notes are ♭3, ♭5, and ♭7). Figure 2-1 shows the C major scale (the familiar do, re, mi — and so forth) with the blue notes shown below their unaltered counterparts.

Figure 2-1:
The C major scale with blue notes.

C major:	C	D	E	F	G	A	B	(C)
Blue notes:			E♭		G♭		B♭	

When discussing scales, you don't include the octave note, in this case, the second, higher C. That's why it's in parentheses. So a major scale is a 7-note scale, though in practice musicians usually include the octave eighth note.

When playing the blues, guitarists incorporate aspects of both the major scale and the blue notes to come up with two new scales of their own: the 6-note blues scale and the 5-note minor pentatonic scale (covered in detail in Chapter 8). Figure 2-2 shows both scales in letter names and in music notation.

If all this talk of scales, intervals, and flat this and that are making your eyes roll, don't worry. You don't need to know any of this to play the blues or to even hear it. Plus, you get a scalar workout in Chapter 7 on blues lead!

C blues scale

C   E♭   F   G♭   G   B♭

Figure 2-2:
The 6-note
blues scale
and 5-note
minor
pentatonic
scale.

C minor pentatonic scale

C   E♭   F   G   B♭

The expression that invokes your senses

One of the best things about the blues — and a huge relief to beginning guitarists — is that the blues isn't all that hard to play, technically speaking. Playing lead or rhythm in most blues songs requires only intermediate technique. What is harder to do — in fact, you never stop figuring out how to do it better — is to play expressively. Expression in the blues is what turns craft into art. Check out these ways to make your music more bluesy:

- ✔ **Use bent notes.** *Bent notes* are notes where the pitch is raised slowly upwards in a continuous fashion, and this element is closely identified with the blues.

- ✔ **Make your music shake.** *Vibrato* is a technique that makes the notes of the music quiver by using left-hand finger wiggling, which gives blues a signature sound. B.B. King is well known for his expressive and soulful vibrato. Because much of the blues is set to medium tempos, players hold notes for long periods of time. Vibrato is a great way to bring notes to life, so they don't just sit there.

- ✔ **Give it some slide.** If you don't hit notes straight on and rather slide into notes from above and below, you give music a bluesy feel and breathe some life into your notes. Guitarists often draw their inspiration from vocalists and horn players (saxophone, trumpet, trombone, and so on), who exercise the slide technique on a regular basis.

- ✔ **Slur your notes.** Connecting notes through *slurs* — where you don't restrike the second note with the right hand — is a good way to loosen up your playing in the typical way a blues player does.

- ✔ **Allow the rhythm to flow.** Blues also allows a certain rhythmic liberty to be taken with melodies and especially letting the melody notes deliberately fall after, or behind, the beat. *Backphrasing* is actually more of a rhythmic alteration, or *rubato,* but it's generally thought of as a phrasing technique. It's been described as *lazy, devil may care,* or *cavalier,* but it sure makes the notes sound more bluesy.

The groove that sets the pace

Groove is often used informally to mean "on the mark" or "in sync with," but the term refers to the meter, rhythmic feel, tempo, and the instruments' role in providing the accompaniment, or backing figures. Several different grooves exist within the blues:

- ✔ A *shuffle* is a type of groove that uses triplet eighth notes with the emphasis on sounding just the first and third notes played at a medium tempo. "Sweet Home Chicago" is an example of a song in a shuffle groove.

- ✔ A *slow 12/8* blues (the "12/8" refers to the time signature) is another type of groove that's also based on three-note groups, but the tempo is slower and all three notes of the beat are pronounced. "Stormy Monday" is a song in a slow 12/8 feel.

- ✔ A *straight-four* groove is where the eighth notes are evenly spaced apart, rather than in the long-short scheme of a shuffle. "Johnny B. Goode" is in a straight four.

- ✔ *Jump* is another groove that is an uptempo shuffle, but it requires a slightly different approach in phrasing and rhythm.

Given the infinite forms of expression the blues takes, it's nice to know that at least from a technical standpoint, only a few grooves need to be mastered to play most of the blues music out there.

Dissecting an Acoustic and an Electric

Anatomically speaking, guitars come in two sexes: *acoustic* and *electric.* Since solidbody electric guitars do not make sound acoustically, but through electronics, they have more chromosomes — er, components — than do acoustics. Some of the functions of these gizmos aren't even obvious until you plug in and start messing around with them. So electric guitars may seem more complicated at first, but really, you learn very quickly what all the stuff does, and it's more about technique than anything else.

It's true, though, that about the only thing that can go wrong with an acoustic is that a string breaks. On an electric, there are more moving and electronic parts that are subject to failure, so you have a little more to keep track of on an electric. And all guitars, being made of wood and moving parts, can go out of whack and need periodic adjustment to keep them humming and happy.

Even though electric guitars are more complicated from a technological standpoint, making an acoustic guitar is harder than making an electric guitar. That's why, pound for pound, a quality acoustic guitar will cost just as much or more than its electric counterpart.

But both types follow the same basic approach to neck function and string tension. That's why acoustic and electric guitars have very similar constructions, despite a sometimes radical difference in tone production. Figures 2-3 and 2-4 show the various parts of an electric guitar and an acoustic guitar.

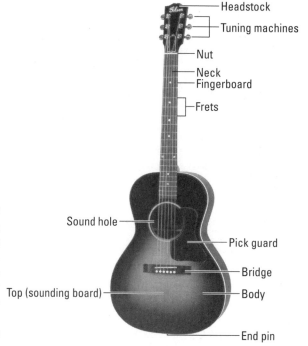

Headstock

Tuning machines

Nut

Neck

Fingerboard

Frets

Sound hole

Pick guard

Bridge

Top (sounding board)

Body

End pin

Figure 2-3: A typical acoustic guitar with its major parts labeled.

The following list tells you the functions of the primary parts of a guitar:

- ✔ **Back (acoustic only):** The part of the body that holds the sides in place; made of two or three pieces of wood.

- ✔ **Bar (electric only):** A metal rod attached to the bridge that varies the string tension by tilting the bridge back and forth. Also called the tremolo bar, whammy bar, vibrato bar, and wang bar.

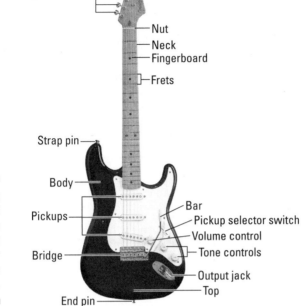

Tuning machines — Headstock
— Nut
— Neck
— Fingerboard
— Frets

Strap pin —
Body —
Pickups —
Bridge —
— Bar
— Pickup selector switch
— Volume control
— Tone controls
— Output jack
— Top
End pin —

Figure 2-4:
A typical electric guitar with its major parts labeled.

✔ **Body:** The box that provides an anchor for the neck and bridge and creates the playing support for the right hand. On an acoustic, the body includes the amplifying sound chamber that produces the guitar's tone. On an electric, it consists of the housing for the bridge assembly and electronics (pickups as well as tone and volume controls).

✔ **Bridge:** The metal (electric) or wooden (acoustic) plate that anchors the strings to the body.

✔ **End pin:** A metal post where the rear end of the strap connects. On acoustic-electrics (acoustic guitars with built-in pickups and electronics), the pin often doubles as the output jack where you plug in.

✔ **Fingerboard:** A flat, planklike piece of wood that sits atop the neck, where you place your left-hand fingers to create pitches and chords. The fingerboard is also known as the *fretboard,* because the frets are embedded in it.

✔ **Frets:** 1) Thin metal wires or bars running perpendicular to the strings that shorten the effective vibrating length of a string, enabling it to produce different pitches. 2) A verb describing worry, as in "He frets about how he'll ever recover his lost mojo."

- **Headstock:** The section that holds the tuning machines and provides a place for the manufacturer to display its logo. Not to be confused with "Woodstock," the section of New York that provided a place for the '60s generation to display its music.

- **Neck:** The long, clublike wooden piece that connects the headstock to the body.

- **Nut:** A grooved sliver of stiff nylon or other synthetic substance that stops the strings from vibrating beyond the fingerboard. The strings pass through the grooves on their way to the tuners in the headstock. The nut is one of the two points at which the vibrating area of the string ends. (The other is the bridge.)

- **Output jack (electric only):** The insertion point for the cord that connects the guitar to an amplifier or other electronic device.

- **Pickup selector (electric only):** A switch that determines which pickups are currently active.

- **Pickups (electric only):** Barlike magnets that create the electrical current, which the amplifier converts into musical sound.

- **Sides (acoustic only):** Separate curved wooden pieces on the body that join the top to the back.

- **Strap pin:** Metal post where the front, or top, end of the strap connects. (Not all acoustics have a strap pin. If the guitar is missing one, tie the top of the strap around the headstock.)

- **Strings:** The six metal (for electric and steel-string acoustic guitars) or nylon (for classical guitars) wires that, drawn taut, produce the notes of the guitar. Although not strictly part of the actual guitar (you attach and remove them at will on top of the guitar), strings are an integral part of the whole system, and a guitar's entire design and structure revolves around making the strings ring out with a joyful noise. (See Chapter 16 for more information on changing strings.)

- **Top:** The face of the guitar. On an acoustic, this piece is also the *sounding board,* which produces almost all the guitar's acoustic qualities. On an electric, the top is primarily a cosmetic or decorative cap that overlays the rest of the body material.

- **Tuning machines:** Geared mechanisms that raise and lower the tension of the strings, drawing them to different pitches. The string wraps tightly around a post that sticks out through the top, or face, of the headstock. The post passes through to the back of the headstock, where gears connect it to a tuning key. Also known as tuners, tuning pegs, tuning keys, and tuning gears.

- **Volume and tone controls (electric only):** Knobs that vary the loudness of the guitar's sound and its bass and treble emphasis.

Getting Down with the Blues: A Quick How-To

The practical differences between the two types of guitars is, in sum, that an electric guitar needs to plug in to an amp and have electricity to be heard, but it's easier to play than an acoustic. An acoustic works with nothing but the fingers nature gave you, but its loudness is limited to a range of a few feet, and in a quiet environment — unless it has a mic, of course. Acoustics can't sustain like electrics can, so their lead qualities are more restricted, too. As you can see in the preceding section, though, the bodies are quite different, owing to the way each converts a plucked string into audible sound. In this section, I cover both methods, but take note that the fundamental principles for acoustic guitars, and the way their strings produce notes, apply to electrics as well — acoustic *is* that baby's daddy, after all.

The foundation for all guitar playing: Acoustic guitars

The first blues guitars were acoustic because blues was invented before electricity had lent its powers to music. Gut and steel-string acoustics were used as a means to accompany a singing voice or another melodic instrument, like the fiddle. Gradually the rhythms evolved into single-note figures (riffs), and then finally into a solo instrument, where the guitar would carry the melody. But blues played on the acoustic guitar is a viable style today, as evidenced by the work of Rory Block, Roy Book Binder, John Hammond, Keb' Mo', and Chris Thomas King. So the first step in playing the blues is to understand how acoustic guitars work, and why they're so perfect for playing the blues.

The right hand makes the sound, and the left hand guides it

In blues guitar, as in other forms of guitar playing, the hands perform different functions — unlike, say, the piano or saxophone where the hands work the same way. In guitar playing, the left-hand fingers press down the strings at different frets, which creates different sounding *pitches* — the note names like A, C, F♯, B♭, and so on. But the left hand doesn't make the sound.

The right hand is what actually produces the sound — by strumming or plucking the strings. The left hand make no sound on its own, but decides what pitches will be heard when the right hand plays. The right hand can make sound, but it can't make organized, intelligent sound without the left hand providing the right notes to play. So the two hands need each other, and they must coordinate their efforts so that they move together to create chords and single notes in rhythm. In blues guitar playing, unlike large governmental bureaucracies, the right hand must know what the left hand is doing, and vice versa.

Lines guide your left-hand fingers

Look at the guitar's fingerboard (the top of the neck; refer to Figures 2-3 and 2-4) and you see a gridlike structure of strings and frets (short metal wires underneath the strings, running perpendicular to them). Frets are like the black and white keys of the piano: They provide all the different pitches available on the guitar in half-step increments. Good guitar players, who "know the fingerboard," can identify any string/fret location by its pitch (note name), no matter where it falls. The better guitar player you become the more you're able to look at the neck and quickly see notes and patterns.

Shifting acoustic to overdrive: Electric guitars

As soon as electric guitars were available, blues players of the day made the transition quickly and easily from their acoustic versions. An electric guitar uses the same approach to neck and frets and the way the left and right hands share separate but equally important roles (see the preceding section for the basics), but it provides some aspects that the acoustic guitar can't do or can't do as well, in addition to the most obvious advantage: increased volume through electronic amplification. The amplified electric guitar certainly changed the music world, but in many more ways than just being able to be heard over the rest of the band. The entire tonal character changed, in addition to the way you had to play it.

Technologically speaking, an electric guitar is no more complicated than an eighth-grade science project: A wire (the string) hovers over a magnet (the pickup), which forms a magnetic field. When you set the wire in motion (by plucking it), the vibrating, or oscillating, string creates a disturbance in the magnetic field, which produces an electrical current. This current travels down a cord (the one sticking out the side of your guitar) and into an amplifier, where it's cranked up to levels that people can hear — and in some cases, *really* hear. Figure 2-5 shows a close-up of the sound-producing parts of an electric guitar: the string and pickup.

Figure 2-5:
The makers
of electric
sound,
reporting
for duty.

Naturally, there's a lot more to the way electric guitars make music than what I describe here, but what's significant is that an electric guitar doesn't make its sound acoustically. Even though you can hear the string when the guitar's not plugged in, that's not what the guitar "hears." The guitar converts a disturbance in the pickup's magnetic field to a current. This all-electronic process is different than "pre-electric guitar amplification," which consisted of placing a microphone in front of a guitar.

In an electric guitar, you must use metal strings, because nylon ones don't have magnetic properties. The fact that you need only a metal wire and a pickup to make sound — rather than a resonating chamber — meant electric guitars could be built differently from their acoustic counterparts. And they were played differently, though that took some time to evolve.

Going easy on your pluckers (or strummers)

Many people think that the only difference between electric guitars and acoustic guitars is that the electric versions plug into an amp and are louder. While that's true, it's not the only difference. As a player, what you notice as soon as you pick up an electric guitar is how easy it is to play. As far as physical effort is concerned, electric guitars are much easier because

✔ The neck is shallower.

✔ The fingerboard width is thinner.

✔ The strings are lighter than those found on an acoustic.

✔ The *action*, or distance from the strings to the frets, is lower, so it frets almost effortlessly.

But the lighter strings have another advantage crucial to blues playing, other than being easier to play: They're easier to bend.

Bending strings allows electric guitarists to be more expressive in their lead playing, and to allow the guitar to better emulate the vocal stylings of blues singers, who used their flexible approach to pitch to play blues notes. Figure 2-6 shows what it looks like to bend a string on an electric. The string is physically pushed sideways on the fretboard by the left hand, stretching it.

Figure 2-6:
A left-hand string bend stretches the string, causing it to rise in pitch.

Getting your sounds to be loud and lingering

The primary reason that everyone grabbed electric guitars was for amplification. Electric guitars could be electronically amplified, making the sound heard over the rest of the band, and offering the player a more controllable solution than placing a microphone on an acoustic guitar.

In the process of electrifying a guitar, blues players noticed something else that was different, too: Electric guitars sustained longer. The notes just seemed to hang on longer instead of dying away quickly, as they did on acoustic guitars and banjos before that. As a result of this increased sustain, electric guitars were able to produce more substantial vibrated notes, bent notes, and long notes that held their sound. Along with jazz players, blues players found they could now more closely emulate vocal and horn stylings. This change encouraged a more versatile approach to single-note, or lead, playing. Before the electric version, the guitar was largely a rhythm instrument, with some notable exceptions, such as the jazz playing of gypsy guitarist Django Reinhardt.

What You Need to Get Your Groove On

To be a well-appointed blues guitar player, you need to have not only your acoustic or electric guitar, but also you need other stuff that allows you to play. Check out this list:

- **Picks:** Being able to play with a pick is an important skill, and you should learn to play with one before deciding to be a rebel and go without. (Some traditional players of both acoustic and electric blues don't use a pick. They use the unadorned fingers of the right hand to produce all their blues sounds, from full strummed chords to riffs to leads.)

- **Strap and pins:** If you plan to stand when you play, you need a strap, and your guitar must have strap pins to go through the strap holes.

- **Spare strings:** As far as "string breakage," it's not a question of *if*, but *when*. Strings break all on their own, even if you don't play hard or bend them. Carry spares, so that a sudden "string mishap" doesn't shut down your jam for the night.

- **Tuners:** Most guitar teachers (yours truly included) will tell you that it should be illegal to allow beginning guitarists to roam the earth without a tuner. These days, the word "tuner" should mean "electronic tuner," the battery-operated kind that you can plug into (or use the onboard mic, if you're playing an acoustic).

    An electronic tuner is designed for quick and easy guitar tuning, and you can tune silently to boot. You can use other tuning methods (such as employing a pitch pipe, tuning fork, or the relative method), but the recommended way is to use a tuner, which allows you to use your eyes (by watching a meter or digital display). Don't worry, your ears will catch up in time. A tuner is an essential tool — and courtesy — for all who appreciate in-tune music.

- ✔ **Tools:** Undoubtedly, you'll need to adjust or fix your guitar from time to time, so you need to gather a toolbox. Chapter 18 tells you just what to put in it.

- ✔ **Amplifier:** If you decide to pursue electric blues guitar, you need to have an amplifier and a cord to connect the guitar to it. To help you navigate the amp section of your nearest instrument dealer, I include a whole chapter on choosing amps — flip ahead to Chapter 15 for that information.

- ✔ **Cords:** If you play an electric guitar (or even a plugged-in acoustic-electric model), you need a cable or cord to connect your guitar to your amp. You can buy cables of varying lengths, from about 6 to 20 feet. Cords have a variety of purposes, though, so here's a quick rundown:

    - **Guitar cord, cable, or patch cord:** This cord connects your guitar and your amp.

    - **Effects cords:** If you buy a tuner or additional effects and pedals (see the next bullet), you can connect them to each other with shorter cables — so you need one short cord (just a few inches long) for every effect in your arsenal, plus one to connect your guitar to the first effect. Because you want your effect to be controllable by your foot — and you want to be out front by the audience and not necessarily back by your amp — you also need a long cord to stretch from your effect back to the amp.

- ✔ **Effects pedals:** Many blues players get along with just an amp, but in today's world, most blues guitarists augment their sound with outboard effects — each about the size of a packet of index cards — to get even more sonic possibilities.

Effects can make it sound like your guitar was recorded in a recording studio, or produce other-worldly sounds that might have more of a theatrical application than a musical one. But perhaps the biggest use of effects is to get a distorted sound — the sonic result that occurs when a guitar is pumped through an amp at top volume and maximum power. An outboard effect gives you this quality at low amp volumes. There are more distortion effects available than any other kind, and they'll keep coming. So try out different effects pedals and start amassing an arsenal of them (check out Chapter 16 before you do, so you shop with a working knowledge of what you're buying).

- ✔ **Slide:** To play slide, you need a slide apparatus, in the form of a metal or glass tube, filed-down bottle neck, or medicine bottle. They're not expensive, so buy a couple of different types and decide which is the best for you.

✔ **Other cool gear:** Besides having the basic hardware essential to creating music, you can find tons of other accessories, doodads, and whatnots to make blues guitar life just a little easier. As you play more and more, you'll find your own life-savers to add to your collection. Here are a few ideas of items people find helpful:

- **Peg winder:** Although not essential to making music, a peg winder is a godsend when you break a string and have to put one back on in a jiffy because you're on stage and in the middle of a song. This handy fellow allows you to bring a string up to tune in about one tenth the time it does by using just your fingers.

- **Metronome:** This valuable practice tool helps you play in time.

- **Miniature tools:** Aside from the fact that they're cute, these tools are fantastic to take with you on a gig in case you're in a pinch and don't have access to the giant toolbox.

- **Polishing cloths:** These babies keep your axe gleaming and looking spiffy.

- **Battery testers:** Effects use battery juice, and when you have a problem or your sound is suffering, it's nice to use a battery tester to quickly determine whether a bad battery is causing the problem.

- **Cord organizers:** Danny from *Full House,* Felix from *The Odd Couple,* and neat freaks the world over would love these organizers. Especially if they have a lot of guitar cords lying around.

Chapter 3

Grab Hold, Tune Up, Play On!

· ·

In This Chapter

▶ Holding the guitar while sitting and standing

▶ Figuring out how to tune your guitar

▶ Understanding guitar notation

▶ Playing your first chord (make some noise, baby!)

· ·

*U*nlike classical guitar playing, blues guitar has no pre-existing beliefs on the right way to play and hold your instrument. This lack of a formal approach frees you from the normal way of learning, which is to listen to someone else tell you how to do something the *right* way — and call you out when you're doing it wrong.

In the blues, you can't really be doing something wrong, unless it either hurts or sounds bad. That's because the blues is a folk art — an art created by ordinary people — and doesn't carry around the baggage of established rules that some other art forms do. But you can observe some simple guidelines that help you play comfortably, efficiently, and, by all means, without pain. For the blues guitarist, any pain associated with playing should come from the heart, not your fingers or lower back!

Holding Your Axe (That Is, Your Guitar)

Holding your guitar should feel as natural as picking up a baby. Don't think too much about it; just treat it with love, and you'll do fine. Once you have your baby — er, your guitar — in your arms, use the info in the following sections so you're comfortable while you figure out how to fret notes and strum strings.

Grabbing your guitar's neck

When you grip your guitar, your left hand surrounds the neck, with the neck between your thumb and index finger. Your fingers are above the strings; your thumb is on the back of the neck. ***Note:*** *left hand* here means *fretting hand* for the right-handed guitarist. If you play left-handed (where you're fretting with your right hand), just make the mental conversion each time I use *right* and *left* when referring to hands.

To create notes and chords, clench your fingers toward your palm, pushing the strings to the fretboard. The chords and notes dictate which way your hand moves to get the optimum leverage, but the ball of your hand (the knuckles at the base of your fingers) should be against the treble side of the guitar most of the time. This position is shown in Figure 3-1.

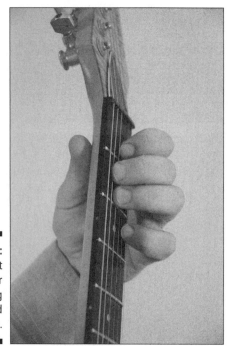

Figure 3-1:
The correct position for creating notes and chords.

Press your thumb against the back of the neck to maximize your squeezing effort when playing chords.

Muffles, buzzes, and dead skin

Buzzes and muffles are the bane of beginning guitarists, and they're especially hard to avoid when playing chords, which I discuss later in this chapter. A *buzz* results if you don't press down hard enough on the string, and a *muffle* occurs if your fretting finger comes in contact with an adjacent string. Don't worry too much if your strings buzz and muffle a little bit; the buzz corrects itself over time without you doing anything consciously, just like a bad haircut. As

your fingers become stronger and more agile, buzzes and muffles gradually heal themselves.

Left-hand fretting can make your fingertips hurt a little until you develop calluses on them. Don't worry, though; the calluses are barely noticeable, so you won't look like a tree frog. But the little bit of extra padding you develop eventually allows you to play all night without the slightest bit of pain or discomfort.

Pushing down on the strings

To know where to place your fingers, remember that the thin metal bars running horizontally on the fingerboard are the *frets,* and you place your fingers between the frets to make a note. To make the definition more complicated, in music notation, *fret* refers to the *space between the frets*, where you place your fingers.

To fret a string, press it to the fingerboard with the tip of a left-hand finger. Place your finger in the space between the two fret bars, but a little closer to the higher-numbered fret. Playing chords requires multiple fingers fretting simultaneously. Keep your knuckles bent and your fingers rounded as you apply pressure, making sure to press straight down on the string rather than from the side. This produces maximum pressure and ensures that you don't prevent adjacent strings from ringing.

When you first start playing, your left hand will have trouble keeping up. You may find it takes considerable strength and concentration to play notes and chords that ring out clearly and that don't buzz. Your hand may hurt after only a few minutes of playing, and you may wonder how you can ever play one song, let alone a whole evening of songs.

Left-hand strength develops over time, and you gain the endurance you need just by playing the guitar a lot. Don't worry about trying to build up the strength of your left hand through independent exercises. Just playing the guitar is enough to develop the appropriate and necessary muscles in your left hand. Playing the blues is physical. As with any physical activity, don't push it, especially in the beginning. Keep at it, but take frequent breaks. When something starts to hurt, stop for a few minutes — or for the day — and rest.

Getting sound to come out

All the positioning in the world doesn't do you any good unless you can get your guitar to make some noise. When you have your guitar in the right position (see "Getting Situated" later in this chapter for proper positions), swing your right arm from the elbow so your right hand crosses the strings. This is the correct movement for striking the strings whether you're strumming, playing lead with a pick, or brushing chords with your fingers.

Figure 3-2 shows right-hand placement over the strings. Notice how relaxed and natural the hand looks.

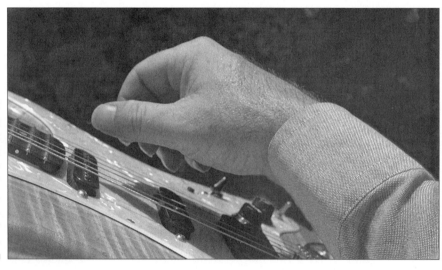

Figure 3-2:
The right hand crosses the strings for picking, strumming, and finger-picking.

Once you're looking all natural and like you were born to play the guitar, you need to actually strike the strings to make sound. Guitarists have three ways to coax sound from the strings:

- ✔ **Use a pick:** The most popular way to play electric blues is with a *pick* — a stiff piece of plastic or nylon that you hold tightly between your right-hand thumb and index finger (head to the next section for a look). For pounding out driving rhythms and digging in for aggressive single-note riffs and leads, picks are the tool choice — they attack the strings with power, authority, and accuracy.

  Playing electric blues with a pick is the best way to start, but some players don't use a pick and manage to do just fine. Albert Collins, Albert King, and Otis Rush all play electric blues guitar using just their fingers.

- ✔ **Use your fingers:** For acoustic blues, fingerstyle is the preferred approach because separating the functions of the right-hand thumb from the fingers allows you to play independent bass lines against the treble voices. Even though most of blues is played with a pick, you can play electric guitar with your fingers, though it's unusual and challenging.

Listen to the music of Robert Johnson, Skip James, and Blind Blake to hear some masterful fingerstyle acoustic blues.

✔ **Use a thumbpick:** Some fingerstyle players use a plastic thumbpick for increased power in the thumb. So if you plan to play fingerstyle, try acclimating yourself to a thumbpick. It allows you to get a stronger attack on the string due to the angle of the thumb striking the strings. Figure 3-3 shows how to wear a thumbpick.

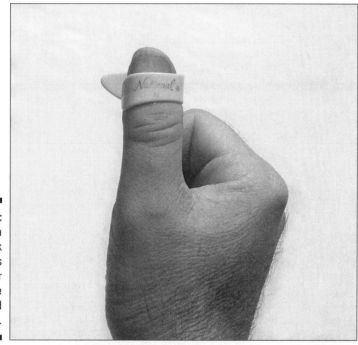

Figure 3-3:
Using a thumbpick increases the power from the right-hand thumb.

All thumbs

Look at your thumb while you try to play fingerstyle and notice that it hits the strings in a glancing blow — unlike the fingers, which contact the strings at a more perpendicular angle. A thumbpick solves the problem by enabling the tip of the pick to strike the string at more of a right angle. Thumbpicks aren't for everyone, but many electric blues players (including Albert King, Albert Collins, and Freddie King) and fingerstyle players (such as Chet Atkins and Merle Travis) have used them.

Holding the Pick, Attacking the Problem

Some blues players don't use a pick, but the majority of electric guitarists who play lead do. A pick provides force, precision, and speed that fingers can't muster as easily and efficiently. If you've never played with a pick, try following the suggestions in this section.

Hold the pick in your right hand between the index finger and thumb, as shown in Figure 3-4. The point of the pick sticks out perpendicularly from your thumbnail, and only the top third of the pick shows.

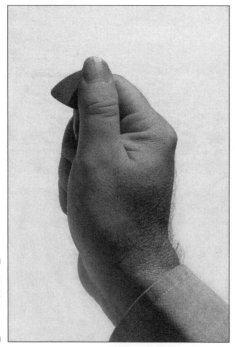

Figure 3-4:
The correct way to hold a pick.

Don't grip the pick too hard when playing lead, but don't let the string push it loose from your fingers either. Play the notes lightly at first to get the hang of playing notes with a pick.

Picks come in different *gauges* or thicknesses, so if playing with a pick is awkward for you at first, play around with different gauges until you get a feel that doesn't *fight back* as much (thinner or medium gauge picks are more flexible). As your playing develops, try to play with a stiffer (heavier gauge) pick for the fastest response from the string and for the strongest sound.

When starting out with a pick for single-string playing, many people wonder whether they're exerting too much effort, going too far past the string, or not going far enough. Really, these problems work themselves out without thinking about them too much.

Generally, as long as you don't accidentally hit the adjacent string in your single-string picking, you're not going too far. And after you clear the string and it rings out clearly, you've gone far enough. However, your pick strokes do become smaller and your wrist motions more efficient the more you play. Also, the tempo dictates how closely you need to restrict your strokes: Fast songs require a small range, but slow songs don't require you to turn-around-on-a-dime, so you can be a little more expansive.

Getting Situated

I bet you've seen those classic pictures of Delta blues players seated, usually on a stool or chair, and often on a porch. They're strumming away on their guitars and singing about their woes. Many early blues players did just that — they sat — not only while jamming or playing for a small group but also while performing in concert. But you don't have to sit; in fact, whatever's most comfortable for you is the way you should play. You can play the blues sitting or standing (or lying down if it makes you feel good).

Current stage practices often demand that performers stand whenever possible. And when you're standing, you certainly enjoy a freedom of movement in your whole body that allows you to be more demonstrative with your music. Standing doesn't necessarily give you any technical advantage when playing the blues, but anyone who plays for an audience generally stands.

But standing and sitting have different ways for the guitar to rest in your arms, so make sure you can play comfortably in both positions. If you practice a lot while sitting, make sure that you get up and walk around the room as you play. If nothing else, this stretches your legs — so your fingers and hands don't get *all* the exercise.

Sitting down . . .

Just because you're playing the blues doesn't mean you can get *too* casual about your approach. You're still trying to master a musical instrument after all, and that requires a serious and consistent approach to holding the instrument — even if you opt to do it off your feet.

To play the blues properly while sitting down, stick to the following steps:

1. **Sit in a comfortable desk chair (one without arms), stool, or straight-back chair.**

   A couch is too relaxed for serious study (though you can certainly have fun with your guitar as a sofa spud — after you've put in your serious practice time)!

2. **With feet apart, sit up straight and forward in the seat of the chair so that you place some weight on your feet.**

   Because the exact position is largely a matter of personal comfort, you can experiment to find the best position for you.

3. **Put the waist of the guitar on your right leg, pull the guitar up against your body, and place your right arm over the guitar's top edge to hold the guitar in place.**

   When you're sitting, your right arm holds the guitar to keep it from falling forward or tipping to the side toward the headstock. You won't have this problem if you wear a shoulder strap, which balances the guitar in place. But take care when adjusting your sitting position so you don't let the guitar fall.

Don't support the neck with your left hand because you want this hand to be free to move up and down the neck without the burden of also holding up the guitar.

. . . *or standing up*

If you want to stand when you play your guitar, follow these few steps:

1. **Attach a guitar strap to your guitar's two strap pins.**

   The strap pins are on the bottom edge of the guitar and on the bass-side edge (this placement differs depending on your particular model).

2. **Put your head, right arm, and shoulder through the strap, letting the weight of the guitar fall on your left shoulder.**

   Then straighten up to a normal, erect, standing position.

3. **Adjust the strap to get the guitar at a comfortable playing height.**

   Take the guitar off before adjusting the strap because trying to adjust it while holding the guitar is sometimes awkward.

The higher the guitar sits, the easier it is to play. But there's a catch: If the guitar is too high, you can look uncool — more a like a do-goodin' folksinger from the '60s than the gritty, hard-scrabblin' blueser that you are.

No amount of looking cool can make up for a position that's not comfortable, and each player knows what *comfortable* is by the way the left hand feels when trying to finger notes and chords. If you have to curl your hand around too much to play, you may feel strain — typically on the back of the hand. Prolonged strain like this, may make your hand hate you later! So hike up that axe and be friends with your guitar!

You may find that the guitar rides a little lower when you're standing than when you're sitting. This is natural. You can test whether your guitar sits lower when standing by wearing your adjusted strap when you sit. Chances are, the strap slacks a bit. If this happens, it's just an indication that what feels natural standing is a little lower than what feels best for sitting.

Tuning Up

The first notes to play on your guitar are the ones that get your guitar in tune. Don't play anything — not a lick, not a rhythm figure — until your guitar is perfectly in tune with itself and the other instruments in the band. Playing out of tune can peg you as an amateur and cause musicians and non-musicians alike to cringe. So learn how to tune your instrument quickly, correctly, and painlessly, and everyone will be happy — especially you.

Basically, you have two ways to tune your guitar:

- **To an outside reference:** These sources include electronic tuners, a tuning fork, a pitch pipe, or another instrument (such as a piano, organ, electronic keyboard, or even a harmonica).

- **To itself:** By using the *relative method,* you tune all the strings to one string. (This method is covered in the section "Helping your guitar get in tune with itself.")

  In the relative method, your guitar may or may not be in tune with another instrument or concert pitch (A = 440), but the strings are in tune with each other. Anyone who doesn't have perfect pitch (which is most of the world, including the world of musicians) won't know.

Each of these methods is explained in more detail in *Guitar For Dummies,* 2nd Edition, but most guitarists, after achieving a certain level of proficiency, prefer an electronic tuner. After you get the hang of using electronic tuners, they're the quickest, most reliable, and quietest ways to tune.

One additional source for tuning exists in the back of this book: the CD-ROM! Track 1 plays the six open strings on the guitar, and you can use these to tune, repeating the track as necessary.

Helping your guitar get in tune with itself

You can tune the guitar so that all six strings play in tune with each other, even if it's higher or lower than other fixed-pitch instruments (like the keyboard or harmonica). Tuning the strings to each other is called *relative tuning*. Start by establishing one string as the reference point, the string to which you'll tune the others. ***Note:*** The low E, or sixth string, is easiest to use. Because this is your reference point, you don't touch its tuning key.

To tune the other five strings, follow these steps:

1. **Play the fifth fret of the sixth (low E) string and, while the string rings, play the open fifth string (A).** Listen closely to determine whether the fifth string is higher or lower than the ringing, fretted sixth string. If the fifth string sounds lower in pitch, or *flat,* turn its tuning key in the appropriate direction to raise its pitch slightly until it matches perfectly the ringing sixth string. If the fifth string is higher, or *sharp,* turn the tuning key to lower the pitch.

2. **Play the fifth fret of the fifth (A) string and the open fourth (D) string.** Let the strings ring together. If the fourth string is flat compared to the fifth string, turn its tuning key to raise the pitch. If the fourth string is sharp, turn its tuning key to lower the pitch.

3. **Play the fifth fret of the fourth (D) string and the open third (G) string.** Let the strings ring together. If the third string is flat, turn its tuning key to raise the pitch. If the third string is sharp, turn its key to lower the pitch.

4. **Play the fourth fret (not the fifth fret) of the third (G) string and the open second (B) string.** Let the strings ring together. If the second string is flat, turn its tuning key to raise the pitch. If the second string is sharp, turn its key to lower the pitch.

5. **Play the fifth fret of the second (B) string and the open first (high E) string.** Let the strings ring together. If the first string is flat, turn its tuning key to raise the pitch. If the first string is sharp, turn its tuning key to lower the pitch.

It's a good idea to back up and repeat Steps One through Five because some strings may slip out of tune slightly during the tuning process.

Holding your guitar to an electronic standard

Electronic tuners can be as small as a deck of playing cards and cost as little as $25. You plug your guitar into it, or, if you're using a non-electrified acoustic, you can use the tuner's built-in mic. When you play a note, it registers as a pitch on the tuner's display. This display allows you to use your eyes in addition to, or instead of, your ears to check whether you're in tune. If you want to *hear* your guitar, you need to plug a cord from the tuner's output into your amp. But you don't need to hear the guitar to tune it with an electronic tuner.

Many people tune silently out of courtesy to fellow musicians and other listeners, and, of course, because the sound of guitars tuning up can annoy some people. But tuning silently is required in some situations — like televised concerts, where the musicians must wait in absolute silence until the cue to come in with bold, in-tune music. By keeping your tuner on and having it between your guitar and amp (or, if you're using effects, between your guitar and first effect), you can tune by turning down the volume on your amp.

A tuner senses which pitch you're playing and tells you, by way of its meter or *LEDs* (light-emitting diodes), the closest pitch (A, B♭, B, C, and so on) and whether you're flat or sharp of it. It's a great system because you can also use a tuner to get into alternate tunings, such as open G, for the times you have to retune the guitar to play slide — doing it quickly and silently.

A tuner can occupy a permanent berth in your signal chain, or you can plug it in at will, just putting it in your guitar case or on top of your amp when you're done. Either way, an electronic tuner is the most fundamental electronic device you need to own — more important than any other outboard effect. You can play a guitar in tune without effects and still make music, but you can't play out of tune and make (tolerable) music, no matter how many effects you own.

Even though you can get the guitar in tune with itself (using the relative method) and can, therefore, play by yourself with no problems, it's a good idea to check often that you haven't strayed too far from concert pitch. Playing flat or sharp of concert pitch isn't bad for the instrument, but you can condition your ears to hear flat or sharp if you stay out of tune for too long.

Who let the cats out?

If your harmonica player's out of tune, guess what? *You're* out of tune. Or more precisely, you're the one who has to adjust to him because you can change your tuning and he can't. The same is true with any fixed-pitch instrument. Some older organs have tuning problems, too, and tend to play below standard-pitch, which means you may have to adjust to them. I once played in a club with a house organ that played flat, but the house harmonica player's instruments were sharp. Worse, the harmonica player was the club's owner and you couldn't refuse his sitting in! The organ was flat, the harmonica was sharp, and the musicians were stuck in the middle. Talk about having the blues!

Playing a Chord

A chord is defined as the simultaneous sounding of three or more notes of different-named pitches. On the guitar, you can play chords in three basic ways:

- ✔ **Strum:** To strum, drag a pick across the strings in a single, quick motion
- ✔ **Pluck:** To pluck, use the individual right-hand fingers
- ✔ **Smack:** Smack the strings with your open right hand or closed right fist

When you play the strings with your right hand, position your hand over the soundhole (if you're playing acoustic) or over the pickups (if you're playing electric). You can't, however, just play *any* group of notes, like all six open strings — the notes must form a musically meaningful arrangement. To a guitarist, that means learning chord forms.

To play the E chord, follow these steps:

1. **Place your first finger (index) on the third string, first fret.**

2. **Place your second finger on the fifth string, second fret.**

   Here, you have to skip over the fourth string. Be careful not to touch the fourth string as you reach over it.

3. **Put your third finger on the fourth string, second fret.**

   You may have to wriggle your third finger to get it between the first and second fingers, which are already in place. Don't grip the guitar too tightly; you want to relax your fingers so you can add fingers as needed.

4. **Press down firmly on all three fretted strings.**

   Make sure to keep your knuckles curved, with none of the fretted fingers covering the open strings — especially the first and second strings, which must ring out to help the E chord sound in all its resplendent, six-string glory. Your hand should look like the one in Figure 3-5. Now, quick, keep reading before your fingers fall off!

Okay, your fingers won't really fall off, but if your left hand is set, you may as well give your right hand something to do. Using a pick, strum all six strings at once with a smooth and firm motion, but don't strum too forcefully.

Listen to Track 2 and try to match the level of intensity (which isn't very intense at all, so relax) and evenness. Note, too, that the four strokes aren't only smooth and even, they're also consistent — one stroke sounds like every other. When you can strum the E chord with four even strokes, try doubling the number to eight, then to 12.

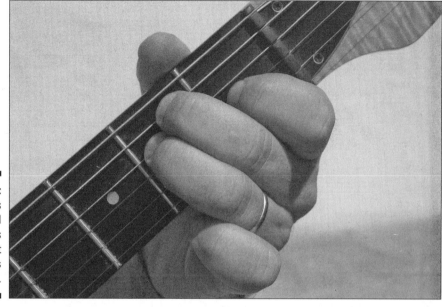

Figure 3-5:
With fingers curved and knuckles bent, the left hand fingers the E chord.

Music Notation: Not Just for Geeks

You don't have to read music to play the blues. In fact, most of today's great blues artists don't read music at all or can't read it well enough to make an impact on their playing. So, you ask, why bother with notation? Because it can make learning more efficient. And it's not going to take away from your ability to play (although some superstition exists in this regard). The following sections introduce you to the music notation used in this book.

Guidance for your aimless fingers: A chord diagram

A chord diagram (shown in Figure 3-6) represents the strings and frets of the guitar as a grid of six vertical lines for the strings and five horizontal lines for the frets. Dots on the horizontal lines indicate where your fingers go. Reading a chord diagram isn't like reading at all. It's more like looking at a map and giving your fingers the directions. A chord diagram has a certain anatomy, and the following list defines each of its elements:

✔ **Grid:** The six vertical and five horizontal lines correspond to the strings and frets on the guitar neck — as if you stood the guitar up on the floor and looked straight at the front of it.

✔ **Vertical lines:** The left-most vertical line is the low sixth string; the right-most line is the high first string.

✔ **Horizontal lines:** The horizontal lines represent the guitar's fret wires, and the space between the horizontal lines is the fret. The top line is thicker because it represents the nut of the guitar.

✔ **Dots:** The numerals directly below each string line indicate which left-hand finger you use to fret that note:

- • 1 = index

- • 2 = middle

- • 3 = ring

- • 4 = little

✔ **X's and O's:** An *X* above a string means the string isn't played. An *O* indicates an open string that's played.

If a chord starts on a fret other than the first fret (which happens a lot in blues guitar because of its reliance on *barre chords*, discussed in Chapter 4), a numeral appears to the right of the diagram, next to the top fret line to indicate in which fret you actually start.

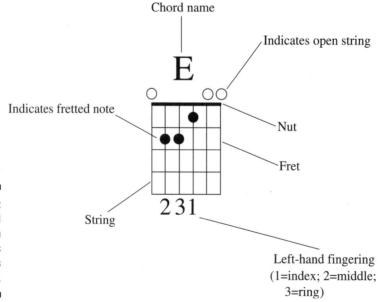

Figure 3-6:
A chord diagram with its parts labeled.

Mapping out your short-term path: Rhythm notation

Musicians often use a simple rhythm chart (like a road map) to convey the basic form of a song, which avoids the issue of reading or writing out more formal music parts. *Rhythm*, in this case, means playing to the beat and keeping a consistent strumming or picking pattern going in your right hand.

Following are some basic shorthand techniques that help you navigate the music figures in this book:

- ✔ *Rhythm slashes* (/) are the diagonal marks that simply tell you to play "in the style of the song," but they don't tell you exactly what rhythm to play.

- ✔ *Chord symbols* (letter name with a quality, such as *7* or *m*) determine what you play, and some other indication, like a simple performance note at the beginning of the piece (such as *Shuffle* or *Slow blues*), tells you the style.

Here's how these techniques work: If you see the chord symbol *E* above a staff with four slashes, you grab an E chord with your left hand and strike it four times with your right hand in a rhythmic manner that is consistent with the song's feel.

Rhythm notation isn't an exact science because whoever wrote this *chart* (as music on a sheet of paper is called) assumes you know what that style is without seeing the exact notes. Figure 3-7 shows a typical bar of music that uses rhythm slashes and a chord symbol. Practice the exercise a few times so you can begin to associate symbols on a page with sounds from a guitar.

Figure 3-7:
One bar of
an E chord
with rhythm
slashes.

In the example in Figure 3-7, the slashes indicate four pick strokes on the guitar. But in general, slashes don't dictate any particular rhythm, only that you play an E chord for the duration of the bar.

Guiding you all the way through a song: Tablature

Tablature (*tab* for short) also shows the frets and strings of the guitar. Tab is more like standard music notation because it tells you how to play music over time.

In this book, every music example has a tab staff underneath a corresponding standard music staff, and it's visually aligned with its top half, so you can use whichever one you're comfortable with. The tab shows you the strings and the fret numbers; the music staff shows you the pitches and the rhythms. This way, you have the best of both worlds. And you still have the CD-ROM to check what you see with what you hear.

You can use both the music and tab staffs simultaneously, or you can elect not to use them at all (relying instead on using the CD-ROM to learn the songs by ear). But you'll most likely employ a method using all three systems. Each system has its strengths, and you're not limited to using any one or two (nor do you even have to tell anyone your secret formula). What's important is that you do get the examples under your fingers and get comfortable with them.

Figure 3-8 shows the anatomy of a tab staff. The horizontal lines represent the strings, as if you faced a guitar that was sitting upright and you rotated it 90 degrees counterclockwise, positioning the high E string on top and the low E string on the bottom. Numerals placed on a line tell you the fret number and string location. *Note:* Tab doesn't tell you which fingers to use, just which frets to play.

Figure 3-8:
Three examples of guitar tablature, with the parts labeled.

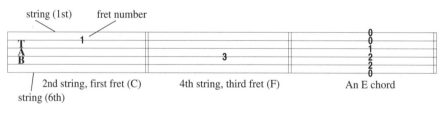

Part II
Setting Up to Play the Blues

The 5th Wave   By Rich Tennant

In this part . . .

Part II gets you working with your hands, so you don't look awkward just standing there with a guitar around your neck. In Chapter 4, you tackle chords and figure out exactly how to finger them with your left hand. But Chapter 5 addresses the right hand, which bangs out the strums, rhythms, single notes, and other joyful noises that your guitar is capable of producing. Chapter 6 takes a look at blues forms and moves — those special devices and tricks that separates the blues from other types of music. The last chapter in this part, Chapter 7, presents riffs — the cool moves that get your feet to tappin' and the joint a-jumpin'.

Chapter 4

Getting a Grip on Left-Hand Chords

*I*f you're going to play the blues, the first step is figuring out the chords. *Chords* are the simultaneous sounding of three or more different-named pitches (such as the notes in a C major chord: C, E, and G). You finger chords with the left hand and hold these fretted notes while the right hand strums or picks the strings.

Other instruction methods may begin by teaching single-note melodies, but in *Blues Guitar For Dummies,* you cut to the chase and start off with chords and how to play them. Chords provide the framework for the vocals and lead instruments to do their thing and are what you need to play rhythm guitar. And rhythm guitar is the backbone of the blues.

Starting Out Simple: Blues Chords Even Your Mom Could Play

The simplest guitar chords are called *open-position* chords (or *basic* chords), and they occur down the neck (close to the nut) within the first three frets. They combine open and fretted strings. If you've never played open-position chords before, this book gives you a brief how-to. For an in-depth discussion and detailed instructions, you may want to check out *Guitar For Dummies,* 2nd Edition.

In blues, like rock, open-position chords are used in acoustic blues, while electric blues favors barre chords (which I cover later in this chapter). In particular, though, the blues seems more liberal with regard to mixing open-position and barre chords. Chords are classified by their *quality,* such as

- Major
- Minor
- 7 (also known as dominant 7)
- Minor 7
- Suspended (abbreviated "sus")
- 7 suspended

More qualities exist, but the blues tends to limit itself to just the above-mentioned choices.

Figure 4-1 shows a chart of 20 chords that provide all the vocabulary you need to play almost any blues song. Please flip back to Chapter 3 if you need the rundown on reading a chord diagram. *Note:* Alternate fingerings appear below the primary ones in parentheses.

The chart in Figure 4-1 is duplicated on the yellow perforated Cheat Sheet located at the front of this book. You can detach this chart and keep it close to you at all times. Tape it to a wall, prop it up on a music stand, or set it on a table top next to any charts, sheet music, or song books you work on.

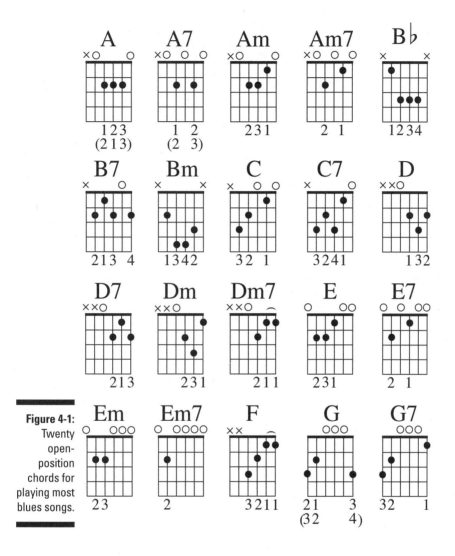

Figure 4-1:
Twenty open-position chords for playing most blues songs.

Going to the Next Level: Barre Chords

Barre chords are so named because you use your left-hand index finger as a bar to cover five or six strings at a given fret. The rest of the chord is formed with your remaining fingers.

You say bar, I say barre; Let's call the whole thing off

Barre is the Spanish word for bar, and guitarists use the Spanish form for two reasons:

✔ It distinguishes *barre* from the word *bar*, which guitarists use for two other meanings in guitar: as a synonym for *measure* and for the arm that moves the floating bridge on some electric guitar models.

✔ Guitar music uses Spanish words for much of the notation in the same way Italian is used for other musical terms (*forte* for loud, *piano* for soft, and so on).

Barre chords may be physically difficult to master for the beginner, but conceptually they're very easy to understand. A barre chord is like a "human capo," in that it allows you to play familiar basic chords all over the neck of your guitar to change keys and transpose music by using only a few forms. Unlike a *capo* (a mechanical device that wraps around the neck at a particular fret), a barre chord can move quickly and in time with the music.

Because barre chords contain no open strings, you can move them around the neck, allowing you to play any chord by using just one fingering form. The letter names of the chord change (from A to B to C, and so on), but the fingering and the quality stays exactly the same. Because all the strings in a barre chord are fretted, you have more control over the sustain (or ringing out) of the strings, which is why barre chords sound less folky or cowboy-like than open-position chords.

Barre chords are harder to play than open-position chords — and even harder on an acoustic than an electric guitar. But luckily playing these chords gets easier quickly, and before you know it, you can't even distinguish between a barre chord and an open-position chord. You simply chose the right chord for the job, and if it happens to be a barre chord and not an open-position chord, you just play it and don't even think about the agony you endured while learning it.

Playing barre chords is much, much easier on electric guitar, so if you have both an acoustic and electric, consider mastering barre chords on an electric before transferring over.

Most barre chords used for the blues use only two forms, the E form and the A form. The next sections focus on building barre chords, naming them, and using these two popular forms.

Forming a barre chord

To form a barre chord, follow these steps:

1. **Place your index finger on the appropriate fret.**

2. **Form the rest of the chord with your remaining fingers (second, third, and fourth left-hand fingers).**

   Don't apply too much pressure to any of the fingers until you have them all roughly in place.

3. **Press down with your fingers, keeping them curved with the knuckles bent.**

Figure 4-2 shows an F chord, which uses the first (index) finger as a bar, covering five or six strings, while the remaining fingers make an E chord-form above it.

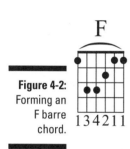

Figure 4-2: Forming an F barre chord.

Here are three tips for getting good sound out of your barre chord:

- ✔ **Thumb it.** Keep your thumb placed directly in the center of the neck's back. This grip helps you get your chord-gripping power.

- ✔ **Relax your arm.** Don't let your elbow stick out at your side like you're doing the chicken dance, and check to see that your left shoulder stays down and relaxed and doesn't hunch up.

- ✔ **Become economical.** Make small adjustments in your finger placement, ensuring that you're not touching adjacent strings, which causes muffles. Keep your knuckles rounded and press straight down on the strings.

Try to produce a buzz-free sound out of each chord you finger. Test your left-hand chord-fretting technique by dragging the pick (or your thumb) across the strings slowly enough that you can hear the individual strings ringing out. If you hear a buzz or muffled sound, try to rectify it with small finger movements only in the trouble spot, without moving your whole hand or other fingers that affect the position or sound of the notes that do sound good.

If you're having trouble with one of your barred notes, make sure that one of the strings isn't getting creased between your knuckles.

Left-hand chording takes work and patience. You need to build up both muscle strength and fine-motor movements to play chords successfully. But after you get it, it's like riding a bicycle — instinctive and effortless, and you never forget how.

Naming barre chords

When you move your barre chord up and down the neck, the name of the chord changes. The E-form barre chord corresponds to the note on the sixth string — the one your index finger covers. So if you know the notes of the sixth string all the way up to the twelfth fret, you know what chord you play as you move it to various frets. As you move your E-form barre chord up and down the neck, practice saying the name of the chord aloud to help memorize each one.

Figure 4-3 shows five common locations for barre chords in playing the blues. Those chords are G, A, B, C, and D. As you reference Figure 4-3, move between the positions, saying the names of the chords. For example, the B chord falls on the seventh fret.

To help get you started, I include a hint in the music by putting the fret number under the staff, but of course you won't see these indications in regular music, so you need to be able to use just the chord's name (E, D, B♭, and so on) to recognize where to place the chord.

Figure 4-3:
Five common major barre chords are found in the blues.

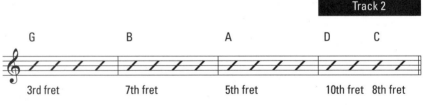

Track 2

G   B   A   D   C

3rd fret   7th fret   5th fret   10th fret 8th fret

The idea isn't just to move your left hand up and down the neck; it's to play clear-ringing chords at these various locations. Make sure that as you move your left hand to different positions, you also play the chords with your right hand and listen to the strummed notes to ensure that all six notes of the chord sound out.

For most of your blues guitar chording efforts, you use the E and A forms. But some other forms do exist and spice up your rhythm playing and give you some options:

- ✔ The C chord is sometimes used in a barre configuration, but C7 — because it's a movable chord on the inner four strings — is used a lot.

- ✔ The D form is a good form for rhythm playing when you want to empha- size the upper strings of the guitar and produce a higher, scratchier sound than the E and A forms provide. Great for R&B-type blues!

- ✔ The B7 form is often used for jazz- and rock-based blues because the highest string, fretted by the fourth finger, can slide around to produce jazz-like dissonances.

Figure 4-4 shows the C7 form played at the fifth fret, which makes it an E7 — a very useful chord for the blues in A.

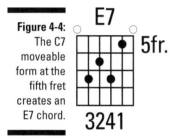

Figure 4-4: The C7 moveable form at the fifth fret creates an E7 chord.

Playing E-based barre chords

Because barre chords, in their true from, are really open-position chords with the barre added on, you can form them by using an F barre chord as an exam- ple. Try out the following steps:

1. **Finger the E-form barre chord.**

   Use fingers two, three, and four for the chord part instead of how you fret for an open-position chord.

2. **Slide the E chord up one fret.**

   Make sure to slide as a unit, so your middle finger is now on the second fret and the third and fourth fingers are on the third fret.

3. **Place your index finger across the first fret, covering all six strings.**

   The sixth string should fall under the tip of your index finger so you can fret it. The first and second strings must also be fretted with the fleshy part of your index finger. Your left hand should look like Figure 4-2.

4. **Strum the chord slowly from the sixth string to the first letting each note sound by itself.**

   Congratulations on making it through the hardest part of barre chords: getting the barred notes to ring clearly!

If you're still having trouble getting all the strings to ring out, try rotating your index finger slightly so the strings fall under the side of your finger rather than the flat, fleshier part. This method may help you get a clearer sound because the side of your finger is harder than the fleshier, flat part and can press harder with more consistency.

Practice and patience can get you through this difficult time where the barred part of your chords can sound mushy, and it seems to take inordinate effort to sound decent. Every guitarist goes through it, but every guitarist conquers it. Consider it a rite of passage.

After you get a barre chord under your fingers, and it starts to sound acceptable, start moving the chord up and down the neck. Moving chords is more about thinking than playing, because you're trying to memorize the names of the notes on the neck. So this adjustment may take a little getting use to.

After you've gotten the basic E-major form under your belt — or should I say, fingers — and are comfortable moving along the neck, familiarize yourself with the other E forms: minor, dominant 7, minor 7, 7 suspended (Em, E7, Em7, and E7sus). These are also based on their open-position counterparts, so the concept should come quickly. Moving barre chords of all qualities around — quickly and accurately with clean sounds coming from all six strings — is the most important concept for successful left-hand blues rhythm technique.

Figure 4-5 shows four different E-based forms at the fifth fret — Am, A7, Am7, and A7sus. Note that these forms, like their open-position counterparts (see Figure 4-1 for all the open-position A forms), require fewer fingers than the major form. Hopefully, they're easier to play, too.

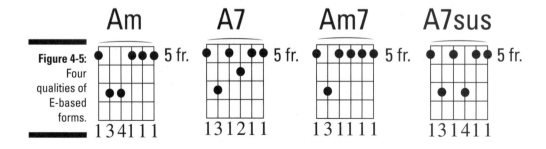

Figure 4-5: Four qualities of E-based forms.

Figure 4-6 is a progression that uses the new chord qualities from Figure 4-5. Remember to say the names of the chords, according to their corresponding note on the sixth string, as you change positions.

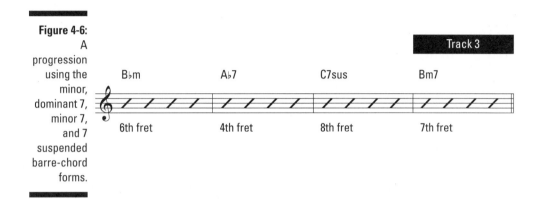

Figure 4-6: A progression using the minor, dominant 7, minor 7, and 7 suspended barre-chord forms.

Playing A-form barre chords

A-form barre chords are based on the open-position A chord. Follow these steps to form the A-form barre chord:

1. **Fret the A chord with fingers two, three, and four.**

2. **Slide the whole chord up one fret, so your A chord rests on the third fret.**

   Sliding an A chord up one fret, or half step, produces a B♭ chord. See Figure 4-7 for the fingering diagram, and note that the sixth string isn't used in the A-based barre chord (indicated by an *X* above the sixth string).

3. **Place your index finger across the first fret up to and including the fifth string.**

4. **Slowly strum the chord with your right hand, from the fifth string to the first, and listen to make sure that all five strings ring out clearly.**

When faced with an A-form barre chord, there's a twist. To maximize the quality of this chord, make sure to play it two ways:

✔ With three individual fingers and the index finger as the barre

✔ As a two-finger, "double barre" chord, using just the first and third fingers

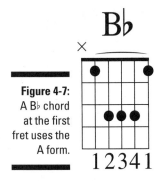

Figure 4-7:
A B♭ chord
at the first
fret uses the
A form.

Most blues guitarists play the chord by using the double-barre version because it's easier and faster. Figure 4-8 shows the alternate fingering.

Figure 4-8:
The
alternate,
double-
barre
fingering for
the A-form
barre chord.

Even if you opt for the four-fingered version of the chord in the lower frets, you find you must resort to the double-barre version as you venture up the neck (past the fifth fret or so) because the frets become too small to cram three fingers in the space of one fret. So though it's possible to play the A-form barre chord with the top string sounding, most people play just the inside four strings, using the double-barre method.

Moving the A-form around the neck

The A-form barre chord corresponds to the open fifth-string A, so when moving this chord around the neck, you can determine the chord's name by its fifth-string note. Memorize the names of the notes on the fifth string up to the 12th fret, just as you did with the E-form barre chord and the sixth string.

Figure 4-9 is an exercise that uses only the A-form barre chord. I've put in the fret number under the staff, but you should be able to use just the chord's name to tell you where to place the chord.

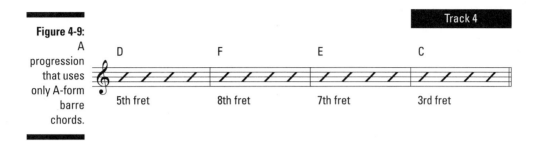

Figure 4-9: A progression that uses only A-form barre chords.

Other A forms: Minor, dominant 7, minor 7, and 7 suspended

Just as you can play different A chord qualities in open position, you can apply these chords to their barre forms, too. Finger these new chords as you did with the major form: Either place the barre down and form the rest of the chord with your remaining fingers or take the alternate approach by placing your second, third, and fourth fingers on the open position chords, sliding the whole form up a fret, and then pressing down across the top five strings with your first finger for the barre.

After you get familiar with forming barre chords, you find yourself grabbing the entire chord form at once — not finger by finger — just as you do with open-position chords.

Figure 4-10 shows four different qualities of A forms and provides a chord progression designed to get you moving around the neck. The fret numbers have been added in the staff to help you orient yourself.

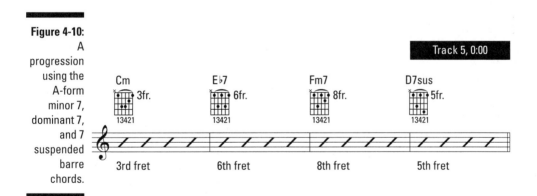

Figure 4-10: A progression using the A-form minor 7, dominant 7, and 7 suspended barre chords.

Combining forms

If you want to move efficiently up and down the neck of your guitar, use a combination of forms. For example, to play the chords A, D, and E (a common grouping of chords for songs in the key of A) in barre form, you wouldn't use just the E form or just the A form, because you have to make large leaps up and down the fretboard.

Instead, use a combination of the E- and A-forms that yield economic movement — distances of only two frets or so. For example, if you substitute the E form for the A chord, you wind up at the fifth fret — a good, central location on the neck. But instead of jumping up to the tenth fret to play the D chord, use the A-form barre chord, which allows you to play D at the same fret as the A chord. Then to play the E chord, simply move the A form up two frets to play the E chord at the seventh fret.

Figure 4-11 shows an exercise with mixed E- and A-forms in the progression described in the previous paragraph. This task gives you practice in switching forms as well as moving around the neck.

Track 5, 0:21

Figure 4-11:
Combining
A- and E-
form barre
chords in a
progression.

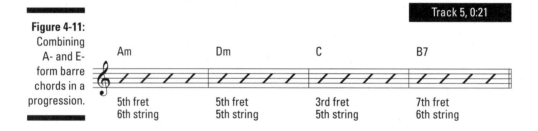

Am	Dm	C	B7
5th fret	5th fret	3rd fret	7th fret
6th string	5th string	5th string	6th string

Taking Advantage of Versatile Power Chords

After you master barre chords (see "Going to the Next Level: Barre Chords" earlier in the chapter), you may want to try power chords. *Power chords* aren't barre chords; they're two- and three-finger chords that are movable. The "power" part of the chord makes these chords sound like rock 'n' roll, because they're neither major nor minor, and they use a lot of distortion — a major staple of the rock sound (for more on distortion, see Chapter 15). But blues players since Muddy Waters and Chuck Berry have recognized the usefulness of power chords in blues, too.

The power chord gets its name from rock-guitar vocabulary, because it sounds better than saying "G no third," although that's technically what this chord is.

A power chord is used for distortion because it doesn't have a lot of notes that can sound noisy when subjected to the extreme overdrive treatment of a lot of rock effects. However, power chords are useful in blues because they have a versatile, open sound that lacks the interval that defines whether a chord is major or minor (also called a third).

Figure 4-12 shows the two forms — the E form and the A form — of the three-note power chord (consisting of the root, fifth, and octave root but no third).

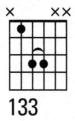

Figure 4-12:
The E- and A-form power chords.

For distorted, rock-based blues, use power chords and not full five- or six-string barre chords. Distortion emphasizes the higher harmonics of a chord, and major and minor thirds — and other intervals other than the root and the fifth — tend to make the sound noisy and muddy.

Chapter 5

Positioning the Right Hand for Rhythm and Lead

Chords, which I explore in Chapter 4, don't by themselves convey anything meaningful. They're just raw building materials of music until you arrange and play them in a certain way. For guitarists, the *playing* part comes when you add in the right hand. By playing chords with the right hand in a certain tempo, rhythm, and strumming pattern, you enter into the world of rhythm guitar — an indispensable part of the blues.

Strumming Along

One of the most basic ways you can play chords is with a *strum*. Strumming involves taking your right hand and, with a pick, thumb, or the back of your fingernails, brushing it across several or all the strings, sounding them simultaneously. A strum can be slow, fast, hard, or gentle, or any of the infinite shadings in between. When you strum, bring your hand from the top of the guitar (closest to the ceiling) to the bottom (toward the floor) in one motion, striking the strings along the way.

If you've never played with a pick before, you may find it takes a little time and practice to figure out how tightly to hold the pick when strumming (see Chapter 3 for the correct way to hold a pick). If you grip it too tightly, the pick gets tripped up in the strings and your right hand doesn't flow smoothly. On the other hand, if you hold the pick too loosely, it may spring out of your fingers when you strike the strings! The important thing is to keep the right hand and arm flowing smoothly while you find just the right grip.

Stroking down . . .

You may not have thought of basic strumming as "executing a downstroke," but that's what you're doing when you go to naturally strike the strings on a guitar. When you get to more complex strumming patterns — especially ones involving syncopation — you distinguish between downstrokes and upstrokes (see the next section). But for now, focus on the more popular and prevalent downstroke strum.

A *downstroke* (indicated with the symbol ⊓) is played with a downward motion of the pick, toward the floor — the way you naturally strike a guitar. You can strum multiple strings or pick an individual string with a downstroke; here you focus on many, but later in the book you play single notes with downstrokes.

. . . And stroking up

An *upstroke* (indicated by the symbol V) is played upward, toward the ceiling, in the opposite direction of a downstroke. So instead of dragging your pick down toward the floor, as you did in a downstroke, you start from a position below the first string and drag your pick upward across the strings, from first to sixth.

This motion may seem a little less natural and comfortable than a downstroke, but with practice, you can perform upstrokes as easily and with as much control as downstrokes.

In an upstroke, you don't need to worry about hitting all the strings. The top three or four strings are usually sufficient. For example, when playing an E chord with an upstroke, you don't have to strum the strings all the way from the first to the sixth, just up to about the third or fourth string. There are exceptions to this rule, but generally, in the blues, you don't hit as many strings on an upstroke strum as you do in a downstroke.

Upstrokes don't get equal playing time as downstrokes do. You typically use upstrokes only in conjunction with downstrokes, but you use downstrokes by themselves fairly often in blues playing.

Combining down and up

In certain fast lead passages, upstrokes alternate with downstrokes, making them appear in virtually equal numbers. For fast eighth notes, the strict observance of upstrokes following downstrokes is called *alternate picking* and is the key for playing fast leads smoothly. So for now, practice upstrokes as they occur in their natural state — in an eighth-note rhythm in between downstrokes (see the section "Eighth-note striking, twice per beat," later in this chapter).

Striking to a beat

Regardless of whether your hand moves up or down when it strikes the strings, the important thing to remember is that you're striking in a rhythm — or in sync with the beat. If you strike the strings once per beat, you're playing quarter notes. If you play two strokes per beat, you're playing in eighth notes, which come twice as fast as quarter notes.

If you need help hearing just what the beat is, get a *metronome* — an electronic device that taps out the beat for you. You can buy a metronome at any music store, and many models are small enough to fit right in your guitar case.

Quarter-note striking, beat by beat

Figure 5-1 shows two bars of an E chord with quarter-note slashes. You play four strums for each bar for a total of eight strums. The quarter notes tell you that the strums occur once per beat. Listen and play along with the CD, and before long, your sound can sound just like the recording.

Figure 5-1:
Strumming
an E chord
in quarter
notes for
two bars.

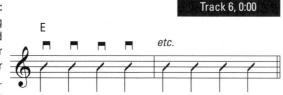

Track 6, 0:00

Eighth-note striking, twice per beat

Eighth notes come twice as frequently as quarter notes, in the same tempo, or two for every beat, instead of one. Instead of the previously used slashes, you now face slashes with *stems* (the vertical lines attached to the *slash noteheads* — not the round, normal noteheads) and *beams* (the horizontal lines that connect the stems). Quarter notes have just a stem attached to them; eighth notes have stems with beams connecting them to each other. An eighth note by itself has a flag instead of a beam: ♪.

For the eighth notes that appear in Figure 5-2, you strum twice as fast (two per beat) as you do for the quarter notes (one per beat). You can do this easily with downstrokes at most blues tempos, which are slow to moderate (between 60 and 160 on your metronome). To make things interesting, change chords and introduce A and B7 into the mix. Note that in the figure, the last note of each bar is a quarter note, which gives you a little more time than two eighth notes would for changing chords. Aren't I a nice guy?

Figure 5-2:
Playing eighth-note and quarter-note strums in down-strokes.

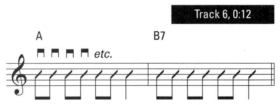

Track 6, 0:12

Figure 5-3 combines downstrokes and upstrokes in an eighth-note rhythm. As you practice this passage, keep a relaxed, free-swinging, up-and-down arm motion going. Also work to get equal emphasis on the downstrokes and upstrokes. You may notice that your downstrokes naturally include more and lower strings, while the upstrokes play just the top strings and fewer of them. Remember, this is perfectly natural.

At a moderate tempo, you can easily play Figure 5-3 with all downstrokes, but that variation gives the figure a different feel — more driving and intense. It may be a subtle difference, but playing an eighth-note figure in all downstrokes — versus playing it with alternating downstrokes and upstrokes — is a *musical* choice, not a technical consideration.

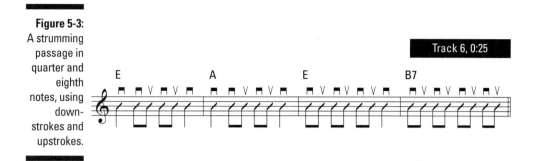

Figure 5-3:
A strumming passage in quarter and eighth notes, using down-strokes and upstrokes.

Track 6, 0:25

Mixing Single Notes and Strumming

Downstrokes and upstrokes are used for playing single notes as well as for strumming. Combining single notes with strums is an important part of rhythm guitar playing and gives the guitarist more options than just strumming. For example, a piano player doesn't plunk down all her fingers at once every time she plays, and guitarists shouldn't have to strike all the strings every time they bring their picks down (or up, for that matter).

In fact, guitarists share a technique with their keyboard-pounding counterparts — they play bass notes with the left hand and chords with the right hand. When guitarists separate the bass notes from the chord, they do it with just the right hand, but the principle is the same.

Separating bass and treble: The pick-strum

Separating the bass and treble so they play independently is a great way to provide rhythmic variety and introduce different textures into your playing. In the *pick-strum* pattern, the *pick* refers to picking the single bass note, and the *strum* refers to the upper-string chord that follows. Both the *pick* and the *strum* are played with the pick in downstrokes.

Figure 5-4 is a simple pick-strum pattern that's used in many folk blues and country blues songs. This notation mixes single notes (which appear with normal, rounded noteheads) and rhythm slashes (with the narrower, elongated noteheads).

Playing common pick-strum patterns

Most strumming patterns in blues are either all strums or a pick-strum combination, and which approach you use depends on the instruments in your ensemble at the time. A *pick-strum approach* is good for solo playing or if you're the only rhythm instrument, because the bass notes fall on different parts of the measure than the chord parts.

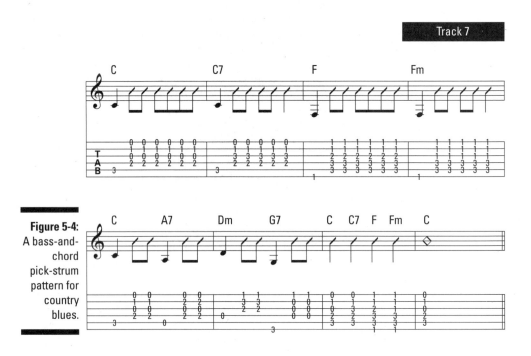

Figure 5-4: A bass-and-chord pick-strum pattern for country blues.

If you're playing solo guitar, you play a lot more pick-strum patterns. In a band setting, you usually have a bass player who handles the bass duties, and it's more appropriate to play all strumming patterns, so as not to get in his way.

The following sections include other pick-strum patterns for the most common blues feels.

Two-beat or cut shuffle

The two-beat or cut shuffle is sometimes referred to as a *boom-chick* pattern because the bass note and chords alternate, as shown Figure 5-5. A two-beat feel is common in other forms of music (Dixieland and big-band jazz, polka, samba, and country), but it has its place in the blues, too.

Track 8

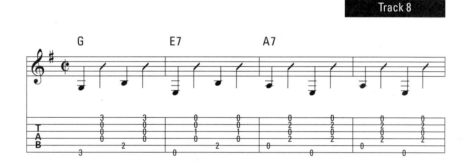

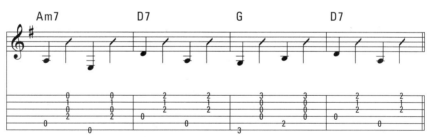

Figure 5-5: A two-beat, or cut shuffle, feel alternates bass notes with the chords.

The 12/8 groove

The 12/8 groove is the slowest pattern of the blues, so it helps to have the bass note play twice on beats one and three, while the chords play on beats two and four, as shown in Figure 5-6.

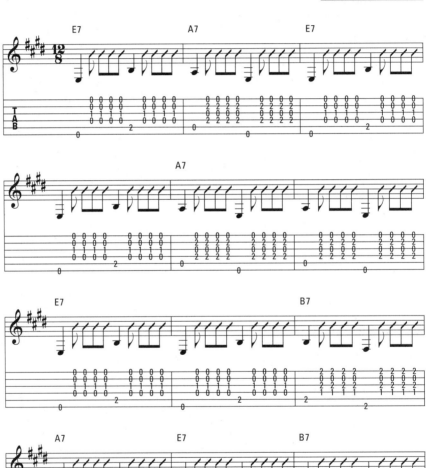

Figure 5-6: A pick-strum pattern in a slow 12/8 feel.

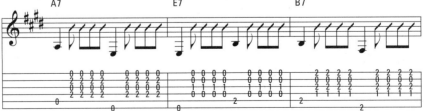

Shuffling the Beats with Syncopated Strumming

After you develop a feel strumming in different combinations of eighths, quarters, and 16ths (which come four per beat, or twice as fast as eighth notes), you can increase the rhythmic variation to these various groupings by applying syncopation. *Syncopation* is the disruption or alteration of the expected sounds of notes. In blues rhythm playing, you can apply syncopation by staggering your strum and mixing up your up- and downstrokes to strike different parts of the beats. By doing so, you let the agents of syncopation — dots, ties, and rests — steer your rhythmic strumming to a more dramatic and interesting course.

A bit of notation: Dots that extend and ties that bind

A *dot* attached to a note increases its rhythmic value by half the original length. So a dot attached to a half note (two beats) makes it three beats long. A dotted quarter note is one and a half beats long or the total of a quarter note plus an eighth note.

A *tie* is a curved line that connects two notes of the same pitch. The value of the tied note adds to the original, so that only the first note is sounded, but the note is held for the duration of the two notes added together.

Figure 5-7 shows a chart of how dots and ties alter the standard note values of eighth, quarter, and half notes.

Syncopation: Playing with dots and ties

So how do dots and ties actually make syncopation in a musical context? There are two progressions — one in a straight-eighth feel and another in a shuffle — that you can practice playing in this section. They both have common syncopation figures used in the blues.

The normal flow of down- and upstrokes is interrupted in syncopation, so it's important to remember which stroke direction to play a note to avoid getting your strums out of sync.

Figure 5-7:
A chart
of dots,
ties,
rests and
common
syncopation
figures.

➖ whole rest, 4 beats

➖ half rest, 2 beats

𝄽 quarter rest, 1 beat

𝄾 eighth rest, 1/2 beat

𝄿 16th rest, 1/4 beat

In both Figures 5-8 and 5-9, pay close attention to the downstroke (⊓) and upstroke (∨) indications. Figure 5-8 is a straight-eighth-note feel, in the key of A. The use of dots and ties signals a syncopated rhythm. If the tied figures present a problem, practice the figure by first ignoring the ties (in other words, play the tied note).

Figure 5-9 is in a *shuffle* feel in the key of A. A shuffle rhythm divides the quarter note into two eighth notes, but the first eighth note is held longer than the second, producing a swinging, lilting feel. The same syncopation scheme appears here as it did in Figure 5-8, but the shuffle feel makes it fall in a slightly different place in the beat.

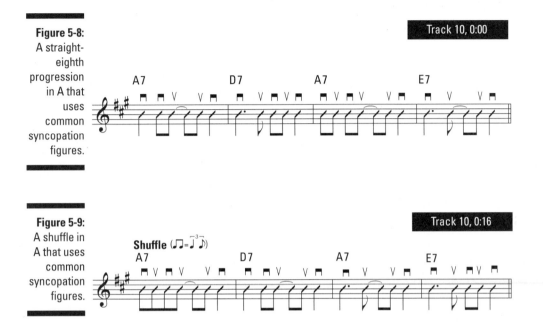

Figure 5-8: A straight-eighth progression in A that uses common syncopation figures.

Track 10, 0:00

Figure 5-9: A shuffle in A that uses common syncopation figures.

Track 10, 0:16

Stopping the String Ringing (Just for a Sec)

Listen to blues rhythm guitar and you hear that it's not one repetitive wall of sound, but an open, varied sound with breathing room and subtle breaks. It's these breaks that prevent the chord strums from running into each other and creating sonic mush. The little gaps in sound keep a strumming figure sounding crisp and controlled.

To create a rhythm guitar part with some breathing space between the notes, you need to stop the strings from ringing momentarily. And I'm talking *very small* moments here — much smaller than can be indicated by a rest symbol in the music. You can stop the strings instantly with the left hand — letting the left hand go limp is the best and quickest way to stop a string from ringing — far faster and more controlled than anything you can do with the right hand.

This left-hand technique may seem out of place in a chapter devoted to the right hand, but it belongs here because it's a coordinated effort between the two hands, which can only occur when the right hand plays.

Muting the sound between two chords (left hand)

To get the left hand to mute (indicated by an X notehead) the in-between sound between any two chords, just relax slightly the fretting fingers enough to release pressure on the fretted strings. The strings instantly deaden, completely cutting off the sound. If your right hand keeps going in the established strumming pattern, you produce a satisfying *thunk* sound as the right hand hits all these deadened strings.

The muted strings intermixed with the sounding strings create a percussive and syncopated rhythm. Allowing your left hand to mute means you don't have to stop and start your right hand to produce syncopation. You can keep it going uninterrupted, in alternating down- and upstrokes.

Simulating syncopation with left-hand muting

Left-hand muting gives you the means to control the strings' sound. Figure 5-10 is technically a straight-ahead down-up eighth-note strum in the right hand. But because you employ left-hand muting, the sound seems to cut off in just the right places, creating a syncopated sound. Your right hand isn't performing *true* syncopation, because it's playing straight through. It's just that some of the notes don't come through audibly.

Figure 5-10:
A strumming pattern that employs left-hand muting to simulate syncopation.

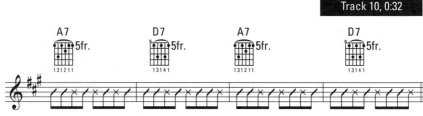

Track 10, 0:32

Guitarists seem to develop left-hand muting naturally, almost as if it wasn't a technique you had to learn but a way of playing that evolves. So don't try to analyze it too much, or slow your playing down as you're learning; just strum and relax and tighten your left hand in the context of a medium-tempo groove. Eventually, your two hands sync up without even thinking about it.

Muting the sound of a note (right hand)

Right-hand muting is a technique entirely separate from left-hand muting (see the previous section) and produces a totally different effect. When you mute with your right hand, you still hear the pitch and tone of the vibrating string but in a subdued way — more like a true mute, in the musical sense. Right-hand muting keeps the string from ringing freely and reduces the volume and ringing of your strings while still maintaining drive and intensity. This technique is a great way to add dramatic variation to your playing.

Two ways to play the right-hand mute include the following:

- **Palm mute:** The *palm mute* is another name for the right-hand mute and is executed by resting the heel of your right-hand on the strings just above the bridge.

  If you place your hand too far forward, you completely deaden the strings, so place it just forward enough of the bridge that the strings still sound but are dampened. Keep your hand in position through the duration of the strum.

- **Accent:** The *accent* is the opposite of a palm mute: It highlights a strike and lets the resulting sound ring out. To accent a chord, just strike it harder than usual and allow the strings to ring free. The result is that the accented strum stands out above all the rest. An accent is indicated with a > just above or below the notehead.

Palm mutes are usually applied to only one or two strings, because the right hand is restricted when you rest it directly on the strings above the bridge. Figure 5-11 is a rhythm figure where you strike only the lowest two strings of the chord during the palm mutes and the upper strings on the accents. Play this progression by using all downstrokes to add intensity.

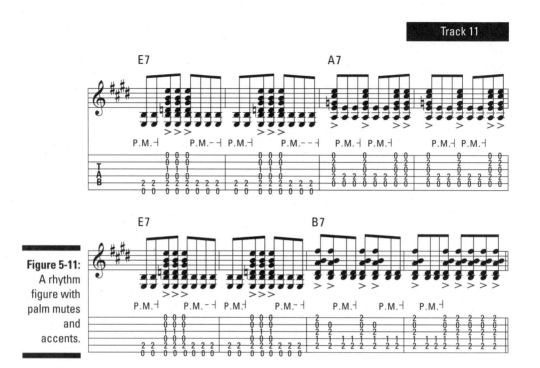

Figure 5-11: A rhythm figure with palm mutes and accents.

Copying the Classics: Plucking Fingerstyle Blues

If you want to make money playing the blues, you should probably get yourself an electric guitar and play it with a pick (make sure to practice the styles presented in the following section). But if you want insight into the roots of the blues, grab an acoustic and play it fingerstyle. Acoustic fingerstyle blues is a wonderful tradition, populated with such immortal figures as Robert Johnson, Skip James, Lightnin' Hopkins, Mance Lipscomb, Leadbelly, Mississippi John Hurt, Reverend Gary Davis, John Hammond, Rory Block, Roy Book Binder, Bob Brozman, Jerry Reed, and Chet Atkins.

Early solo blues guitar players quickly realized that separating the thumb and fingers was a great way to get the bass line going independent of the chords and riffs above it. So acoustic fingerstyle blues is best played with an independent thumb. And more than just using the thumb to hit the bass notes while the fingers brush the treble strings, *independent thumb* means that the thumb and fingers can play separate musical roles — almost like a mini rhythm section. The thumb can be the bass player, and the fingers can provide chords like the guitar's traditional role.

Figure 5-12 shows a basic fingerstyle pattern where the thumb drives out a steady quarter note rhythm on the low strings, and the thumb plays chords on the offbeats. Listen closely to the CD to capture the shuffle feel in this figure.

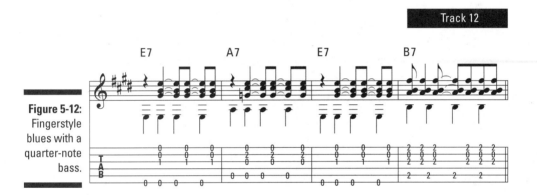

Track 12

Figure 5-12:
Fingerstyle blues with a quarter-note bass.

The Right Hand's Bliss: Different Rhythm Styles to Play

Blues consists of a few different feels, and if some songs sound like others (as *some* people say), it's partly because of the relatively few feels. Table 5-1 is a list of the common blues feels and well-known songs written in that feel (and if you don't know these songs, find them and listen to them).

Table 5-1	Blues Songs by Groove	
Feel	*Song*	*Artist*
Shuffle	Sweet Home Chicago	Robert Johnson, The Blues Brothers
	Blue Suede Shoes	Carl Perkins, Elvis Presley
	Midnight Special	Leadbelly
	Hide Away	Freddie King, Eric Clapton, Stevie Ray Vaughan
12/8	Stormy Monday	Allman Brothers, T-Bone Walker
	Red House	Jimi Hendrix
	At Last	Etta James
	The Sky Is Crying	Elmore James, Stevie Ray Vaughan
Two-beat	Maybellene	Chuck Berry
	Got My Mojo Working	Muddy Waters
	I Found a New Baby	Charlie Christian
Straight-four	The Thrill Is Gone	B.B. King
	Killing Floor	Howlin' Wolf, Mike Bloomfield, Jimi Hendrix
	Crossroads	Robert Johnson, Cream
	Born Under a Bad Sign	Albert King, Cream
16 feel	Hard to Handle	Otis Redding, Black Crowes
	Little Wing	Jimi Hendrix, Stevie Ray Vaughan
	Mary Had a Little Lamb	Buddy Guy, Stevie Ray Vaughan

The shuffle groove

The *shuffle groove* is certainly the most common feel in blues — more common than the straight-four and slow 12/8 feel. There's one small hurdle to get over: A shuffle feel uses a triplet-based rhythmic division, where each quarter note is divided into eighth-note triplets. The typical melodic division is two eighth notes, where the first note is held for the duration of the first two notes of the triplet, and the second eighth note is the third note of the triplet. This yields a lopsided, lilting feel in the eighth-note flow that's the heart of the shuffle sound.

Figure 5-13 is a progression in a shuffle feel. Practice while listening to the CD on this one to make sure that you get the sound of the shuffle.

The driving straight-four

The *straight* in straight-four refers to the eighth notes being evenly spaced, just as they are in most *normal* music forms you encounter. The *four* is four-four time, which is the most common time signature for blues. This explanation may sound mundane, except when you consider that most blues is in a shuffle feel, so the word *straight* indicates that you're doing something a little uncommon for the blues. Figure 5-14 shows a driving straight-four groove.

The slow 12/8, with groups of three

The *slow* part of the slow 12/8 feel is easy to grasp. The 12/8 is related to the shuffle, because a shuffle is a four-four feel based on triplet divisions of eighth notes. But in 12/8, the feel is slower, and the individual eighth notes (they're not triplets, because their grouping of three is built into the time signature) are given more prominence.

Don't be intimidated by the 12/8 part of this feel. There are twelve eighth notes to the bar, and each eighth note gets one beat. In practice though, the eighth notes are grouped in four units of three each. So it's a lot like 4/4 time with eighth-note triplets on every beat. If it's a slow blues, and you can hear note-groupings of three, it's probably a 12/8 feel.

Famous blues songs in 12/8 include T-Bone Walker's "Stormy Monday," covered by the Allman Brothers on their *Live at Fillmore* album. Figure 5-15 is a passage in the style of "Stormy Monday."

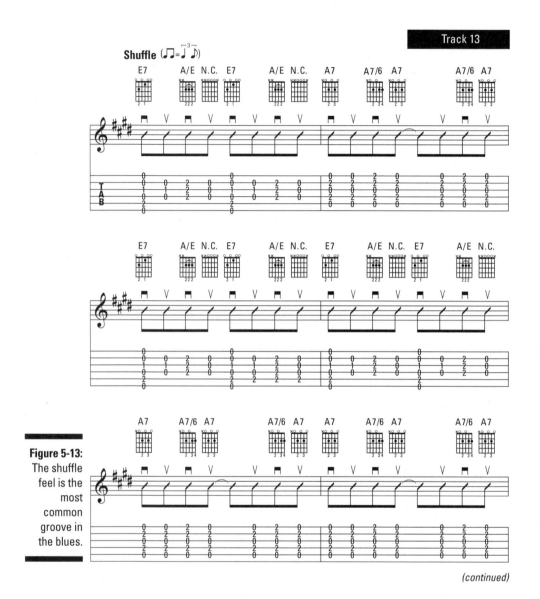

Figure 5-13: The shuffle feel is the most common groove in the blues.

(continued)

(continued)

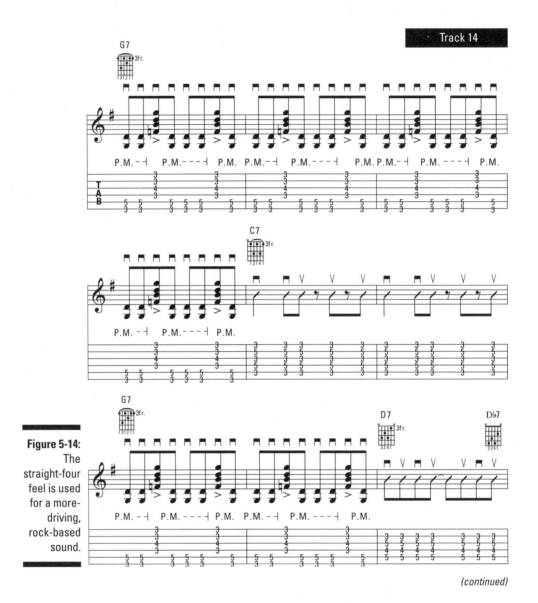

Figure 5-14: The straight-four feel is used for a more-driving, rock-based sound.

(continued)

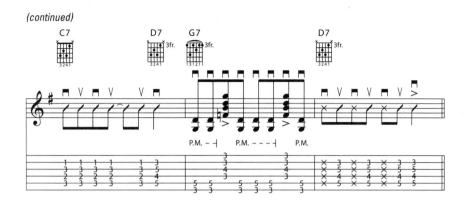

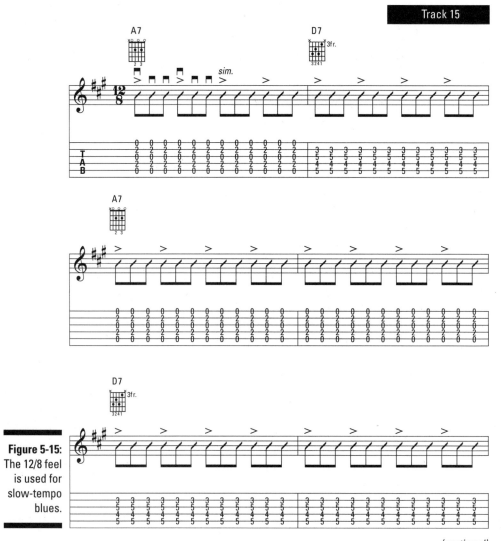

Figure 5-15:
The 12/8 feel
is used for
slow-tempo
blues.

(continued)

(continued)

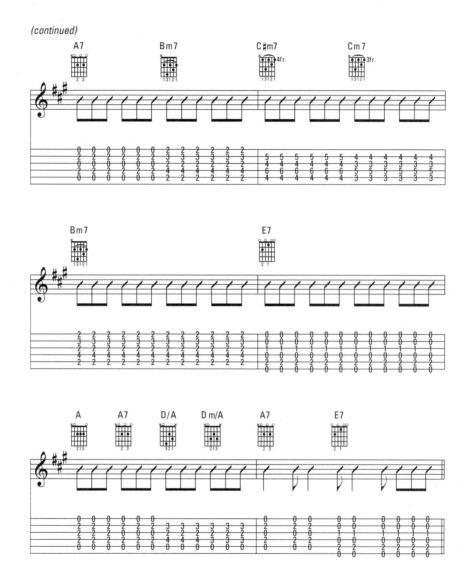

The two-beat feel

The two-beat feel came to the blues from Dixieland and big-band jazz and from novelty tunes. The lively pace of this style makes you want to jump, unlike the more sedate blues grooves. The two-beat feel, also called *cut time* or *cut shuffle,* is characterized by a pronounced *boom-chick, boom-chick* feel, where the *booms* are bass notes (usually alternating between the root and the fifth of the chord), and the *chicks* are the chords, shown in Figure 5-16.

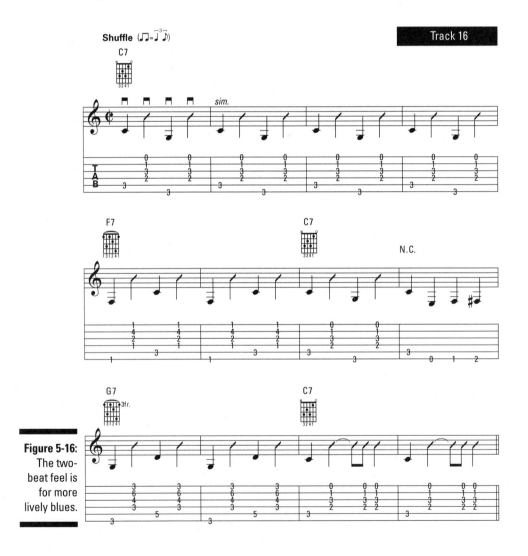

Figure 5-16: The two-beat feel is for more lively blues.

The slow and funky 16 feel

More modern blues grooves include the 16 feel, which has a slower tempo but funkier sound due to the 16th-note subdivisions. (James Brown's "I Feel Good" and "Papa's Got a Brand New Bag" are classic examples of 16th-note based funk.) "Hard to Handle," written by Otis Redding and covered by the Black Crowes, is a famous example of 16-feel blues. Figure 5-17 is medium tempo, funky groove in a 16 feel.

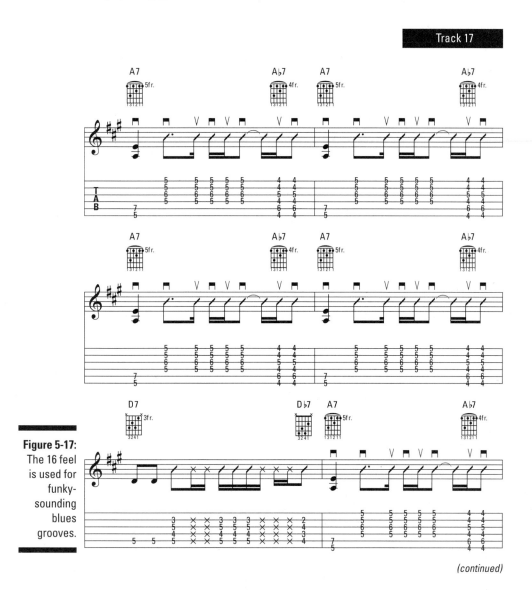

Figure 5-17: The 16 feel is used for funky-sounding blues grooves.

Track 17

(continued)

(continued)

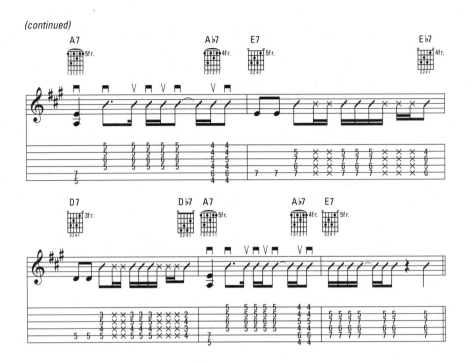

Chapter 6

Blues Progressions, Song Forms, and Moves

*B*lues is a welcoming, beckoning music for both listener and performer that says, "Join in and start contributing!" The blues' repetition and call-and-response qualities — derived from its forebears, the work song and field holler — make it easy for people to join in a song on the fly. Musicians can grasp the form quickly, and listeners have an expectation that's set up by each phrase, which is then satisfied by the lyrics or the chord progression. Best of all, these simple, infectious, and ingenious devices that make the blues so relatable are easy to understand and master, and are covered in this chapter.

Blues by the Numbers

You can learn music a lot quicker if you associate chords and keys by their numerical equivalents. In any key, the root or tonic (the tone that names the key or chord) becomes *one,* and subsequent pitches become *two, three, four,* and so on. These numbers are expressed in Roman numerals. So in the key of C, the numbers are broken down like this:

▶ C is I

▶ D is II

▶ E is III

▶ F is IV, and so on

As keys change, so do the letter names, but the numbers, or relationships, remain the same, allowing you to treat all keys equally. The number system works well for building chords by intervals, too, but in the blues, you're more concerned with chords formed on the notes of the scale of a key.

If you memorize the chord formula in numbers (I, IV, V), then you can figure out the progression in any key because the numbers — and therefore the relationships — don't change even if the letters do. Many people realize that since there are only seven letters in music (A through G), you can just memorize the keys without converting numbers to letters. And the more experienced you become, the more your ears take you to the right chord without having to memorize anything! But the numbers reveal the underlying structure, and are important in understanding the function of the chords.

Musicians often refer to chords by their numerical designation instead of their actual letter name. For example, when a musician says, "In that song, listen to what B.B. does when he goes to the IV chord," you know exactly where in the song that is (bar five). If the musician had said, "When B.B. goes to the D chord," you'd have to know what key he was in first, and you or the storyteller may not have that information. By viewing music through numbers, the key is irrelevant. Or more precisely, the key can change, but the function doesn't, and that's the important point of the exercise.

Recognizing the Big Dogs: Primary Key Families and Their Chords

Whether you play folk, rock, or blues, sooner or later you notice that certain chords seem to cluster together. If you think of these chords by their numerical assignments, or function, you see this phenomena is common to all keys. In every key, the main chords are the one, four, and five, represented by the Roman numerals I, IV, and V. These groupings of I, IV, V are known as *families*. It's a virtual certainty that whatever other chords you may find in a song, you always have a I, IV, and V. And many songs have only these three chords. Here's an example of how to figure out the I, IV, and V of different keys:

✔ In the key of A, A is the I chord.

- Count on your fingers up to your fourth finger, saying the letters of the alphabet as you go, and you find that the IV chord in A is D.

- The V chord, then, is E.

✔ In the key of C, C is the I chord.

- The IV chord is F.

- And the V chord is G.

Try it yourself with other keys, starting on I with the letter that names the key (in the key of G, G is I). Table 6-1 shows common blues keys and their I, IV, and V chords. There are other keys (for example, B and A♭), but these are the most commonly used keys for blues guitar.

Table 6-1	The I, IV, and V Chords in Common Blues Keys		
Key	*I*	*IV*	*V*
A	A	D	E
B♭	B♭	E♭	F
C	C	F	G
D	D	G	A
E	E	A	B
F	F	B♭	C
G	G	C	D

For guitarists, some keys and chords lend themselves certain movements that sound especially good for the blues; other keys are less successful. In the following section, I mix up the keys so you get familiar with the different families. But the blues is most accommodating to the keys of E and A, especially when using open-position chords.

The Structure of a Blues Song, Baby

It's time to give your hands some direction — to organize sounds into chord progressions and song forms. These larger organizing principles make the blues come alive and build a meaningful experience for the player and the listener. You watch techniques turn into expressions and patterns into musical messages. In this section, you take the shorter phrases of the right-hand patterns (covered in Chapter 5) and make them into actual songs.

A *song* is made up of a chord progression. The song's form and chord progression are concepts that can be used almost interchangeably, with chord progression describing more often the harmonic architecture of the song. Many people can recognize a song form — such as the 12-bar blues — but as a guitarist, you need to know the corresponding chord progression that makes up that 12-bar form (covered in the next section). And you need to be able to identify the actual chords going by as well as any variations to that form. In the blues, the progression is part of what makes the blues the blues. So the progression is synonymous with the form. In other words, saying "the blues" implies a 12-bar structure with the chords falling at specific bars within that structure.

A chord progression isn't the only aspect of a song, but it's a pretty important one, because it forms the framework or structure that supports the other elements: melody, lyrics, riffs, and the solo sections (something guitarists care deeply about).

Playing the 12-bar blues

The 12-bar blues is by far the most popular form for the blues. It consists of 12 measures and observes a particular scheme as shown in Figure 6-1.

I use Roman numerals instead of letter names in Figure 6-1, because the progression is the same in every key. For example, if you play blues in E, then E is the I chord, A is the IV chord, and B or B7 is the V chord. So with the corresponding letters substituted for the Roman numerals, the progression looks like Figure 6-2.

B7 replaces B because B7 is the easier of the two chords to play. Technically, you could play B as a barre chord on the second fret. But I want to convey the letter names dictated by the I, IV, and V, so playing either B7 or B is acceptable for this case.

Because the slashes (///) leave some interpretation in what you're playing, try this exercise *with shuffle eighth notes* (eighth notes that have a long-short rhythm scheme, which are explored in detail in Chapter 5) in alternating downstrokes and upstrokes. You hear this version on the CD, so see if you can match the rhythm of the performance on the audio.

Figure 6-1:
The 12-bar blues using Roman numerals to represent chords in a key.

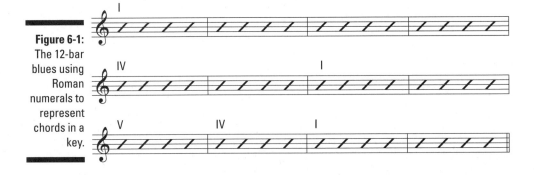

Track 18, 0:00

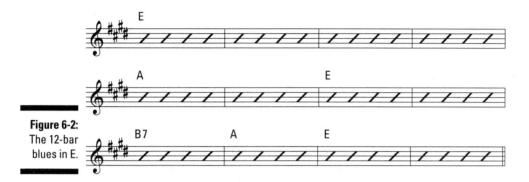

Figure 6-2:
The 12-bar
blues in E.

If you're a little shaky on the eighth-note strum for Figure 6-2, try first playing
this blues with quarter-note downstrokes (covered in Chapter 5). Don't
worry, you're still in sync with the CD, but the guitar on the CD strums two
chords to your one. After you can play that comfortably, try playing with
eighth-note downstrokes in a shuffle feel. After that, try the alternate-picking
approach, which is discussed in Chapter 5.

The quick four

The *quick four* is a variation on the 12-bar blues that occurs in the second bar,
where you go to a IV chord — for example, A in the key of E — for one bar, and
go back to the I chord for two bars. The quick four, as shown in Figure 6-3,
provides an opportunity for variation and interest in an otherwise unbroken
stretch of four bars of the same chord.

Track 18, 0:37

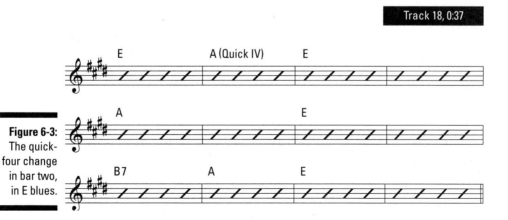

Figure 6-3:
The quick-
four change
in bar two,
in E blues.

The quick four happens just about as often as not in blues songs. Some songs that use the quick-four method include "Sweet Home Chicago" and "Hide Away." Songs such as "Hound Dog" and "Johnny B. Goode" don't use this variation. Most blues guitarists don't think too much about whether a song has a quick four. They just look at someone else in the band who knows more than they do to see if they're going to make that move in bar two or not.

The quick four happens very soon after you start the song, so if you're at a jam session, or are playing along with a song for the first time, you must be on your toes to anticipate its use.

The turnaround

The turnaround is the last two bars of the progression that point the music back to the beginning. At the end of the 12-bar blues, you can repeat the progression or end it. Most of the time you repeat the progression to play additional verses and solos. To help get the progression ready for a repeat, you employ a turnaround that sets up the repeat. At the most basic level, you can create a turnaround by just substituting a V chord for the I chord in the last bar — bar 12.

Practically all songs (blues or otherwise) end on a I chord (the tonic chord of the key), so the substitution of the V chord creates a strong pull that brings the song back to a I chord, which occurs at bar one of the progression. When the V chord occurs at the end of the progression, it tells musicians and listeners that "we're going back around again." While the most basic application of a turnaround is just playing a V chord in the last bar, to most guitarists, a turnaround presents an opportunity to play a riff or lick. Riffs are covered in Chapter 7. Figure 6-4 shows the last four bars of a 12-bar blues with a turnaround bar added .

Figure 6-4:
The turnaround can be a V chord substituting for I in the last bar.

Track 19

Bar 9 of 12-bar blues

The 12-bar blues in song

If you're wondering how musical charts and symbols relate to the actual songs (melody and lyrics), here's the quick version:

✔ The 12-bar blues breaks down neatly into three lines of four bars each. These three lines correspond to the vocal phrases.

✔ The vocal scheme of the blues is A-A-B. Each letter represents a sentence, complete thought, or phrase of the lyric.

✔ Think of any 12-bar blues, such as "Hound Dog," "Stormy Monday," "Kansas City," "St. Louis Blues," "Easy Rider," or "Corrina, Corrina." Each song has three lines per verse, with the first line repeated.

Even though the first vocal line is repeated, it never sounds repetitious, because the chords underneath the lyric and melody change, which provides interest. You can actually sing any of these songs along to any 12-bar progression.

You may see the V chord in the turnaround bar with parentheses around it. This method is shorthand for saying that you use the turnaround optionally or whenever you decide to repeat the progression. When you want the progression to end, you ignore the parentheses and continue playing the I chord from the previous bar.

Slow blues

Slow blues is usually a 12-bar blues, but played in 12/8 time, using three strums to the beat. Because of the slower tempo, there's often more opportunity to put in additional chords — especially with the use of ninth chords (for more on ninth chords, see Chapter 12), a common slow-blues hallmark.

Figure 6-5 is a slow 12-bar blues in 12/8 time with its own moves added — moves that consist of adding chords a whole step higher before the main ones. But it's still a 12-bar blues. You can hear a lot of this quality in the playing of T-Bone Walker.

One irony of slow blues is that while the tempo is slower than a shuffle, and the changes come more slowly and are therefore more manageable, the lead playing is often very intricate, especially with regard to rhythm. If you ever get a chance to see transcribed guitar solos in print, look at the ones in a slow 12/8. The notation can get quite hairy!

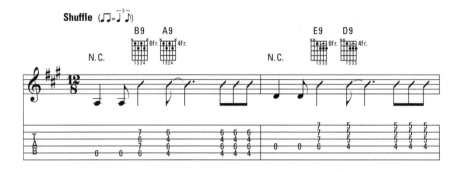

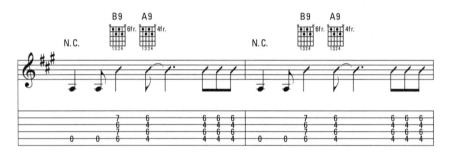

Figure 6-5: A slow blues in 12/8 with added chords.

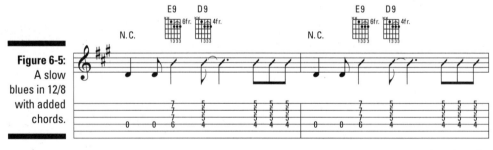

(continued)

(continued)

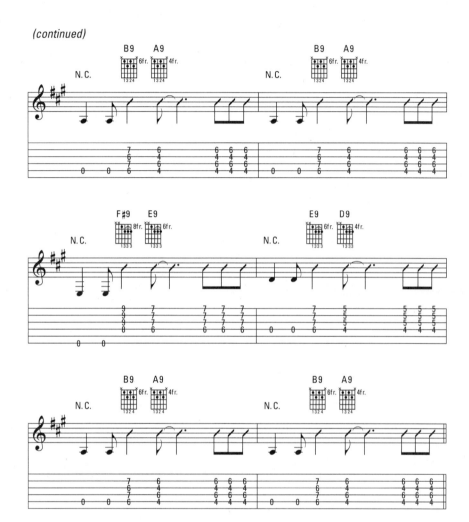

The 8-bar blues

The 8-bar blues is four bars shorter than the 12-bar blues, but the 8-bar blues doesn't really follow a strict form the way the 12-bar blues does. The 8-bar blues encompasses several feels, tempos, and qualities — often an 8-bar blues has more chords in it than just the basic I, IV, and V, making it more "songlike" than a 12-bar blues. Figure 6-6 is an 8-bar blues played with a bass-strum pattern by using a variety of chords.

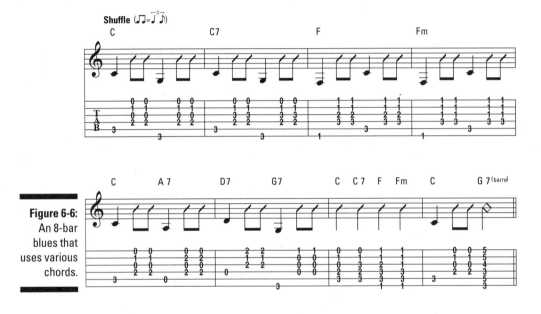

Figure 6-6:
An 8-bar blues that uses various chords.

Straight-four (or rock blues)

Straight-four is sometimes called *rock blues* or *rock feel* and means that you play even eighth notes supported by a heavy *backbeat* (emphasis on beats two and four, usually courtesy of a cracking snare drum). Most blues is in a *non-straight feel,* meaning it's either in a shuffle (a long-short scheme that derives from triplets) or a slow 12/8 feel (with three notes to the beat). So a straight-four, which is common in rock, is actually rare in traditional blues.

Some examples of well-known songs in a straight-four include "Roll Over Beethoven," "Johnny B. Goode," and Albert King's "Crosscut Saw." Figure 6-7 shows a straight-four progression in A with a variation on the 5-to-6 move (also called the Jimmy Reed, covered in the next section). This variation has the moving voice occasionally going up to the flat seven. (G in the A chord, C in the D chord, and D in the E chord.)

Track 22

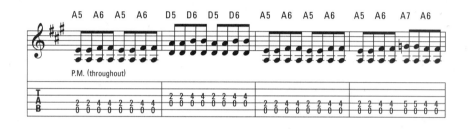

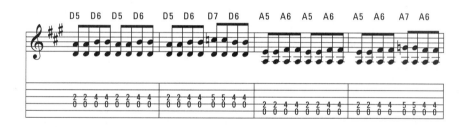

Figure 6-7: A straight-four progression with a variation.

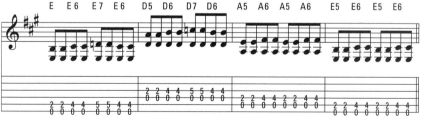

Applying Structures to Keys

Although every key is treated equally when discussing function and music theory (see "Blues by the Numbers" earlier in this chapter), the reality is that different keys and chords on the guitar present different moves. What you can do easily in E, you may not be able to do in G, and G has other options that E may not have. These variations are a delight (and frustration!) of playing the guitar. Each key has something idiomatic that can't be performed comfortably or convincingly in another key. Composers and musicians write and play songs in different keys to exploit these little differences that each key provides.

A move with many chords: The Jimmy Reed move

If you have the basic 12-bar blues under your belt, including the quick four and turnaround bar, it's time to shake things up a bit. (See the corresponding sections earlier in the chapter if you look under your belt and nothing's there.) I like to start off with a move that's been a blues and rock staple forever. It's known by many different names, but because this book is a blues book, I attribute it to one of its most famous practitioners — Jimmy Reed.

The *Jimmy Reed move* — named after the Chicago harmonica player, singer, and guitarist — involves going from the fifth to the sixth degrees in each chord (the note E in a G chord, A in a C chord). Chuck Berry made this technique famous in a straight-eighth, rock 'n' roll setting in the late '50s and '60s. For now, don't worry about converting numbers to notes for the I, IV, and V chords; just figure out the left-hand part.

To play a "move," you put your left hand in motion. Figure 6-8 shows the Jimmy Reed move in the key of E, using E, A, and B power chords (for more on power chords, see Chapter 4). The chord diagrams are given above the tab, allowing you to think of this move in two ways: as an extra chord inserted in between the ones you already know or as a simple one-finger move in the left hand. Whichever way works for you is the right one!

One of the best things about the Jimmy Reed move is that it works so well in different chords and keys. When played in different keys, the figure preserves the original relationship of the notes in the new key, but because it's in a different key, it just sounds, well, different. Not better or worse, perhaps, just different — and still very cool! It's like singing "Happy Birthday" in the key of G or E♭: You can recognize the melody in any key setting — but the Jimmy Reed move is so much hipper than "Happy Birthday."

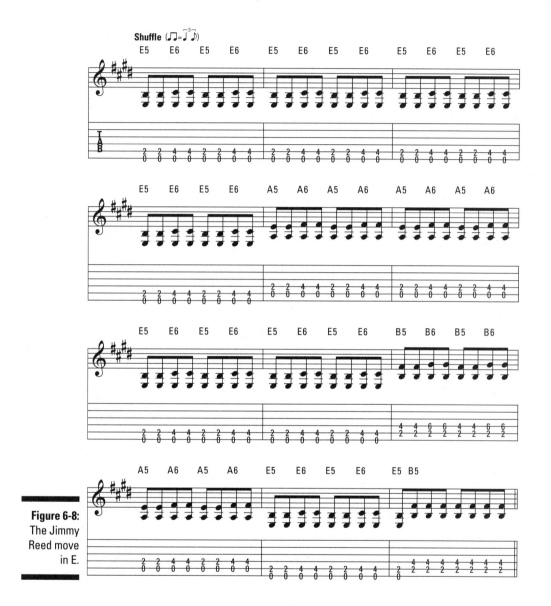

Figure 6-8:
The Jimmy
Reed move
in E.

Jimmy's move in G

If you had to play in the key of G, and you wanted to throw in the Jimmy Reed move from earlier in this section, it would look like Figure 6-9. This move has a different character and is a little easier to play than the same move in E (in the previous section). The chord diagrams in the figure are presented above the staffs, so you can view the move as either a new chord inserted between the ones you already know or as just simply moving a finger over to play a previously open string on beats two and four.

Figure 6-9:
The Jimmy Reed move in G.

(continued)

(continued)

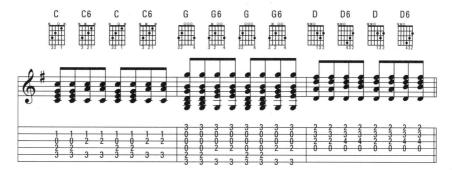

In the blues move in G, you have to mute the open string that your finger just left to play the new chord (indicated by an *X* in the chord diagram).

Jimmy's move in A

In this section, you familiarize yourself with the Jimmy Reed move in A. The move travels up the neck of the guitar to grab the IV and V chords (the technique is shown in Figure 6-10). This sound is very rock 'n' roll (and I mean that in a good way), and has a less folky character than the G progression in the previous section. The blues move in A has an entirely different feel than the same move in G, yet they're only one letter away — the basis for Chuck Berry's sound and for much of the "boogie" rock 'n' roll played by rockabilly artists of the '50s, '60s, and today. (For more info on rockabilly, see Chapter 11).

The sound of sadness: Minor blues

For a different flavor of blues, consider the blues in a minor key setting. Minor keys in music sound sad or menacing or mysterious, and what better way to give the blues a double dose of trouble than to put it in a minor key? Putting the blues in minor also provides some variety. A *minor blues* doesn't say much about the form, only that it uses minor chords instead of the usual major or dominant-seven chords. A minor blues can be a 12-bar blues with minor chords or a straight-eighth (or non-shuffle feel), 16-bar format (instead of the more common 12-bar format).

Track 25

Figure 6-10: The Jimmy Reed move in A.

(continued)

(continued)

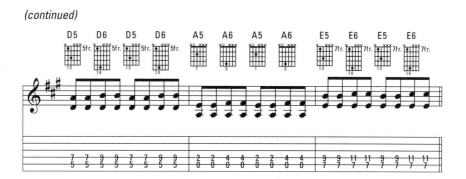

"St. James Infirmary" and "The Thrill Is Gone" are two minor blues songs. "The Thrill Is Gone" is a popular format for more contemporary blues, and Figure 6-11 shows a progression more along the lines of this song. Notice the addition of minor-seventh chords, which help give a jazzier feel.

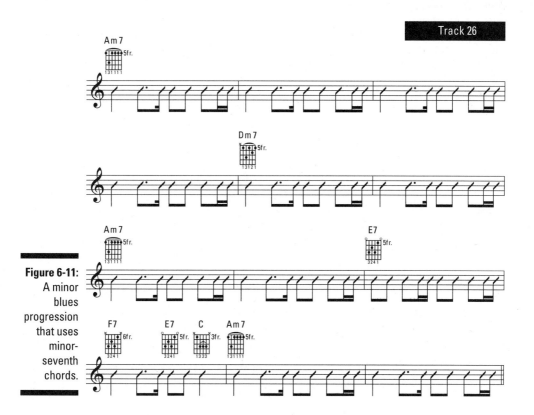

Figure 6-11: A minor blues progression that uses minor-seventh chords.

Track 26

Accessorizing the 12-Bar Blues: Intros, Turnarounds, and Endings

Intros (short for introductions), turnarounds, and endings are all enhancements to the 12-bar blues. They're used to steer the song toward repeats or resolutions and are all related. There are countless variations for these three devices, and they're often reworked versions of each other, where the only difference is how they end.

Intros

An *intro* often features a solo lick by the guitar, piano, or other instrument (think of "That'll Be the Day" by Buddy Holly). But sometimes the whole band plays the intro, and the guitar is expected to play rhythm guitar (licks and riffs are covered in Chapter 7).

Intros often borrow from their turnaround cousins, because the whole idea is to set up the I chord and the beginning of the progression — the same duties that the turnaround has. Turnarounds are covered in the next section.

Figure 6-12 shows a basic two-bar intro. The rhythm features a syncopation and then a held note, which creates a musical space (or hole) before the downbeat of the 12-bar progression. This space allows room for a vocal or instrumental melodic pickup — a phrase that starts before bar one.

Figure 6-12:
A simple
two-bar
intro.

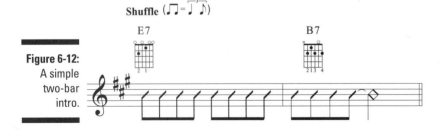

Figure 6-13 is a four-bar intro that is just the last four bars of the 12-bar blues. This intro is popular and is often announced by a musician saying, "Let's bring it in from the V," or "Let's walk it down from the V."

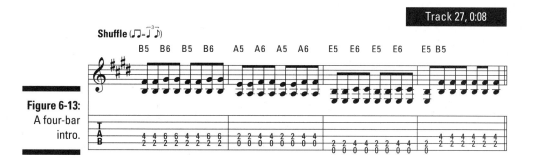

Figure 6-13:
A four-bar intro.

Turnarounds

A turnaround bar is a bar that substitutes a V chord for a I chord in the last bar of the progression — bar 12 in a 12-bar blues (see "Playing the 12-bar blues" earlier in this chapter). A true, full turnaround is, at minimum, a two-bar phrase that goes from the I chord to the V chord. *Note:* Entire books could be written on just turnarounds, but I'm only going to cover a few rhythm approaches in this section.

Figure 6-14 shows a simple two-bar turnaround using the Jimmy Reed move and syncopation.

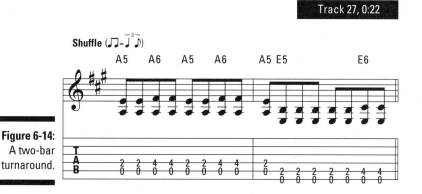

Figure 6-14:
A two-bar turnaround.

Figure 6-15 shows a more elaborate turnaround using one chord for every two beats or five different chords in all: C, C7, F, Fm, and G7 — all in the space of two bars.

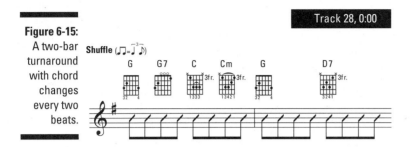

Track 28, 0:00

Figure 6-15:
A two-bar turnaround with chord changes every two beats.

Figure 6-16 is a variation of Figure 6-15, with a chromatic move in the last part. It's also in an unusual key — B♭.

Track 28, 0:10

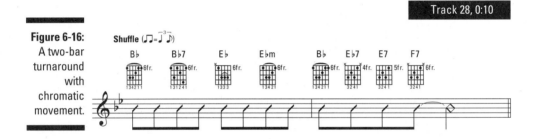

Figure 6-16:
A two-bar turnaround with chromatic movement.

Endings

Endings are closely related to turnarounds, except for the last part of the last measure. The last measure terminates on a I chord of some type. Figure 6-17 shows an ending that a slow blues often uses — a ninth chord for the final chord of the piece.

Track 29, 0:00

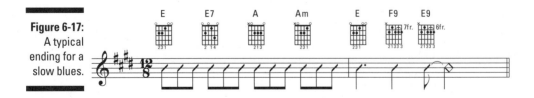

Figure 6-17:
A typical ending for a slow blues.

Figure 6-18 is an ending that's typical for medium-tempo shuffle tunes.

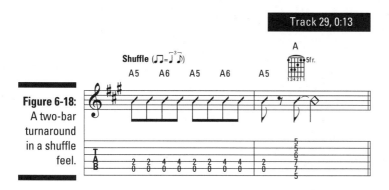

Track 29, 0:13

Figure 6-18:
A two-bar
turnaround
in a shuffle
feel.

High Moves

All the moves that are covered in the rest of this chapter have taken place on the lower strings. But you can play moves on the higher strings, too. These strings often involve the same notes that are played in the lower strings (the fifth and sixth of the chord featured in the Jimmy Reed move — covered in "Applying Structures to Keys" earlier in this chapter), but when played up high, it sounds more like a riff than a chord figure. This creates a bridge between chord figures and riffs and licks, which are explored in Chapters 7 and 8.

Think of these new, higher moves as chord forms added to your basic eighth-note strumming. As you play these added chords, notice that the sound produces a melodic motif. Figure 6-19 shows the first high-note move in the key of E. The two added chords are E7 chords with your fourth finger of the left hand playing notes on the second string.

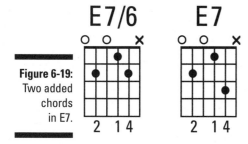

Figure 6-19:
Two added
chords
in E7.

Now add two chords to the A7 chord sequence. The notes are the same relative ones you added to the E7 chord — the sixth and the seventh. Figure 6-20 shows the fingering with the added notes played by the fourth finger of the left hand.

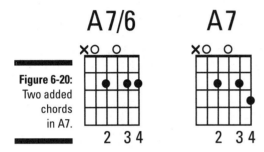

Figure 6-20:
Two added
chords
in A7.

For the B7 chord, in Figure 6-21, the fourth finger again plays the added note, but because the finger is already in place — on the second fret, first string — you must move it up to the third fret briefly. This may seem a bit awkward at first, and the stretch between your fourth and third fingers may take a while to get smoothly, but it will come in time.

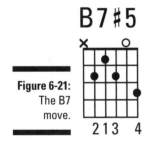

Figure 6-21:
The B7
move.

Figure 6-22 shows all three moves in a 12-bar blues. If some of the moves seem difficult, or come too fast, try leaving them out at first. As long as you don't break the rhythm in your right hand and you change left-hand chords where you're supposed to, the blues still sound fine. That's the beauty of the blues: You can play any variation on the basic structure — from simple to complex — and it always sounds good!

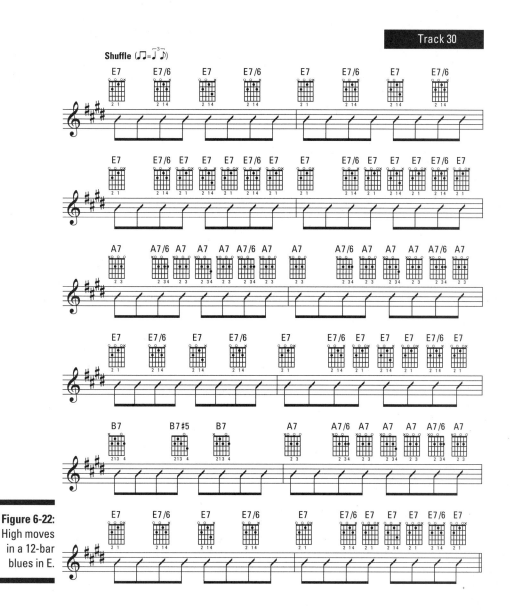

Figure 6-22: High moves in a 12-bar blues in E.

Chapter 7

Musical Riffs:
Bedrock of the Blues

....

In This Chapter

▶ Mastering the basics: Single-note riffs

▶ Exploring double-stop riffs

▶ Shooting for high-note riffs

▶ Taking your skills to the next level: Mastering rhythm figures

....

*I*t can be tough to find your own blues voice because you can't sponta-
neously improvise the blues any more than you can improvise baroque
or bebop; you have to learn the vocabulary. And the vocabulary for blues
includes licks and riffs.

Although related to chords, riffs aren't tethered to chords the way the rhythm-
based approach is (check out Chapter 6 for more about chords). It's always
good to know where your riffs spring from — especially if they're derived out
of a chord form! But you don't need to grab a chord first to play a riff. In this
chapter, you play riffs with a liberated left hand!

When you learn chords, strumming, double-stops, and single-note riffs, you
have most of the ingredients necessary to start really developing as a player.
In the blues, it's always a delicate balance between cloning the greats and
doing your own thing.

Basic Single-Note Riffs

A *riff* is a self-contained musical phrase, and it can be used to form the basis
for a song. Riffs are the bridge from chords to lead guitar. They're usually
based on single notes, but they can involve *double-stops* (two notes played
simultaneously) and bits of full-chord playing.

You may hear the terms *riff* and *lick* used interchangeably in your blues guitar career. But I like to think of a riff as more of a structural, repeatable phrase, and a lick as a *cliché,* that is, a self-contained lead figure that doesn't necessarily have structural importance (like those short, snappy melodic phrases played by blues and country guitar-players between vocal lines).

The signature guitar parts in the Stones' "Satisfaction" and the Beatles' "Day Tripper" are classic examples of riffs. In blues, the crisp, ascending, horn-like melodic bursts in Freddie King's "Hide Away" are riffs as is the repeating pattern in Bo Diddley's "I'm a Man."

In the next few sections, you look at riffs in order of increasing rhythmic activity, starting with quarter notes, advancing through eighth notes (the straight, shuffle, and triplet varieties), and moving to the more complex 16-note-based and syncopated riffs (which involve eighths and 16ths). Just as you do when playing chords, you must play riffs with a solid and consistent approach to articulation (attack), rhythm, and dynamics (overall loud and soft) to help keep the drive in the guitar part.

Use a metronome to help keep yourself playing along with the beat, and use a combination of your ears and muscle memory to make sure you strike the strings with the same force for achieving consistent dynamics.

For the low-down bass notes: Quarter-note riffs

You may think that you can't do much to groove hard with the boring ol' quarter note, but the quarter note drives a lot of boogie-woogie basslines. Boogie-woogie and blues are close cousins, and you can always throw in a boogie bass as a variation to almost any medium- to uptempo shuffle. Figure 7-1 shows a common quarter-note boogie pattern that you can play easily with just downstrokes.

Track 31, 0:00

Figure 7-1:
A boogie bassline in quarter notes.

The big daddy of riffs: Eighth-note riffs

Most riffs in blues are eighth-note based, so there's a wide range of music you can play in an eighth-note groove. But to start off, jump into eighth-note riffs by taking quarter-note riffs (from Figure 7-1) and doubling them up — that is, play two notes per beat instead of one. Figure 7-2 is a boogie-bass pattern in shuffle eighth-notes.

Track 31, 0:16

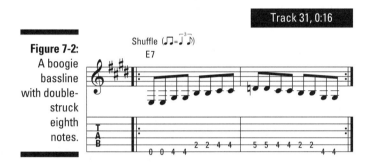

Figure 7-2: A boogie bassline with double-struck eighth notes.

Another popular riff is the stop-time feel. It features the low notes of the guitar. The entire band plays a figure in unison and stops at the downbeat of each measure in the phrase, like in "Blue Suede Shoes." This approach is used famously in the Muddy Waters tunes "Mannish Boy" and "Hoochie Coochie Man." A tribute to the stop-time riff is featured in Figure 7-3.

Track 31, 0:32

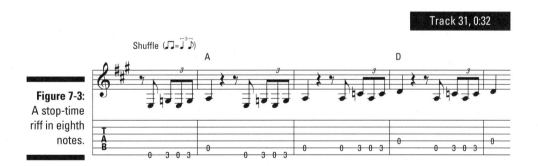

Figure 7-3: A stop-time riff in eighth notes.

Figure 7-4 shows a riff in the style of Freddie King's "Hide Away" — one of the most recognizable eighth-note riff-based songs in the blues repertoire!

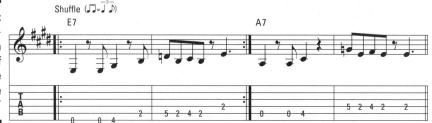

Figure 7-4: An eighth-note riff in the style of Freddie King's "Hide Away."

Adding a little funk: 16th-note riffs

Funky blues usually sound that way because 16th notes are in the mix. In a 16th-note groove, the tempos tend to be moderate. But because the beats use 16th-note subdivisions, the groove sounds quite active. Often the bassline and drums (particularly the hi-hat) employ 16th notes to lend support to the scratchings laid down by the guitar. Figure 7-5 is a 16th-note riff on the low strings that you play with strict alternate (down-up-down-up) picking.

Figure 7-5: A 16th-note riff, using alternate picking.

Throwing rhythm for a loop: Syncopated eighth-note riffs

Although syncopation isn't a huge influence in the blues (compared to, say, jazz, R&B, and funk), it's used sometimes and is always a welcome treat. For more information on syncopation and its mechanisms, flip back to Chapter 5. Figure 7-6 shows a syncopated blues line consisting of a dotted eighth, a tie, and 16th notes.

Track 32, 0:32

Figure 7-6:
An eighth-
note riff
featuring
common
syncopation
figures.

If you're practicing the syncopation in Figure 7-6 and it gives you trouble at first, try practicing the line without the tie (so you're playing both notes in the tie). Then, when you're confident with the figure, practice the tie by letting the note ring through.

Double the Strings, Double the Fun: Two-Note Riffs (or Double-Stops)

Riffs aren't restricted to single notes. In this section, I explore double-stops, a technique that doesn't strictly involve single notes. The term *double-stop* means *two strings*.

A double-stop applies to all string instruments when two notes are stopped or played together. Even when guitarists don't have to fret a string, they still refer to simultaneous two-string playing as *double-stops*. But more than just playing two strings (like in the Jimmy Reed figure in the next section), double-stop playing implies moving in lock step — and even performing bends, slurs, and vibrato (discussed in Chapter 10) on two strings at once.

Part of the versatility of a two-note figure is that it can be played on any two strings — low, high, and in the middle — all for a slightly different effect. When you get tired of playing chords and single-note leads, a two-note riff can be just the ticket to give your playing (and your listeners) a much-needed dose of dual-string diversity!

The 5-6 riff is a blues-rhythm hallmark of going from the fifth to the sixth degree in a chord (E to F♯ in an A chord) and is technically a double-stop, although the string motion doesn't proceed in parallel motion. But the right-hand coordination is the same: You strike two strings as if they're one every time your right hand comes in contact with the strings. The 5-6 riff is also known as the Jimmy Reed move, which is covered in Chapter 6.

In the following sections, I cover two 5-6 riffs, each in a different feel.

Straight feel

Straight-eighth notes are unusual in blues. But in blues-rock, classic rock 'n' roll, and rockabilly — all closely related to the blues — the straight-eighth feel rules. *Straight eighths* are spaced equally apart, whereas *shuffle eighths* follow a long-short scheme.

Chapter 6 tackles the basic 5-6 move, but Figure 7-7 shows an expanded version that uses linear movement instead of the more static, back-and-forth 5-5-6-6-5-5-6-6. Also think of the riff to Roy Orbison's (and later Van Halen's) "Oh, Pretty Woman" for a classic straight-eighth approach to a low-note riff.

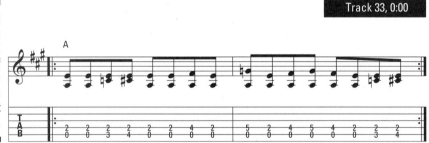

Track 33, 0:00

Figure 7-7: An expanded version of the classic 5-6 move in straight eighths.

Many eighth-note riffs sound equally good in a shuffle or straight-eighth feel. And in many early rock and R&B recordings, such as Chuck Berry's "Johnny B. Goode" and "Carol," you can actually hear some instruments playing straight eighths and others playing shuffle eighths! Try the passage in Figure 7-7 in a shuffle feel to see if it translates. Some riffs will work, and some won't. You don't really know until you try, and there's no harm in that, even when it doesn't work out.

Shuffle, or swing, eighths

Most blues are in a shuffle feel, and shuffle-based eighth-note riffs (also called swing eighths) are the most popular and numerous types of blues riffs. Countless tunes employ eighth-note riffs, including such hits as "Dust My Broom," and "Sweet Home Chicago." Figure 7-8 show you a classic shuffle rhythm that employs swing eighths and the occasional eighth-note triplet.

Track 33, 0:13

Figure 7-8:
A variation of the 5-6 move in swing eighths.

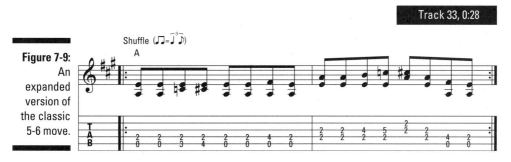

Figure 7-9 is an eighth-note riff with the melody weaving in and out of the low and high strings. This riff, once mastered, is tons of fun to play because it takes your left hand up and down and makes you look like you're really movin' on those strings!

Track 33, 0:28

Figure 7-9:
An expanded version of the classic 5-6 move.

Figure 7-10 brings together chords, double-stops, swing eighth-notes, and eighth-note triplets. Practice this at various tempos to make sure that you're playing all the elements with equal precision and command.

Figure 7-10:
A progression fusing chords, single notes, and double-stops.

High-Note Riffs, the Bridge to Lead Guitar

A high-note riff is very close — in words and in music — to a lick (see "Basic Single-Note Riffs" early in this chapter for more on these two terms). So, just forget the whole idea of strictly defining terms in such a forgiving and nonjudgmental form as the blues. But if you're mastering all that low-note stuff, you deserve to see what awaits you when you ascend the cellar stairs into the sunshine of high-note, melodic-based playing.

Keith Richards's borrowed trademark: Quick-four riffs

A quick-four (in this section) refers to a double-stop riff that you play on the second and third strings within a measure of a I or IV chord. (Don't get this quick-four confused with the kind of quick-four that happens in bar two of a 12-bar blues; I cover that version in Chapter 6.) When you play this riff during a chord, you create a temporary IV chord.

The Rolling Stones' Keith Richards carved out a very successful career exploiting this riff, and he learned from the great American blues masters. Figure 7-11 shows a four-bar phrase where the quick-four riff is applied at the end of each bar of an E and A chord.

Keith Richards's signature riffs in Stones classics like "Brown Sugar," "Honky-Tonk Women," and "Start Me Up" are actually in open-G tuning, which makes the quick-four easy to access. Open tunings in G, A, D, and E were used extensively by prewar acoustic guitarists — such as Charlie Patton, Son House, and Robert Johnson — especially for slide.

Intro, turnaround, and ending riffs

Intros, turnarounds, and ending riffs fill out the chord structure with melodic figures. As you play the figures in this section, try to hear the underlying structure — the rhythm guitar in your mind — playing along with you. You can play the chords according to the chord symbols above the music, but in this case the symbols identify the overall harmony and don't tell you what to actually play at that moment.

Track 35

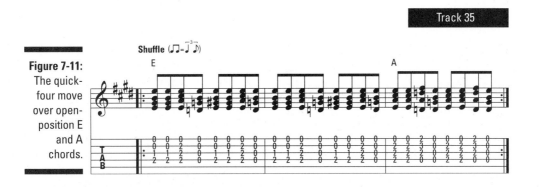

Figure 7-11: The quick-four move over open-position E and A chords.

Intro, turnaround, and ending riffs have very similar DNA, so they can be mutated ever so slightly to change into one of the other two functions. I provide examples (in the figures) in this section that you can easily adapt and add your own flavor to, so take a stab at converting the intro in Figure 7-12 into an ending that borrows from Figure 7-17. These practices get you used to taking other people's ideas and fashioning them into your own. That's how pre-existing riffs and licks get turned into an individual and original voice.

Intro riffs

Figure 7-12 is a snappy, triplet-based intro riff. The lower voice descends while the top voice stays fixed. Try playing this riff fingerstyle or with a pick and fingers.

Track 36, 0:00

Figure 7-12: A triplet-based intro riff in E.

Figure 7-13 is related to Figure 7-12 in that the lower voice descends against a fixed upper-note. But here, the notes are played together as double-stops for a more obvious and dramatic harmonic clash of the two notes. This blues lick and the one in Figure 7-14 are borrowed from a famous pop song — Johnny Rivers's version of Chuck Berry's "Memphis." Play this lick fingerstyle or with pick and fingers.

Track 36, 0:11

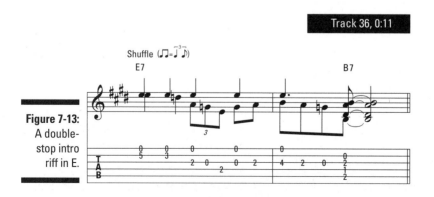

Figure 7-13: A double-stop intro riff in E.

The varying motion of the riff in Figure 7-14 makes it unpredictable and dramatic. The figure shows an all-single-note riff in triplets, ending in a B7 chord that comes on beat two. The melody here changes direction often and can be a little tricky at first. But I'm confident that you can get the hang of it with some practice.

TIP

The last note of the melody, low B, is actually the root of the B7 chord that you play one moment later. So play that B with your left-hand second finger.

Track 36, 0:21

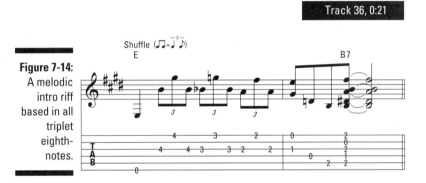

Figure 7-14: A melodic intro riff based in all triplet eighth-notes.

Turnaround riffs

Figure 7-15 can be used as an intro or a turnaround, but I've cast it as a turnaround. This is a double-stop riff in A with a descending lower voice, reminiscent of the playing of Robert Johnson.

Track 36, 0:30

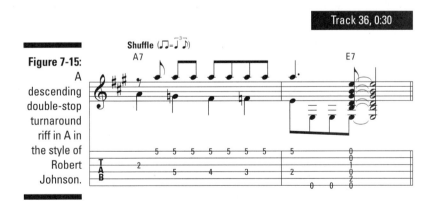

Figure 7-15: A descending double-stop turnaround riff in A in the style of Robert Johnson.

Figure 7-16 is a wide-voiced double-stop riff where the voices move in contrary motion (the bass ascends while the treble descends). This riff is great for any fingerstyle blues in E because it highlights the separation of the bass and treble voices — a signature feature of the fingerstyle approach.

If the double strikes in the bass give you trouble at first, try playing them as quarter notes, in lock step with the treble voice.

Track 37, 0:00

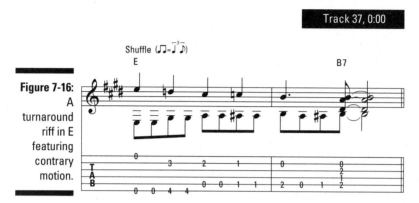

Figure 7-16: A turnaround riff in E featuring contrary motion.

Figure 7-17 is an open-chord turnaround riff in C — the key for fingerpicking country blues like Mississippi John Hurt. The last chord is a treat: a jazzy G7augmented (where the fifth of the chord, D, is raised a half step to D♯), which gives the progression a gospel feel with a little extra flavor.

Track 37, 0:12

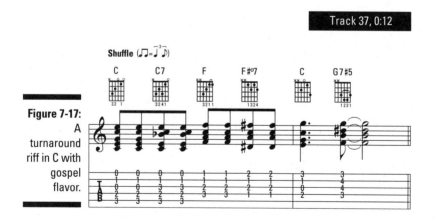

Figure 7-17: A turnaround riff in C with gospel flavor.

Ending riffs

Ending riffs are similar to both intros and turnarounds, except ending riffs terminate on the I chord, not the V. Figure 7-18 is a triplet-based riff in sixths, where the second string isn't played.

You can play this riff with just the pick, but it's easier with fingers or a pick and fingers. The open B string on the last triplet of beat one gives you a bit of a head start to get your hand up the neck to play the F9–E9 ending chords.

Figure 7-18: A triplet-based ending riff.

Figure 7-19 is a low note ending in E, using triplet eighths and a double-stop descending form. This riff is meaty and doesn't sound too melodic because it has more of a low, walking bass feel.

Combining single notes and chords

One way to get the best of both worlds — the lead and rhythm worlds, that is — is to combine single notes and chords. Many blues players don't make clear distinctions between chord playing, riff playing, or lead playing. Their technique just melds aspects of all these approaches into one cohesive style. And many of them do this while singing! Here are two examples:

 ✔ Stevie Ray Vaughan was a master of this style. He created full-sounding, active, and infinitely varied parts under his vocals as well as when he was just vamping along with the band.

 ✔ Eddie Van Halen, when in rare blues-mode (as opposed to his tapping, metal rock-god mode) was also an excellent practitioner of the integrated single-note-and-chord approach.

Today's students of the guitar tend to look at rhythm versus lead guitar as a black-and-white issue. But the history of blues shows that, until the advent of modern rock (from about the late '60s and beyond), players didn't really think of guitar-playing in those terms.

Be sure to also listen to the traditional players who sang and accompanied themselves on guitar:

 ✔ Robert Johnson

 ✔ John Lee Hooker

 ✔ Mississippi John Hurt

You hear the best examples of how to combine single notes and chords in the above players' styles, and the musical playing is some of the best you may ever hear.

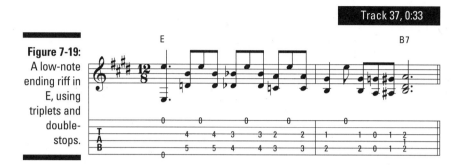

Track 37, 0:33

Figure 7-19:
A low-note ending riff in E, using triplets and double-stops.

Figure 7-20 is something completely different: a ragtime or country-blues progression in A. The more complex-sounding chords and the *voice leading* (where each note resolves by a half or whole step to the closest chord tone) give the riff a tight, barbershop sound. You hear this type of progression in the playing of the great country-blues fingerstyle-players like Mance Lipscomb, Fred McDowell, Mississippi John Hurt, Reverend Gary Davis, and Taj Mahal.

Track 38

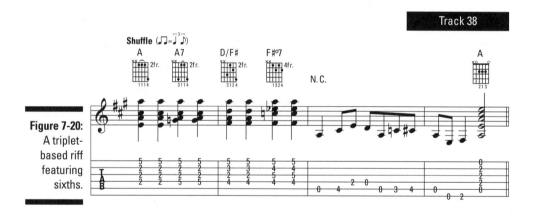

Figure 7-20:
A triplet-based riff featuring sixths.

Mastering the Rhythm Figure

After you have a handle on the components of rhythm guitar — left-hand chords, right-hand strums, riffs, and combinations thereof, it's time to put them all together in various ways.

In this section, you master the *rhythm figure*, which combines all the components of rhythm guitar: left-hand chords, right-hand strums, riffs, and combinations of the three. In some musical circles, a rhythm figure — usually longer than a riff — describes any repeatable passage of music that forms the basis for a song or section of a song.

Rhythm figures can be as simple as a quarter-note chord strum, an eighth-note boogie pattern, or a wild hybrid containing everything but the kitchen sink, as evidenced by the complex, integrated rhythm work of Magic Sam, Freddie King, Jimi Hendrix, and Stevie Ray Vaughan.

Figure 7-21 is a 12-bar blues that uses chords, single-note bass runs (to bring you in and out of those chords), and single-note riffs that go into flights of blues fancy.

Figure 7-21: A rhythm groove over a 12-bar blues in E.

Part III

Beyond the Basics: Playing Like a Pro

"First you play a G7 diminished, followed by an augmented 9th, then a perverted 32nd chord ending with a mangled 11th with a recovering 3rd."

In this part . . .

This part dives right into the nitty gritty of blues: lead guitar, up-the-neck playing, and expressive techniques that make your guitar sing, wail, and cry. Chapter 8 explores single-note technique, pentatonic and blues scales, and solo playing (with improvisation), which put your guitar center stage and in the limelight. Chapter 9 opens up the entire neck for your exploration by introducing position playing and moveable versions of the pentatonic and blues scales. Chapter 10 shows you how to milk the most emotion from your playing through the expressive techniques of hammer-ons, pull-offs, slides, vibrato, and the mother of all blues techniques — string bending. Get ready to weep!

Chapter 8

Playing Lead: Soaring Melodies and Searing Solos

● ●

In This Chapter

▶ Perfecting your picking patterns

▶ Deciphering between the pentatonic scale and the blues scale

▶ Exploring your expressive opportunities in the blues scale

● ●

*B*lues rhythm-guitar and riff-playing are pretty exciting in themselves, but blues lead-guitar usually gets the joint on fire. It's the lead guitarist who gets to play the really soulful, expressive stuff, and the best-known blues guitarists — T-Bone Walker, Albert King, Albert Collins, Freddie King, B.B. King, Stevie Ray Vaughan, and Eric Clapton — are known for their leads. When you think of their solos and their stylistic hallmarks, you may think of their lead-playing first. But they all started out the way you're going to in this chapter: by eking out single notes in open position against a backdrop of a 12-bar blues progression.

Lead-playing involves not only playing single notes but also taking a creative leadership role. As a lead guitarist, you're expected to step up, step out, and take center stage when it's your time. Part of being prepared is having a solid picking technique and the confidence to relay your expressive impulses — both in your choice of notes and in your execution of them.

In this chapter, you take the first step and start playing the guitar melodically, where you're the featured instrument — the big dog on the stage. In Chapters 9 and 10, I cover playing up the neck and incorporating articulation and expressive techniques — the next two steps.

Mastering Your Picking Technique

Lead technique requires you to get a little more precise and scientific about your approach. The rhythm, articulation, and dynamics are more varied in lead than in riff-playing (see Chapter 7 for more on that technique), so I focus on the more subtle aspects of coaxing out single notes from the guitar.

When you play with a pick, you can use either downstrokes or upstrokes (see Chapter 5 for an explanation of the two). In rhythm- and riff-playing, downstrokes are more important and usually suffice. In lead-playing, your down and up picking must be equally matched and of a certain technical proficiency to make your solos as controlled and expressive as possible.

In this section, I help you master the technique of alternate picking so you can apply it to all your single-note playing, even when all downstrokes will do.

Every musical instrument has note combinations or fingering sequences that are harder to execute than others. But melodies are indifferent to these mechanical quirks and difficulties. Part of mastering your instrument is making sure that the listener isn't aware when you're making a difficult move versus when you're having an easy time of it.

To begin, work on playing both types of strokes with equal ease and facility.

Becoming smooth with your simple downs and ups

The best way to begin alternate picking is to simply play steady down-up-down-up patterns on an open string. If you can maintain a steady rhythm and experience no glitches or hesitations in either direction, you're doing well.

However, many people initially have trouble making their upstrokes as smooth and loud as their downstrokes. This is natural, because you play many more downstrokes in guitar than upstrokes. Also, upstrokes go against gravity and require a little more effort to maintain smoothness all through the stroke. Just keep practicing, making sure that your upstrokes come up with the same swift confidence that your downstrokes have.

Don't think too much about your pick strokes, though — simply play as much as you can with a pick, and your picking will be smooth as butter in time. Smoothness in picking is the same as achieving gracefulness in dancing or skiing. You get there by doing it — over and over.

In notation, a downstroke is indicated by the symbol ⊓. An upstroke is indicated by the symbol ∨. Be sure to pay close attention to the down- and upstroke indications in this chapter.

Figure 8-1 shows an exercise that uses alternate-picked downstrokes on the open high-E string. The rhythm is straight eighth-notes. Work to get your picking as rhythmic and *dynamic* (loud and soft) as the example on the CD. You should hear no difference between the downstrokes (which are a little more comfortable and natural to play) and the upstrokes (which require a little more finesse and confidence to bring them up to the level of downstrokes).

Figure 8-1:
Alternate
picking on
the open
high-E string
in straight
eighth-
notes.

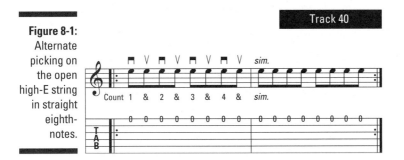

By first playing alternate picking in even, straight eighth-notes, you gain better control of your picking pattern. Before moving on to the next section, practice the exercise in Figure 8-1 until you can play it confidently.

Tackling tricky alternate-picking situations

After you have the concept down of moving your pick in a strict, alternating, up-and-down motion, you can apply that motion to different situations on the strings of the guitar. In real-life situations, the melody isn't affected by whether you have to change strings on an upstroke or downstroke or whether you're stronger going from the higher strings to the lower strings.

Don't think about the stroke — just think about the next note, and the stroke will take care of itself. You've drilled so much, the strokes are second nature. When you get really good, you won't even be aware of what stroke you're using — your right hand will just naturally play the right stroke. In this section, you apply alternate picking to a couple of different passages in a variety of settings to make sure you can keep the alternate-picking scheme intact.

Figure 8-2 features two notes — the open second string and the first-fret C — and may look similar in rhythm to Figure 8-1. In fact, this exercise is in swing eighths, or a shuffle feel. In a shuffle feel, the long-short rhythm corresponds to the down-up order in pick strokes, so the time between the downstroke and upstroke is shorter than between the upstroke and downstroke. Don't think about it too much; just try to get the feel and don't make your upstrokes too wide.

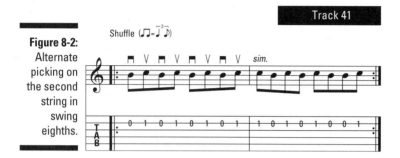

Figure 8-2:
Alternate picking on the second string in swing eighths.

Try adding some left-hand movement into the picture so you get used to fretting the left-hand fingers in sync with the right-hand alternate-picking pattern. Figure 8-3 is an alternate-picking pattern on the third string, using left-hand fretting.

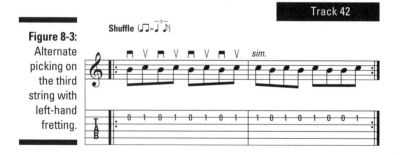

Figure 8-3:
Alternate picking on the third string with left-hand fretting.

Figure 8-4 is a single-string alternate-picking exercise that uses fretted notes on all six strings. The feel of playing on the six strings differs slightly because each string is a different thickness and has more or less tension. The strings are in different locations, too, which requires a slight adjustment in your right hand.

Figure 8-4:
Alternate
picking with
notes on all
six strings.

You can use either the tab or the standard music notation to play the notes in Figure 8-4. You can even memorize the sequence of notes by ear if you listen to the CD enough times. The point here isn't to get you reading music but to practice alternate picking. (But reading music is often an efficient way to accomplish other musical goals.)

The Universal Lead Language: The Pentatonic Scale

Many scales exist in music, including the two most popular: the seven-note *major scale* (the familiar *do re mi fa sol la ti do*), and the seven-note *minor scale* (the major scale's mournful and mysterious counterpart). But many other scales exist too, and each sounds a little different and performs different melodic functions.

One common scale is the *pentatonic scale*, which consists of five notes drawn from the members of the major or minor scale. Many melodies are written with the pentatonic scale, especially folk songs in many cultures, because of the scale's open and gentle quality. "Amazing Grace" and "Auld Lang Syne" are two examples of familiar songs that use the pentatonic scale for their melodies. The pentatonic scale is simpler than the major or minor scale, but it has some important uses that musicians from such cultures as Chinese, Japanese, European, African, Polynesian, and Native American have put to good use.

The five black notes on a keyboard form a natural pentatonic scale. If you play just the five black notes (G♭, A♭, B♭, D♭, and E♭) on any keyboard, you produce the G♭ pentatonic scale — without even trying very hard! Try it yourself: Go to the nearest keyboard and play "Auld Lang Syne" and "Amazing Grace" using just the black notes (and your ear, of course). Then improvise your own melody.

Why the pentatonic is the perfect scale

The pentatonic scale is probably the greatest thing to happen to the blues since the Mississippi Delta. The scale was born to play the blues. When using this scale, it's virtually impossible to hit a wrong note — meaning all the notes sound good when played over any chord in the key, producing no unpleasant *clashes* (musically discordant results), no matter what combinations you dream up. It works in a blues progression. It works in a minor key. It works over a country-rock progression. The pentatonic scale is easy to memorize and provides you infinite material for melodic expression. It's as close to *plug and play* or *play by the numbers* that blues guitarists have.

Ever wonder why wind chimes always clang in perfectly pleasing tunes? They're often tuned to a pentatonic scale; no matter what random combination of sounds the wind can whip up by pushing the chimes' bells or tines into each other, the results are pleasing.

By a stroke of very good luck (and the blues needs all the good luck it can get!), the minor version of the pentatonic scale — see the next section — fits perfectly over blues progressions; provides some authentic-sounding and expressive, melodic material; and gives blues guitarists an instant solution for playing all the right notes! Wouldn't you have liked to have the pentatonic scale when you had to play your second-grade piano recital in front of all those kids in the auditorium? Or how about a pentatonic scale for talking with your boss so that you never hit a wrong note with him? Real-life conversations may not have a pentatonic scale, but the blues does, and in the following sections, I show you what it is and how to use it.

The two sides of the pentatonic scale

Guitarists use two kinds of pentatonic scales: major and minor. Both use identical fingering and notes, but the keys are referred to by different names. For example, the scale in the following section is called E minor pentatonic. But it's also G major pentatonic and can be used in non-blues progressions in G major (like those used for country and country-rock music). Because blues primarily uses the minor-pentatonic version, the focus here is on the minor-pentatonic keys and applications.

Check out Table 8-1 for a comparison of the notes in the major and minor pentatonic scales.

Table 8-1	Comparing the Major and Minor Pentatonic Scales	
E major	*E minor Pentatonic*	*Interval*
E	E	1
F♯	—	—
G♯	G	♭3
A	A	4
B	B	5
C♯	—	—
D♯	D	♭7

Two notes in particular clash in Table 8-1: the third (G♯ versus G) and the seventh (D♯ versus D). But the tension created when a minor, or *flatted*, third (G) occurs against an expected major third (G♯) in the tonic chord gives the blues its energy and vitality. It's a large part of what makes the blues *blue*.

A common scale for practice: E minor pentatonic

In this section, you start practicing the pentatonic scale in open position (using open strings and the first three frets), and in Chapter 9 you can practice closed position (no open strings), which gives you the opportunity to transpose the scale to any key and any position on the neck. You apply the same approach to the six-note blues scale as well. (See the section on the blues scale later in this chapter.)

An E minor pentatonic scale has five notes and fits the key of E minor (or an E minor chord). Traditional major and minor scales have seven notes (you don't count the octave, or eighth note, as part of the scale), but a pentatonic simplifies life a little by counting just five notes as its members.

Though the minor pentatonic scale has *minor* in its name and fits well in the key of E minor and its related chords, you can also apply that minor quality to the chords in a blues progression, which are *major*. This minor/major combination is what gives the blues its special character.

Minor scales versus major chords

What is often called the *major/minor ambiguity* of the blues is an outgrowth of the pre-blues field hollers and work songs sung in the South before and after the Civil War. Perhaps as an African retention of pentatonic melodies, musicians applied these scales to their songs and then later to riffs, licks, and melodies on the banjo, harmonica, and guitar. When African Americans began to add the harmony of I, IV, and V chords under what would become the blues in the late 1800s, they kept the ♭3rd from the minor pentatonic scale. Though theoretically dissonant, we have become used to hearing a ♭3rd played or sung against a major or dominant chord in blues, rock, and other forms of popular music and readily accept it as a *bluesy* sound.

The pattern

The pentatonic scale has a certain pattern, and Figure 8-5 shows the notes in that pattern. Keep in mind that the diagram isn't a chord form; it's a collection of notes that you play one at a time.

Figure 8-5:
The notes of the E minor pentatonic scale on the guitar neck.

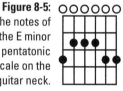

The best way to see and hear which notes you're supposed to play is to start at the highest or lowest note in the pattern and play in one direction (up or down), striking one note at a time until you reach the end of the pattern. Then reverse the process. First try the pattern ascending in eighth notes, beginning with the open low-E string and continuing up to the third-fret G on the first string.

Did your playing match that of the performance on the CD? Did you remember to play open strings along with the fretted ones? Did you manage to maintain your alternate-picking pattern as you crossed strings? This is your first venture into single-note playing, so be sure you've got these basics down cold before moving on.

The notes

In E minor, the notes of the pentatonic scale are E, G, A, B, and D. These notes can be easily found and played in open position, which makes it a great starting point for learning pentatonic-scale concepts. Figure 8-6 shows the notes and tab of the E minor pentatonic scale in open position.

Track 44

Figure 8-6:
The ascending E minor pentatonic scale.

When figuring out a new scale, most guitarists like to see just the neck diagram (instead of the tab written out) because remembering a cluster of notes is quicker. Also, a neck diagram doesn't tell you to play the notes in any order, like music and tab do; it just shows you which notes are in the scale.

The way to make the scale shine

When you can run the notes from bottom to top and top to bottom, it's time to mix up the order of the notes. After all, music is about a lot more than running scales — even if it's a really cool scale, like the minor pentatonic! The minor pentatonic shines when it's played against the chords in an E blues — E, A, and B7.

In Figure 8-7, I mix it up a little for you, and you take the minor pentatonic scale and play a 12-bar blues with it. The lead plays over the rhythm part by using the notes of the E minor pentatonic scale. This exercise is your first official solo. Try memorizing this figure and practicing at different tempos until you can play it smoothly and confidently.

The blues creates drama in part because the melody uses *blue* notes that don't fit in the major scale. In the key of E, the major scale is E, F♯, G♯, A, B, C♯, and D♯. And the chords of the blues progression include these notes. But a quick look at the E major scale and E pentatonic minor scale reveals they have few notes in common.

Track 45

Figure 8-7:
A 12-bar blues with an E minor pentatonic lead over it.

Pentatonic Plus One: The Six-Note Blues Scale

The pentatonic scale is a wonderful invention — and can save you from sounding bad as a blues player. On the flip side, because the scale plays it safe, so to speak, it can lack a little color or *teeth*. If you want to add some blues bite and grit to the pentatonic scale and make it more blues-like, follow a simple process: Just add one note. Then your five-note scale becomes a six-note scale that's tailor-made to bring out the edge in blues. And it's appropriately called the *blues scale*.

You can transform the five-note minor pentatonic scale into the six-note blues scale by throwing in the interval of a ♭5 — B♭ in the key of E minor. Figure 8-8 shows the notes and pattern of the E blues scale. Play through the scale slowly from the bottom to the top and then from the top to the bottom, playing one note at a time. Pay attention to where the added B♭ comes in. It occurs twice in this pattern — once on the fifth string and once on the third string, an octave apart. Notice how it reeks (in a good way) with blues flavor!

O = added note: B♭

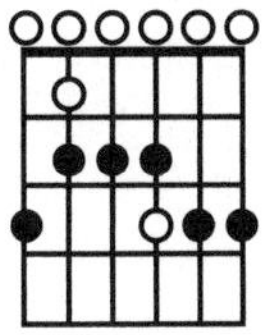

Figure 8-8:
The E blues scale.

Thousands of songs use the blues scale, both in their composed melodies and in their improvised solos. Some famous rock songs, like Cream's "Sunshine of Your Love" and Deep Purple's "Smoke on the Water," use the blues scale as the main riff of the song — and exploit that ♭5 interval. Figure 8-9 may not be as immortal as "Smoke on the Water," but it uses the blues scale as a melodic solo over a 12-bar blues in E.

Figure 8-9: The E blues scale used to solo over a 12-bar blues.

Adding Some Extra Flava to the Blues Scale

The blues scale enables you to create a lot of music, and you can spend a lifetime exploring its expressive possibilities. Although the blues scale sounds good in a 12-bar blues over the entire progression and over any chord, it does leave some of those chord tones out because the notes clash (albeit in a good way!) with tones in the I, IV, and V chords.

By adding just a couple of notes, you can choose to either clash with the tones (as usual) or reinforce the chord tones with the added notes. And, more than just supporting the chords, you can give your playing a different character, one that evokes jazzier, sweet, and Texas-style flavors. And music can never have too much Texas in it (at least as far as I'm concerned)!

Clashing bitterly

The chords that make up the 12-bar blues are *triads* — three-note chords with the intervals one, three, and five. Here's the breakdown:

- ✔ The E chord consists of E (one, or the root), G♯ (three, or the major third), and B (five, or the fifth).
- ✔ The major third of the E chord, G♯, is a half step away from its closest note in the blues scale (E, G, A, B♭, B, D), which is G.
- ✔ The other two notes of the chord, E and B, are already in the scale.

When you play a G lead note (part of the E blues scale), it clashes with the G♯ in the E chord playing underneath you. That interplay creates the tension with the lead voice, pitting a *blue note* within the harmonic framework that's supporting a major-scale note (in this case, G♯). It's that tension, or clash, that gives the blues its uniquely expressive and sometimes troubled character.

If you know your blues progressions, you can also substitute dominant seven chords for the triads. But the added notes in E7, A7, and B7 — the sevenths D, G, and A — are all already contained in the blues scale. So for our purposes, they don't affect the issue of clashing versus supporting tones.

A dash of sweetness

Playing a chord tone is never a bad thing in blues, rock, and jazz because there are times when you want to support the harmony and times when you want to go against the grain. In the case of the major third of a chord, it's a very defining sound in swing and Texas blues and is often nicknamed the *sweet* note.

Figure 8-10 shows a passage using blues-scale notes along with the occasional G♯. In this figure, G immediately precedes the G♯ and is a classic blues move that's encouraged!

○ = sweet note: G♯

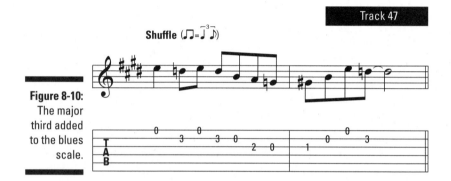

Track 47

Shuffle (♫=♩♪)

Figure 8-10:
The major
third added
to the blues
scale.

Another sweet note is the major sixth of the I chord (C♯ in the key of E). In Texas-style blues, it's quite common to hear the major third and the major sixth used in conjunction with each other. The major sixth has another bonus function: It is also the major third of the IV chord (C♯ in A).

The principles applied in matching up the notes of the blues scale with the major 3rd of the I chord also apply to the IV chord, A. The notes of an A major triad are A, C♯, and E. The notes A and E (the one and the five of the chord) are already in the E blues scale (E, G, A, B♭, B, D). The major third, C♯, is a half step away from the D in the scale. So the C♯ adds a half-step-away alternative for the blues-scale D that clashes with the A-chord C♯. Plus, the C♯ sounds so good against the E chord anyway, so it's doubly supported as a sweet note.

Figure 8-11 uses a C♯ as both a sweet note over an E chord (the I) as well as a chord tone (the major third) in the A chord. This variation is typical of leads that use the sixth (C♯); the major third (G♯) is also included.

Other chord tones appear in lead guitar passages (see the solos in Chapters 11, 12, and 13), but the major third and sixth (which does double duty as the major third in the IV chord) are the most important notes to incorporate after you master the blues scale. These added sweet notes, along with others, will help you break out of the proverbial box so that you don't have to rely on just the blues scale — or any scale — to play from your heart. The entire musical alphabet can be your palette.

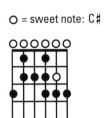

○ = sweet note: C♯

Track 48

Figure 8-11:
The major sixth sweet note added to the blues scale.

Chapter 9

Playing Up the Neck

· ·

In This Chapter

▶ Positioning your fingers with ease

▶ Playing up the neck and changing positions

▶ Checking out the ways to move up and down the neck

▶ Figuring out the five pentatonic positions

▶ Creating a dynamic solo

· ·

*K*nowing the neck of your guitar (and your sweetie) is the secret to playing well (on both fields!). If you played nothing but the notes of the pentatonic scale, and shifted smoothly between positions, you'd never play a wrong note again — and you'd be moving up and down the neck with authority and confidence.

This chapter gives you the tools to break out of the open position to boldly play on the higher frets. The guitar sounds great when played anywhere on the neck, but for brilliant, piercing lead lines, you can't beat the upper frets for their tone and expressive potential.

For Inquiring Minds: Why Up the Neck You Should Go

Melodic lead guitar — especially electric guitar — sounds better in the higher positions for three reasons:

> ✔ **It stands out more than it otherwise would.** Chords from the rhythm guitar and keyboards occupy primarily the lower and middle registers, so the lead guitar distinguishes itself by playing notes in a different region than the ones occupied by the rhythm instruments.

✔ **Going up the neck puts the guitar's sound in a range with other melody-playing instruments, such as the piano, harmonica, sax, and trumpet.** Higher notes (up to a point) just sound better, and the guitar is kind of a low-pitched instrument, so the higher it can play, the more brilliant and vibrant it will sound.

✔ **The strings are more flexible and more responsive to left-hand expressive techniques the higher you go.** This quality makes not only bending easier, but also playing hammer-ons, pull-offs, slides, and applying vibrato (more on these articulation and expressive techniques in Chapter 10).

Positioning Your Digits for an Easy Key Change

In order to make your knowledge transferable, you need to recognize the value of the *closed position.* This term refers to a chord, scale, or lead pattern that uses no open strings. When you play something that doesn't rely on open strings, you can shift the passage up and down the neck without changing the relative sound.

Barre chords (covered in Chapter 4) can be played anywhere on the neck, in all 12 keys. The principle holds true for scales, lead patterns, and licks: Play them in closed position, and they retain their integrity no matter where you place them.

Eyeballing your guitar's neck

You can play the guitar in open position without really looking at the neck. But when it comes to leaving the confines of the lower frets, you must now look at the neck to get your left hand in the correct position. You may have noticed this when you first tried to play barre-chord progressions around the neck. (For more on barre chords, see Chapter 4.)

If you're a singing guitar player who uses a microphone, having to look down at the neck can be disorienting, because you have to move your head — and your mouth — away from the mic to look at the guitar to play reliably up the neck. It's not a huge adjustment, but you must be aware that playing up the neck requires you to adjust your stage posture slightly. Also, if you're used to having unbroken eye contact with your audience, you may have to momentarily unfix your gaze from that attractive person in the third row whom you're trying to impress with your version of "I'm Your Hoochie Coochie Man."

The pros of closed positions

In open position, you usually have only one way to play a chord or series of notes. But in position playing you have the whole neck — that is, all the frets and strings above open position — and that provides several different ways of playing a given passage of music. This is liberating, but it also means that you have to understand a little more about how the music you hear and see (if you're looking at sheet music or tab) relate to the guitar neck. So you have to couple some brain power to your technique to make it all work.

Fortunately, the minor pentatonic scale (covered in Chapter 8) makes that easy to accomplish. But consider the following advantages of playing single notes in closed position, instead of in open position or grabbing the notes randomly by ear:

✔ You can play a passage of music in any key just by moving your hand up or down the neck. You don't have to relearn the melody with a different fingering, as you would in open position.

✔ You can move any piece of music around the neck to find exactly the right key for whatever reason the musical situation calls for — a singer's vocal range, the key the band knows the song in, the position you think looks best for TV, and so on.

✔ You get to know the entire neck of the guitar just by moving the licks you already know into different places.

When you know the five pentatonic positions for a key, a few licks and solo passages that use those patterns, and a sweet-note lick or two to throw in, you'll have a big chunk of the fretboard under your command. And that's just for one key!

The details of closed, numbered positions

To understand exactly where or at what fret to play, look to the strategy known as *position playing* on the guitar. A *position* is the group of frets that can be played by the left-hand fingers in a fixed place on the neck. In *position playing,* the left-hand first finger plays the lowest fret, the second finger plays the next highest fret, and so on, covering a four-fret span. Positions are named by their lowest fret number — the one the index finger plays.

For example, to play in fifth position, move your left hand along the neck until your index finger hovers above the fifth fret. (Most guitars have a fret marker here.) Now you're poised to play in fifth position. Check out Figure 9-1 for the proper position.

Figure 9-1:
The left
hand is
ready to
play in fifth
position.

Playing in fifth position means that you use one finger per fret, from the fifth fret to the eighth fret:

✔ Your first finger plays all fifth-fret notes.

✔ Your second finger plays the notes on the sixth fret.

✔ Your third finger plays the notes on the seventh fret.

✔ Your fourth finger plays notes that occur on the eighth fret.

Playing in a given position means you play all the notes within a four-fret span, the lowest being the fret number that defines the position's name. So playing in fifth position means that you don't play any notes below the fifth fret or any notes higher than the eighth fret.

Easing Into Position: Moving the Pentatonic Up and Down

Your first journey into position playing enlists the minor pentatonic scale (for more on the minor pentatonic scale, see Chapter 8). The most important pentatonic scale position is the one nicknamed *home position.* This position is the one you play most often from, and if you decide to play high notes or low notes, you leave "home," but you eventually return.

The A minor pentatonic scale is just five half-steps higher than E minor, so it's the same as the E minor pentatonic moved up five frets. This puts the A minor pentatonic scale in fifth position, and the open strings used to play the notes of the scale all become fifth-fret notes. You use the closed-position example in A minor as a basis to derive other pentatonic positions.

Figure 9-2 shows the minor pentatonic scale transposed to the fifth fret (where your first finger plays, and is anchored to, the fifth fret).The box diagram above the staff shows the collection of notes in a lead pattern; it isn't a chord.

Figure 9-2:
The A minor
pentatonic
scale at the
fifth fret.

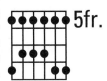

There are a couple of things going on when you play this new scale form:

- ✔ The scale that you originally learned in open position has been transported up the neck, so you now play it by using all fretted notes.

- ✔ The faithful E minor pentatonic scale has been transposed to the key of A, so you have to adjust the chords accordingly to play in the right key. (Moving anything on the neck transposes it to a different key.)

Figure 9-3 is a passage that uses the descending A minor pentatonic scale, starting at the highest note — the first string, eighth-fret C.

Figure 9-3:
A passage
that uses
the
descending
fifth-position
A minor
pentatonic
scale.

Track 49, 0:00

After you practice Figure 9-3 a bit, check out Figure 9-4, which mixes the notes up a little and adds in the blues notes, which occur on the third string, eighth fret, and fifth string, sixth fret. The blues notes are indicated with open circles in the fretboard diagram. (This six-note scale is the *blues scale* that's covered in Chapter 8).

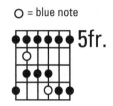

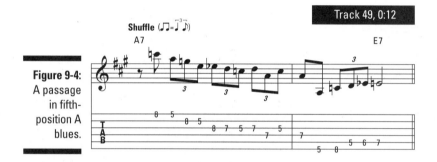

Track 49, 0:12

Figure 9-4: A passage in fifth-position A blues.

Use the pattern from Figure 9-4 to create your own solos. In fact, I encourage you, at any time, to throw down (well, gently place aside) this book and strike out on your own. The only rule is to play just the notes in the six-note blues scale.

Changing Your Position

When you play lead, you quickly figure out that playing in position is cool, but changing positions while you play is even cooler. That's when you really feel like you're in command of the entire neck and that you're playing where you want when you want. If you look at professional guitarists, they move smoothly and gracefully up and down the neck, as if the music is just naturally taking them there. And you can get there, too. But first start by looking at the positions adjacent to home position, and then see how you get in and out of them.

Even though you're extending the home position upward and downward, the notes in the new positions are the same ones found in home position. Some of them are an octave higher or lower, but they belong to the same scale — in this case, A minor pentatonic.

A natural first: Moving from fifth position to eighth

After you can move around in home position with abandon, you're ready to get out of the house — or leave home — musically speaking. The first position to help you out of your lateral tendencies is eighth position — the next position up from fifth for the A minor pentatonic.

Figure 9-5 shows the notes in eighth position. You use just five notes on three strings. You could play the minor pentatonic scale on all six strings in positions other than home, but it's more common for blues lead guitarists to use just some of the notes — the ones that help extend the range. So use just the higher notes of this upper extension pattern in eighth position.

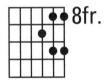

Figure 9-5:
Four notes in the eighth position A minor pentatonic.

Track 50, 0:00

The eighth-position blues bonus

In the position immediately above home, you find another, high blue note on the first string — the eighth position blues. In Figure 9-6, you can see this bonus note, which offers a high blue note on the 11th fret, which is particularly desirable for blues lead guitarists because of its prime location in the highest spot in the position.

The position just above home is sometimes called the _extension position_ instead of the eighth position blues. It was used so extensively by Albert King from the mid-1960s on, that it has come to be affectionately known as the "Albert King box." The other two "Kings of the Blues," B.B. and Freddie, also made regular use of this position along with countless other blues guitarists.

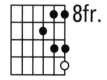

Track 50, 0:12

Figure 9-6:
A lick in eighth position using the high blue note on the 11th fret.

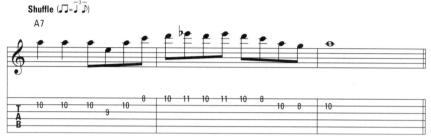

How low can you go? Moving from fifth position to third

The position immediately below the home position in A minor pentatonic is third position. Third position features just four notes on two strings, and these notes are on the two lowest strings of the guitar, extending the notes of the home position downward.

Figure 9-7 shows the four notes of the third-position lower extension of A minor pentatonic.

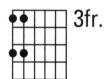

Track 51, 0:00

Figure 9-7:
Four notes in third-position A minor pentatonic.

The Technical Side of Moving

Knowing the different positions is important for extending your range beyond home position, but to really use the other positions effectively, you need to be able to get into and out of the lower and higher positions smoothly. There are several ways to achieve smooth transitions, and I tackle them in the following sections in order of popularity.

Like taking candy from a baby: The subtle shift

A shift is the most common and easy way to change positions on the guitar. The object of this movement is to switch positions without calling attention to it. To shift, you simply glide your finger quickly along a string, up or down, until it reaches the appropriate fret in the new position.

Figure 9-8 shows a shift from fifth position to eighth position on the third string and a shift from third position to fifth position and back on the fifth string. Both shifts use the third finger on the ascent, but the lower shift switches to the first finger on the descent. The movement along the third and fifth strings during the shift must be silent and transparent to the listener.

`Track 51, 0:08`

Figure 9-8:
Shifting
from fifth to
eighth
position and
from third to
fifth
position.

Seeking a bit of attention: The noticeable slide

If you *want* people to hear you move positions on your guitar, you can employ a slide. A *slide* is similar to a shift, except that you don't try to disguise the fact that you're sliding — you make the shift part of the musical phrase. Slides are covered in more detail in Chapter 10, but it's so close to a shift, that I want you to try a slide right now to get you from home position to eighth. Check out Figure 9-9 to help you with that slide.

Figure 9-9 shows the third-string slide on the left-hand third finger going from fifth position to eighth. Play the note on the third string, seventh fret, and while the note is still ringing and while still applying downward pressure on the fretboard, slide your finger to the ninth fret. You should hear the gradual glide in pitch between the two notes.

Track 52

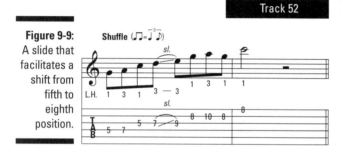

Figure 9-9: A slide that facilitates a shift from fifth to eighth position.

When you don't want to move, just reach or jump

A *reach* involves the stretch of the left-hand finger — usually the third or fourth if you're going up — to grab a note that's in the new position. A reach is handy when you don't want to change positions but need to grab one or two notes from the new position. But you can also use a reach to bridge a position shift if you prefer it over moving your hand.

Because a reach involves stretching the hand, it's not the most comfortable way to grab new notes, and if you have small hands, you may not find it a viable option. Reaches do become more reasonable the higher up you go on the neck because the frets become closer together.

A *jump* or *leap* is like a shift without the sliding action in between. You jump — or let go of the string completely — and grab the new note. You often use jumps when you want to shift to a position that's not adjacent to the one you're currently playing in. In that case, it's often easier to leave the fretboard entirely to land on a distant part of the fretboard.

Five Positions You Should Know: Meanderings of the Pentatonic Scale

When you're based in the home position (fifth position for the A minor pentatonic and blues scales), most of the time you use the upper and lower extensions for their ability to extend your range. That's why you play just the top three strings in the eighth position and the lowest two in third position.

However, you can play the minor pentatonic scale across the entire width of the neck using all six strings. Not coincidentally, there are five positions for the pentatonic scale. Some are more useful than others, but knowing all five in their complete, six-string form allows you to play any scale note on any string in any position on the guitar. It means you know the entire area of the neck — which roughly consists of 140 notes!

Relating the positions to each other

To understand how the five patterns of the pentatonic scale relate to one another, start off by viewing two positions: the eighth and third positions. When you play the full versions, their positions change to seventh and second, respectively, but the notes are still in the same place.

Figure 9-10 shows the full, six-string pattern for the A minor pentatonic scale in seventh and second positions. Note that the home position is indicated in open circles for easy reference. The lower notes of the seventh-position pattern are actually the upper notes of the fifth position, and the upper notes of the second-position pattern are the lower notes of the fifth position. So the patterns really interlock and are related to each other.

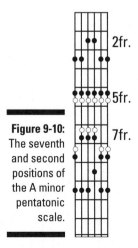

Figure 9-10: The seventh and second positions of the A minor pentatonic scale.

There are two more minor pentatonic patterns above the seventh position to consider. Figure 9-11 shows the home position and seventh-position extension, which are indicated in open circles for your reference.

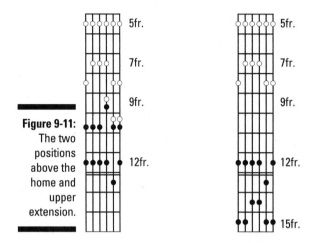

Figure 9-11: The two positions above the home and upper extension.

Figure 9-12 shows all five positions of the minor pentatonic scale. Note how the scale positions overlap and how much of the neck is covered just by one scale in one key. If you can play blues using just this scale, shifting up and down the neck smoothly while playing rhythms and ideas, you have come a long way toward understanding not only the blues, but the potential of the entire guitar neck.

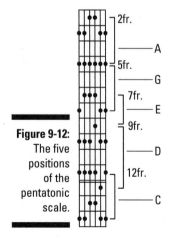

Figure 9-12: The five positions of the pentatonic scale.

The pentatonic positions actually outline specific open-position chord forms, if you try to look at them that way. The home position relates to the G or E minor chord. The lower position outlines an A chord. The position immediately above home is an E chord, and the two above that are D and C or A minor. This relationship is displayed by first playing the scale and then playing the barre chord with the appropriate form at the same fret.

Connecting the positions: Licks that take you up and down

To truly appreciate the scales' interlocking properties, you need to be able to connect the positions together in a seamless way. This combination involves multi-position ascending and descending *licks* (self-contained melodic passages). Licks are even more fun to play moving up and down the neck than scales are, so get ready to really sound (and look) like a blues player. Figure 9-13 is a passage that takes you from eighth to tenth to twelfth position and back down to home position (at the fifth fret). (See "Like taking candy from a baby: The subtle shift," earlier in this chapter for more on shifts.)

Track 53

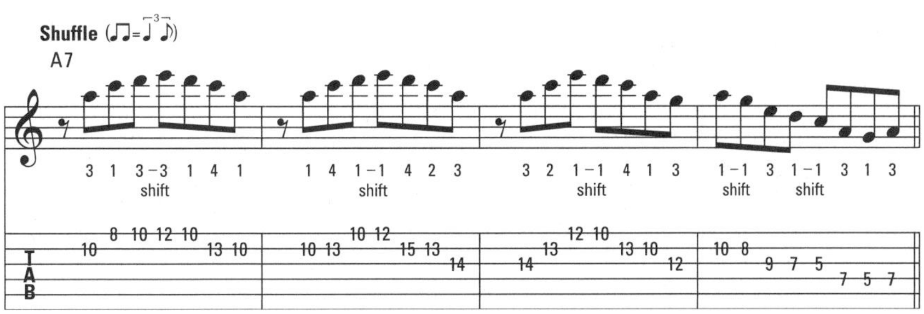

Figure 9-13:
A passage with shifts that take you in and out of multiple positions.

Understanding the Logic behind the Corresponding Shift of Position and Key

You quickly find that when you learn a lick in closed position, transposing it up or down the neck is no big deal, technically. It's the same lick, different location. But for your guitar playing to be meaningful to the outside world, you must know what happens (and why) when you move around. You can't just grab any position to play a lick arbitrarily because there are typically constraints on where you can play something. For example, if you're learning a song that must stay in a particular key.

Many beginning guitarists fall into the trap of not knowing what key they're in when they're playing something. You can learn any motor-skill function by rote, but for playing guitar, you should always know, at the very least, what key you're in.

The following sections help you understand the relationship between keys and positions.

Recognizing common keys and their comfortable positions

Each of the 12 keys has one or two positions ideally suited for playing blues licks. You can venture in and out of these positions for little licks in the extensions, or you can leave a position completely to grab a high or low note, but you generally find yourself anchored in just a couple of positions to play most blues licks in a particular key. And pentatonic positions aren't the only ones that yield "tasty" results, as you see in the next section.

This chapter covers a lot of information about patterns for the pentatonic scale and its close relative the blues scale. But there are other patterns, too, that fit the blues. One sound the pentatonic patterns don't cover is the *sweet notes,* which are discussed in Chapter 7.

But take a look at a pattern that provides you with a sweet note. As it so happens, a nice sweet-note pattern exists on the top three strings, just two frets above the upper extension of the home-position minor pentatonic. And the fingering happens to be the same, except for the added note. The sweet-note pattern has a different sound than the pentatonic scale, but it's very useful in blues. Figure 9-14 shows a solo that uses notes that are different from the ones in the pentatonic scale but that use a familiar fingering pattern.

Mapping keys to positions

In mapping keys to position, if you've already explored the key of A blues, then you notice that it sits well in fifth position. So by reasonable deduction, G blues would fit third position, right?

Your fingers don't have to do any more work to transpose all the A licks to G; it's just your brain that has to make sure that you've made the transfer correctly.

Figure 9-15 is a table that shows all 12 keys, the home-position and alternate pattern, the position name, and chord forms that the patterns correspond to. This chart is handy to have in case you're not sure of how to map a position to a key, and vice versa. You may not need to refer to this chart after you master your keys and forms well enough, but it never hurts to have it around.

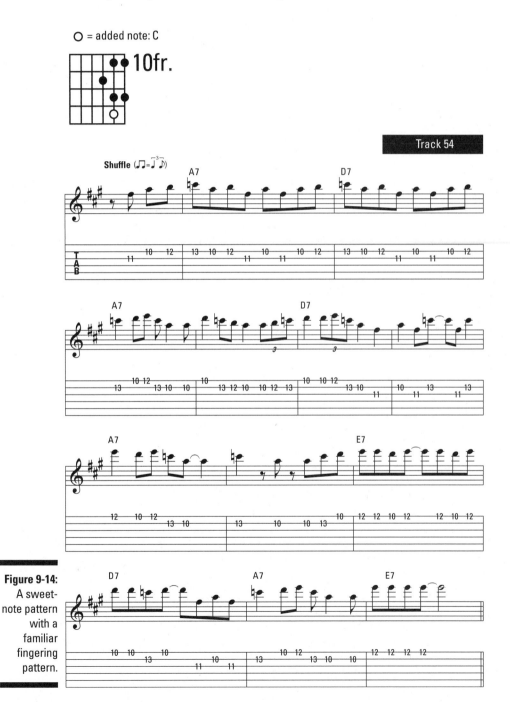

Figure 9-14:
A sweet-note pattern with a familiar fingering pattern.

Song keys	Pentatonic pattern/fret #	Chord forms
A major/F♯ minor	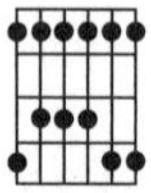 2nd fret	G/Em
B♭ major/G minor	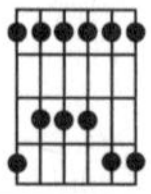 3rd fret	G/Em
B major/G♯ minor	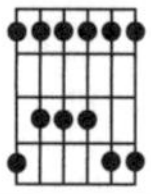 4th fret	G/Em
C major/A minor	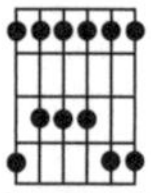 5th fret	G/Em
D♭ major/B♭ minor	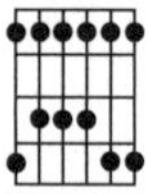 6th fret	G/Em
D major/B minor	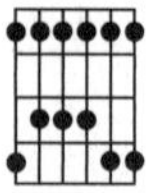 7th fret	G/Em
E♭ major/C minor	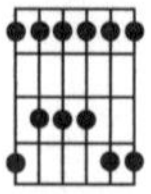 8th fret	G/Em
E major/C♯ minor	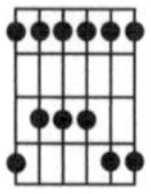 9th fret	G/Em
F major/D minor	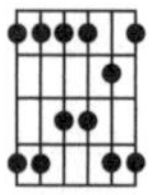 5th fret	C/Am
G♭ major/E♭ minor	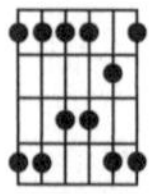 6th fret	C/Am
G major/E minor	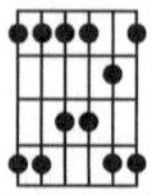 7th fret	C/Am
A♭ major/F minor	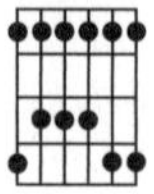 1st fret	G/Em

Figure 9-15:
A table showing the 12 keys and their pentatonic scale patterns.

Chapter 10

Express Yourself: Making the Guitar Sing, Cry, and Wail

In This Chapter

▶ Grasping articulation and putting the pieces together

▶ Discovering the dynamic sounds of your guitar

▶ Adding musical flair to your playing

*I*f all that were required to play the blues was knowing the right notes and scales, anybody — or even a non-body, like a robot — could do it. So what's the difference between the execution of right-sounding notes and music that can change your life? Expression. Soul. Playing from the heart.

These phrases describe what happens when thinking, feeling, red-blooded humans get a hold of some good musical material, make it their own, and communicate that message through an inspired performance. The blues, like any great music, takes a creative interpreter to make it come to life. You have to know the moves — the chords, scales, and notes — but you also have to play coherently and persuasively and with feeling.

In this chapter, I cover articulation and expression, and these expressive techniques help you to connect notes in different ways, shape phrases, and add nuance to your playing. Armed with your note knowledge and some articulation technique, you choose not only what notes to play but also how to play them — as soulfully as your aching heart allows.

Appreciating the Art of Articulation

Articulation is the class of techniques that deals with how notes are sounded. This includes the way you *attack* the notes as well as the way you *produce* notes through non-attacks, such as slides, hammer-ons, pull-offs, and bends.

After you bring the note into existence, though, the job doesn't stop there. As the note sounds, you can still shape and modify it by adding *vibrato* (a wavering quality to the sustained part of the note) and affect its duration (that is, whether the note rings for its full rhythmic value or gets cut off prematurely). Your influence on the life of a note breaks down in the following ways:

- **Attacking the notes:** Accents and mutes are ways of varying your attacks, and the two often work in conjunction with each other. An *accent* makes a note louder and is used to help an important note stand out from those immediately surrounding it. A *mute* (performed with the right-hand heel, which partially stops the string from vibrating) subdues a note, making it softer and percussive and shortening its *sustain* (how long the note rings).

- **Varying sound after the attack:** Beyond how you initially sound the note, you also have to consider what you can do to it once it's ringing. Unlike wind instruments (like trumpets and harmonicas), a guitar (like the piano or other percussive instruments) can't really increase the volume after a note has been sounded except through electronic means (like goosing the guitar's volume control or, better yet, by using a volume pedal to swell a note). You can also apply vibrato to a note, which gives a sustained note a little more life.

- **Phrasing the notes:** The most subtle of all expressive playing is the overall approach to the music. This method is called *phrasing,* and it can mean everything from making the notes shorter or longer (*staccato* versus *legato,* for you music-school types) to varying the rhythmic flow through *laying back* or *backphrasing* (also called *rubato*). For more on music dynamics, see Table 10-1, later in this chapter.

Going In for the Attack

The most important part of a note's existence is its initial sound. This is what gives instruments much of their character. Guitars and pianos have sharp sounds at their outsets because they're struck with a pick and a felt hammer, respectively. But a note from a violin has a softer sound because it's coaxed into life with a bow. Striking a string is called *attacking* in musical terms, but don't let the hostile nature of that word give the wrong impression. An attack can be gentle as well as fierce. In fact you can apply an infinite variety of force to your attacks, making the guitar whisper or shout. In this section I talk about the expressive musical possibilities when you attack notes with varying degrees of intensity.

A little bit louder now . . . a little bit softer now: Dynamics

Dynamics is the degree of how loud and how soft you play. Giving thought to dynamics in your music is the first step toward making your playing more expressive.

Many people think *dynamics* means something else, like when someone says, "His playing was so dynamic!" In that case, they mean he plays with abandon and excitement. But technically, when you're talking musical expression, the word *dynamic* describes only the loud and soft aspects.

Getting accustomed to the road map

Often you get indications, either written or spoken, that guide you as to how loudly to play. For example, someone may instruct, "Play the first line soft and the second line loud," or you may see the symbols that are written directives for playing soft and loud. Table 10-1 lays out the most common dynamics symbols, their full term, and what that term means.

Table 10-1	Dynamics Symbols and Their Meanings	
Symbol	*Spelled-Out Term*	*What It Means*
pp	Pianissimo	Very soft
p	Piano	Soft
mf	Mezzo-forte	Medium-loud
f	Forte	Loud
ff	Fortissimo	Very loud
<	Crescendo	Gradually get louder
>	Decrescendo	Gradually get softer
dim.	Diminuendo	Gradually get softer (similar to decrescendo)

In classical music, dynamics are often written out in the score. (Often these indications come from the original composers themselves.) But popular music isn't nearly as prescriptive. Much of pop music doesn't necessarily employ dynamics in a formal way, except perhaps at the beginning of a piece or at the start of new sections. Generally, in rock, jazz, and blues, dynamics are left up to the discretion of the performer.

Super blues star Buddy Guy is a master of dynamics, especially in live performances, as he careens from a shout to a whisper with guitar and voice. A good recorded example, however, can be found on the epic, cathartic, slow blues "I Smell a Rat" on *Stone Crazy* (Alligator Records).

The techniques of playing loud and soft

Controlling the loudness and the ways to change between two degrees of loudness (and not just loud and loudest!) takes some skill. But really, the concept can't be simpler: To play loud, strike the strings hard. To play soft, strike gently.

Playing dynamics may sound simple enough, but until you master it, playing dynamically can mess with your timing. Specifically, you may find that you tend to rush when playing loud and drag when playing soft. This phenomenon is natural because playing hard requires more speed and strength. In science, force = mass × acceleration, so translating that to a hand striking a string, you get the force you need by exploiting the acceleration side of the equation (the speed at which you downstroke). You have to be careful, though, because you also use quick motions to play fast — so be aware of the timing when you change dynamics.

Fine-tuning your awareness: Playing dynamically across a phrase

Playing certain passages loud and other passages soft isn't so much a technique as an awareness. Simply knowing that the front half of the phrase should be soft and the second half loud makes you play that way naturally. (For more about phrases, see the section "Breaking Down the Music: Phrasing.") What may be less obvious is *which* part of the phrase should be soft. In Figure 10-1, the written music tells you through dynamic marks. A *call-and-response exchange* (where the first phrase *makes a statement* and the second phrase *answers it*) is a typical situation where you use dynamics to differentiate the two repeated phrases.

Track 55

Figure 10-1: A call-and-response exchange can benefit from a contrast in dynamics.

Hitting hard and backing off

Accents and mutes differ from dynamics (I cover dynamics in the previous section) in that the loud and soft forces refer to specific notes or groups of notes instead of to a general volume level. These indications are written above or below the actual noteheads to which they apply.

Striving for an *even* sound is a good goal in the beginning of your blues playing education — especially when strumming, alternate picking, and running scales — but it's not always the most musical achievement. In music you want to emphasize certain notes more than others to give them significance and to better express the meaning of your thought. In guitar playing, you stress certain notes by applying increased intensity to them.

Striking hard to be heard: Accents

To play a note louder than its surrounding notes, you simply strike that string or strings harder (with more right-hand force). Playing with a pick really comes in handy here because the pick is like having a small hammer — you get better leverage with any tool than you do with just your bare hand. When a note appears with an accent mark attached to it, strike the note with more force than the others, taking care to keep control of your hand while doing so. Figure 10-2 shows a passage with the important notes in the phrase accented (indicated by the symbol >).

Track 56, 0:00

Figure 10-2:
Accented notes are struck harder than the surrounding notes.

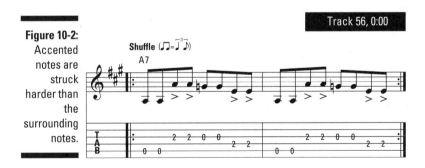

A dull and shortened roar: Mutes

You can play a note softly to de-emphasize it or to make an accented note stand out even more. But you can also mute the note with the right hand, which not only makes it softer but also actually dulls the tone and shortens the sustain. This technique is also applied for chords and riffs in Chapters 5 and 7, but in this chapter, you apply it to single-string lead playing. Figure 10-3 shows a lead passage that uses muted notes (indicated by the letters *P.M.*) along with accented notes to sustain the dramatic interest.

Figure 10-3: Muted notes interrupted by occasional accented notes.

Track 56, 0:15

Another way to play a note short, other than muting it, is to simply stop it dead from ringing through its full, indicated rhythmic duration. Playing short, crisp notes is called *staccato;* this is indicated with a small dot appearing over the notehead.

Breaking Down the Music: Phrasing

Putting notes together in a cohesive *thought* in music is called *phrasing*. Phrasing takes into account how notes are sounded (articulated or not) and how they're grouped together (as part of a unit or detached). The following sections present techniques to help you have more control over phrasing a series of notes and making them more emotionally powerful than just the notes themselves would be.

Connecting notes the slippery way: Slides

A *slide* is a smooth, slippery way to connect notes, and you perform them with just a slide of a finger. Slides come in many flavors and can be used subtly or obviously to gently connect two melodic notes or to enter and exit notes. In a slide between two notes of definite pitch, the first note is picked, but the second note is not picked. The sliding motion of the left-hand finger sounds the second note, and the effect is subtler than if the second note were articulated (attacked with the pick). Slides are a great way to mix up the sound of a series of notes so every note is not articulated — which can sometimes sound mechanical. Unlike some other left-hand techniques that must be practiced and perfected, the slide comes naturally to blues guitarists and needs little introduction.

It's almost impossible to play in a blues shuffle or slow 12/8 feel and not slide into and out of some of the melody notes. If sliding wasn't already an established technique, blues players would invent it every time they picked up the guitar.

Basically, to play a slide, you pick a note and then slide your finger up or down the string to a second note while maintaining pressure on that finger.

You have your pick among three major types of slides, which I cover in the following sections.

First things first: The difference between scoops and fall-offs

An ascending slide before a note is sometimes called a *scoop* and sounds much the same as when a horn player or vocalist enters a note gradually from a slightly lower pitch (rather than hitting it dead on). The scoop's counterpart is a *fall-off*, where the finger is dragged downward after a note ends.

To play an ascending, pre-note slide, pick the note from a fret below the principal note and slide up quick to the destination fret, letting the note ring. For the descending, fall-off slide, play a note in the normal way (hitting it dead on) and let it ring for its full value (or nearly so), and then pull your finger down the fretboard toward the nut for a fret or so and then lift off. Figure 10-4 contains slides into and out of notes as a way to give a little *grease* to a melody.

Track 57, 0:00

Figure 10-4:
Slides into and out of individual notes.

On an ascending slide, the note that starts the slide can be from one or two frets below, but, because you don't really hear it, it doesn't matter. If you want a longer-sounding slide (because the tempo is slow) or if you want to slide a long distance for dramatic effect, you can start four or five frets below the destination note.

An oldie but goodie: Slide guitar

With all this talk of left-hand slides, you may wonder how the genre of slide guitar factors in here. Slide guitar is essential to blues history and the blues repertoire. Prewar acoustic country-blues guitarists often incorporated some left-hand fretting in slide guitar because they generally played solo and needed to accompany their vocals with chords, riffs, and bass lines. Contemporary electric-slide guitarists playing in a band context usually use no fretting at all, relinquishing any left-hand contact with the strings to a metal or glass tube (the *slide*), which is dragged lightly over the strings above the fretboard.

In slide guitar, the bar never fully depresses the strings. Instead, you press down on the strings directly over the fret wires with just enough pressure to make them ring clear and rattle-free but not so hard that they touch the fingerboard. Playing the guitar with a slide produces truly *continuous* (infinitely small-interval) pitch changes, similar to the sliding effect of a fretless bass, violin, cello, or other fretless string instruments, as well as a trombone. Playing slides with a left-hand finger moving on a fretted guitar only approximates this sound. You can play slide guitar in standard tuning, but many guitarists find it more versatile to tune the guitar to an open chord, such as D or G (or their relative equivalents, E and A), which allows for better chord-playing. For more on slide guitar, see Chapters 11, 12, and 13.

A little flair for just one note: Quick slides

Quick slides (like the ones you play in Figure 10-4) are used to adorn individual notes. You just *push* your way into or out of a note from a nearby fret instead of hitting it dead on.

Quick slides in and out of notes are also called *indeterminate slides* because the note of origin (going up in pitch on the ascending slide) or destination (on the descending slide) isn't important.

Slides connecting two melody notes, with some rhythm in between

Sometimes you want to start with one specific note and end up on another specific note, but you want to connect them by using a slide. For these types of slides, you must factor in the rhythm of the slide between the two notes. Slides work equally well ascending or descending and are indicated in notation with a straight line in the appropriate direction with a slur over or under the line.

Figure 10-5 shows slides between melody notes in different rhythms.

Track 57, 0:13

Figure 10-5: A passage with rhythmic slides between notes.

Slides with two strikes (with your pick, that is)

Some advanced players choose to strike the first note, slide up or down to a specific note, and restrike the string just before they reach the second note. This isn't technically a *slur* (a general term for two notes played together where the second note is not articulated), but it's a common technique for advanced players. In this case (where the second note is picked), the curved slur line is omitted and just a straight line connects the two notes. A non-slur slide (one where you pick the second note) gives more authority to the second note but provides just a little bit of grease between the two, courtesy of the slide.

It has been said that the *organic quality* of the blues encourages the sliding into notes (and chords) from below or above. B.B. King is so skilled at the technique that it sometimes sounds like he's playing slide guitar, when in fact he never has.

It's hammer time — get ready to strike a string!

A *hammer-on* is a technique for performing an ascending slur by sounding a higher note on the same string with a left-hand finger without restriking the string. This makes for a smoother connection between two notes than if both notes were picked. A curved line indicates a hammer-on in notation.

The technique of playing hammer-ons

To play a hammer-on, strike the first note with your pick or right-hand finger and fret the second, higher note with a left-hand finger without re-striking the string. Figure 10-6 shows three types of hammer-ons: from a fretted note, from an open string, and a skip (a minor 3rd) between two fretted notes.

Track 58, 0:00

Figure 10-6:
Three types
of hammer-
ons.

Hammer-ons sometimes perform cleaner at faster tempos. So don't practice these passages too slowly when first trying to hear the effect.

Playing hammer-ons like an old hand

Figure 10-7 is a short blues break in a medium shuffle feel containing various types of hammer-ons, including multiple hammer-ons, where two or more successive notes are hammered. You can use multiple hammer-ons in fast passages where it may be difficult to alternate-pick a rapid series of notes. If you have trouble at first, try playing the figure slowly, omitting the hammer-ons, and apply alternate picking so you can hear the sound. Then go back and substitute the hammered notes for pick strokes.

Exposing a note by lifting a digit: Pull-offs

A *pull-off* is a downward slur where the second note is sounded by the quick removal of a left-hand finger that exposes the second, lower note.

A pull-off also has a little twist to its technique that sometimes helps the second note to sound more clearly: Peel away your left-hand finger to the side slightly instead of lifting it straight off the fingerboard. This technique produces a subtle attack sound courtesy of the skin on the left-hand fingertip that grips momentarily and then releases the fretted string.

The technique of playing pull-offs

To execute a pull-off to a fretted note, play the lick in bar two of Figure 10-8 by placing the third finger on the seventh fret and the first finger on the fifth fret. Apply and keep pressure on both fingers. Pick the first note (the seventh-fret D) and then, while the note rings, pull, lift, or peel the third finger off the string, allowing the fifth-fret C (fretted by the first finger) to sound.

Figure 10-7:
A lick using various hammer-ons.

Peeling takes a little practice. Generally, the faster the tempo, the better a pull-off reads without the extra effort. But after you have some pretty good calluses built up, your pull-offs (and your hammer-ons) will sound better.

59, 0:00

Figure 10-8:
Three types of pull-offs.

Pulling off like a pro

Figure 10-9 shows a passage that uses pull-offs in combination with hammer-ons, their constant companions. (I cover these earlier in the chapter in the section "It's hammer time — get ready to strike a string!")

Track 59, 0:14

Figure 10-9:
Pull-off
licks — in
isolation
and with
hammer-
ons.

Giving Your Sound a Bit of Flair

In addition to connecting notes with slurs to vary your expression, you can also add *juice* to notes after you've sounded them. The following sections describe techniques you can apply to a fretted note after you've brought it to life.

Shake that string: Adding vibrato

Vibrato is the wavering, shimmering quality in a sustained note that gives it life and vitality. A vibrato can be wide or narrow, pronounced or subtle, or any one of the infinite variations in between, but you accomplish them all by using the same technique of bending the note slightly and rocking it back and forth across the fretboard.

Technically, a vibrato is performed by slightly bending and releasing a string with a left-hand finger. You can do this a number of ways, but the most common way in blues is to pull or push and release the string across the fretboard at a fast rate.

Figure 10-10 shows a sustained note that's played with vibrato. Listen to the CD to make sure that you can approximate the rate at which you pull and release your finger and the intensity (how far or wide you pull the string) to achieve the pitch-wavering effect. Vibrato is indicated with a wavy line above the note, and it extends for the duration of the note.

The kings of vibrato

Vibrato is a fairly simple technique to acquire, but it can take a lifetime to master. Many expert listeners like to think they can identify a performer just by his vibrato. Whether or not that's true, certain guitarists are known for their particular brand of note-shaking. Consider a couple of techniques of the pros:

✔ B.B. King (born 1925) has stated that he developed his vibrato as a way of imitating the slide guitar of his cousin, Bukka White. If you have a chance to watch him play up close or in videos, you notice that B.B. King removes his thumb from the back of the neck and waves it in the air like a counterweight, especially when applying vibrato with his index finger.

✔ Michael Bloomfield (1943–81), who inherited a great vibrato from B.B. King, said that the trick of vibrato was to keep the pressure on the string consistent from the beginning to the end of the maneuver.

Track 60

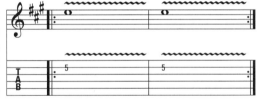

Figure 10-10:
A whole note with vibrato.

To produce a more vocal-like effect, let a sustained note sound without vibrato at first, then introduce it gradually (with slow, gentle bending), getting more intense (by increasing both the speed and width of the bend), and then finally, end the note with a little fall-off slide. Now, *that's* the way to be expressive with a whole note that would otherwise just sit there gathering dust!

Good vibrato, it is said, takes years to achieve. Listening to B.B. King, the master of the blues vibrato, certainly supports that claim. No one can match the soulful quality of his vibrato, and he got better as he got older!

The rubber-band blues: Bends that stretch a string

String bending is perhaps the most important — and certainly the coolest and smoothest — left-hand technique available to a blues guitarist to alter a fretted note. *Bending* is the act of stretching a string with a left-hand finger, increasing its tension, and causing the resulting pitch to rise. Bends are most effective on electric guitars, where the string *gauges* (thicknesses) are lighter and the strings are more flexible than on acoustic guitars, though string-bending on acoustic, while more limited, is still effective. Also, electric guitars are better at sustaining long tones, which enhances the sound of the bend.

In a bend, the pitch changes continuously instead of discretely through the fretted intervals that hammers, pulls, and slides produce. With a bend, you can vary the rate of change between notes, too. For example, if you have a whole-note bend (four beats' time to change from one pitch to another), you can take the entire four beats to bend smoothly up to the new pitch. Or you can wait three and a half beats on the original pitch and bend up suddenly, covering the same distance in just an eighth-note's time. There are endless variations to bending, all up to the musical situation and your personal taste.

The techniques of bending a note

To perform a bend, pick a fretted note and push the string across the fretboard (toward the sixth string) or pull it (toward the first string) with your fretting finger so the string stretches and raises the pitch in the process. Figure 10-11 shows two types of bends on the third string, one fast and one slow.

Track 61, 0:00

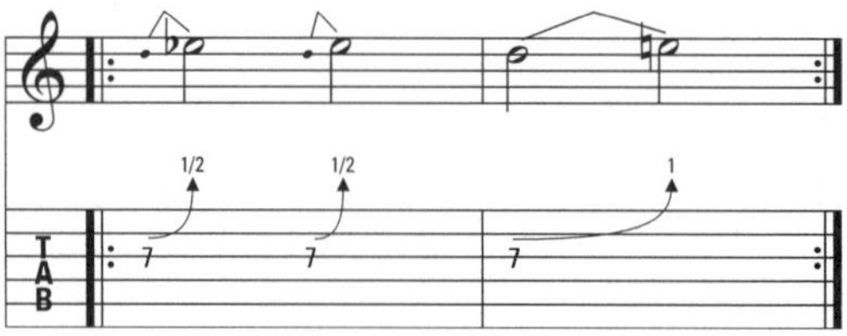

Figure 10-11: Two types of bends on the third string.

If you find it difficult to bend by using just one finger, try supporting the bending finger with another finger behind it (toward the nut). For example, if you use your third finger to bend, use your second, first, or even both of them to help push the string. This assistance affords more control and strength and is especially helpful when bending *and* vibratoing at the same time.

Playing great bends like it's nobody's business

Bends are a great way to add life to an already-sounded note, and they come in a wide variety of combinations: immediate bends, bends in rhythm, bends and releases, and pre-bends. You can even have multiple bends and releases all occurring after just one pick strike. Perhaps most important, though, is that bending distinguishes blues guitar from classical, folk, or jazz, where there's relatively little or no string bending. (Rock guitar has a lot of bending, but much of rock is derived from the blues.) The following sections all describe various ways to bend a string.

Albert King, arguably the most influential postwar, electric blues-guitarist after B.B. King, is widely regarded as the *king* of string benders. Part of his readily identifiable technique was facilitated by his playing upside down and backward, resulting in pulling down, rather than pushing up, to bend strings. His "Blues Power" from *Live Wire/Blues Power* (Stax Records) is a virtual glossary of multiple bends.

Bending in rhythm

Often a bend between two notes occurs in a specified rhythm. This means that you must control the travel of the bend between two notes, arriving at the destination note in rhythm — and in tune! Figure 10-12 shows a passage containing bends with three different variations of rhythms and distances.

Track 61, 0:17

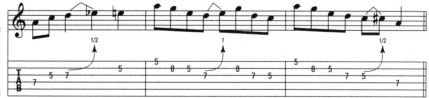

Figure 10-12:
Bending in
rhythm.

Releasing right on time

Letting go of a bend is called a *release*, and you can do this in a specified rhythm just as you do in a regular, ascending bend. Figure 10-13 shows two bend and releases. The first consists of a picked note — a bend of a half step in an eighth note and then a release back to the original pitch in an eighth note. The second is a picked note, a bend of a whole step in a quarter note, and then a release back to the original pitch in a half note.

Track 61, 0:31

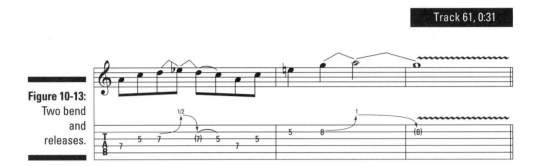

Figure 10-13:
Two bend and releases.

Bending a string before sounding the note

A *pre-bend* is where you bend the string and hold it in position before striking it. When you pick the string and release it from its pre-bent position, the pitch falls (descends) and produces a *downward bend*. Because it's technically impossible to bend down on the guitar, a pre-bend and release is a way of getting around this limitation; it's an expressive technique, especially when mimicking a crying or keening quality.

Figure 10-14 shows two examples of figures that employ a pre-bend and release, each in a different rhythm and interval combination, each requiring a different preparation by the guitarist.

Track 62

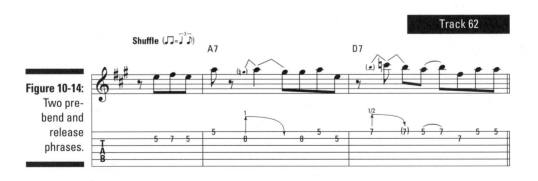

Figure 10-14:
Two pre-bend and release phrases.

Pre-bends can be tricky to master because they require a little more setup and consideration than a normal bend. In a pre-bend, you must have the time to bend up in silence, and you must be able to bend up to the starting note in tune — without hearing it first. Like normal bends, pre-bends can occur on different strings, at many different frets, and with a few different intervals (half-steps, whole steps, minor 3rds, and major 3rds being the most common). Still, you can practice pre-bends to feel your way to create in-tune pre-bends with remarkably consistent results.

The harmonica also bends notes to great expressive effect. But the harmonica can only bend notes down, and the guitar can only bend them up. So when a guitar employs a pre-bend and release, simulating a downward bend, it more closely emulates the characteristics of a harmonica.

Playing a Song with Various Articulations

In this section, you put together all the techniques in this chapter (which means that you may need to review the other methods before tackling this section). Figure 10-15 is a song called "Express Yourself Blues," featuring a smorgasbord of expressive techniques. Follow these steps when starting this piece:

1. **Practice just the notes and the rhythm, without necessarily trying to nail all the left-hand techniques.**

2. **Add the expressive touches one by one until you feel you can perform the techniques, notes, and rhythms with equal confidence.**

It's better to perform the piece with authority and leave some techniques out than to cram all the tricks in and have the result sound shaky. Blues is very unpretentious: It's about playing what you know with heart.

After you can play "Express Yourself Blues" accurately and from memory, then apply different overall dynamic approaches, moving accents around at will, playing loud here, soft there, and so on. Then try varying the rhythm a bit — rushing here, dragging there — until you feel you can play the piece upside down, in a wind tunnel, and under water. When you really know a piece, almost to the point that you're sick of it, you can start providing all the little nuances that can't really be pinned down or notated but that make the song your own. In blues it's those nuances — those indefinable but nevertheless discernible qualities — that can turn your phrasing from serviceable to inspired.

Track 63

Express Yourself Blues

Figure 10-15: "Express Yourself Blues" uses a variety of expressive techniques.

(continued)

(continued)

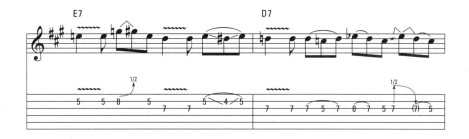

Part IV

Sounding Like the Masters: Blues Styles through the Ages

In this part . . .

Part IV contains the style chapters, which examine the various styles of blues throughout history. Chapter 11 starts with the roots in the Mississippi Delta and the acoustic guitar of Robert Johnson. It then moves East to catch the lively ragtime-influenced strains of the Piedmont school. Chapter 12 is the heart of today's blues: classic electric blues. Chapter 13 visits the other classic period of the blues — blues rock — which started with Eric Clapton, Jeff Beck, and Jimmy Page. Chapter 13 closes with the metal movement (yes, they played the blues, too) and the 21st century players.

Chapter 11

Acoustic Roots: Delta Blues and Its Country Cousins

. . . .

In This Chapter

▶ Hammering out the Delta blues

▶ Discovering the roots of Piedmont blues

▶ Melding Delta and Piedmont blues: Country and folk blues

▶ Producing a new form of blues: Rockabilly

▶ Performing with style: Acoustic slide guitar

. . . .

Acoustic-guitar blues is one of the earliest forms of blues. Before acoustic blues developed into its own instrumental style, the guitar was just a convenient instrument to play and accompany yourself while you sang. A performer naturally played rhythmically when singing and more melodically in between the vocal phrases. So the guitar style was woven into the singer's approach to accompanying himself on the guitar. Gradually, the guitar went from being just a background instrument into a solo, unaccompanied instrument and then evolved into the different branches of ragtime, country blues, and even rockabilly.

In this chapter, you explore the different forms of acoustic blues — Delta blues, Piedmont blues, country and folk blues, and rockabilly. You also take a tour of slide guitar.

Delta Blues: Where It All Began

The Delta is an area of northern Mississippi and Arkansas that was agriculturally and musically fertile. When people refer to the "Delta blues," they describe the music specific to a geographic region and the hard-edged, acoustic blues played by Charlie Patton, Son House, and especially Robert Johnson — its most famous and influential practitioner, who has contributed some of the best lasting recorded examples.

Understanding the Delta technique

The Delta blues style is an acoustic, self-contained approach (rhythm and lead combined) used almost exclusively as accompaniment for a singer. The thumb and fingers often play different parts. The thumb plays either steady quarter notes or a shuffle-eighth-note rhythm, especially when the high notes are laying out. The Delta blues liberally uses the minor pentatonic scale. (For more on the minor pentatonic scale, see Chapter 8.)

Figure 11-1 is a 12-bar blues in the Delta Blues style. The thumb hammers out either quarter notes or shuffle eighths. In the spaces where the vocal rests, high notes are introduced as melodic fills.

Many Delta players use thumbpicks for extra power. For more rhythmic playing, thumbpicks are especially appropriate, even if you don't normally use them.

The more experienced players try to incorporate licks and subtle chordal flourishes while keeping an insistent bass going. Figure 11-2 is an expanded version of the passage in Figure 11-1. It contains more movement in the treble part and bass runs connecting the chords for even more forward momentum.

If you've read through Chapter 8 and you think your knowledge of the open-position E minor pentatonic scale is up to snuff, create your own variations of fills between where the vocal phrases fall. The hardest part may be keeping the thumb going in quarter notes while you play the lick up top — especially if the lick contains rests, syncopation, or triplets mixed with shuffle-eighths.

Ladies and gentlemen, king of the Delta blues: Robert Johnson

Robert Johnson (1911–1938) is universally recognized as the "King of the Delta Blues," and for good reason. His influence is felt not only through those who followed but also in every student who picks up the guitar with a mind to play the blues.

Johnson influenced so many aspects of the blues — through his playing, his songwriting, and his aura. No performer has led — or was alleged to have led — a more mythic or legendary blues life. Some people believe that Johnson gained his talent in a deal with the devil; he died young and under mysterious circumstances, and his songs are haunting with chilling themes about the devil and death.

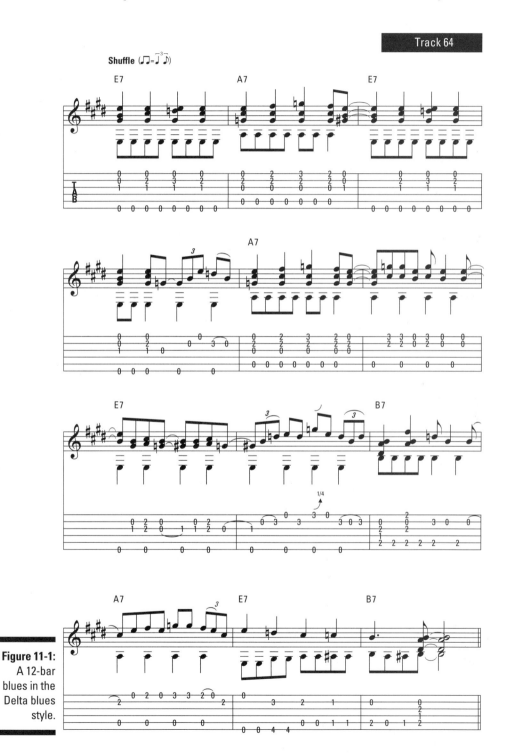

Figure 11-1:
A 12-bar
blues in the
Delta blues
style.

Track 65

Figure 11-2:
A 12-bar
blues in E
with
variations.

(continued)

(continued)

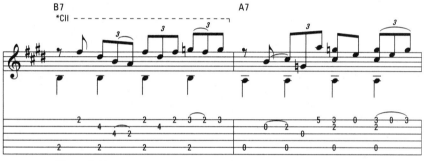

*Barre at 2nd fret.

If you've grown up with blues as interpreted by B.B. King, Eric Clapton, Stevie Ray Vaughan, and other modern electric-blues masters, hearing the scratchy, raw recordings of Johnson can be quite startling at first. Johnson's thin, keening voice, his twangy guitar, and his sometimes irregular meter and quirky phrasing are definitely an acquired taste. But when you make the adjustment, the genius of him in these stark settings is awe-inspiring.

Robert Johnson's music embodied the Delta blues in its finished state. And there was no end to Johnson's innovation. He played with a slide and without, in altered tunings as well as standard, and he shifted from accompaniment to a featured guitar style effortlessly. Actually, only one solo break of Johnson's talent is even on recording. To hear Robert Johnson play his only known recorded solo break, check out "Kind Hearted Woman Blues."

Practicing Johnson's famous style

Johnson played his brand of blues in many keys and in many different tunings, but he's known for his work in the key of open A. Figure 11-3 shows a passage in standard tuning that Johnson frequently used for intros, turnarounds, and endings.

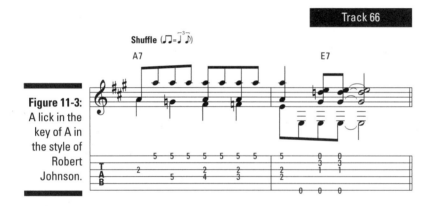

Figure 11-3: A lick in the key of A in the style of Robert Johnson.

Track 66

The lick in Figure 11-3 is similar to others that are covered in Chapter 6 in the key of E. (Don't worry if you haven't looked at that chapter yet.) In this figure I use a device called *oblique motion* — a fancy term for when one voice stays the same (the top) and another moves (the lower, descending).

Grasping the elusive Johnson progression

Johnson's style was complex and hard to pin down. Some of his stylistic hallmarks include the following:

- An insistent bass in quarters and shuffle-eighths
- Up-the-neck chords
- Chromatic movement
- Melodic fills in between vocal phrases
- Classic turnaround figures

Figure 11-4 shows a typical Johnson progression.

Figure 11-4:
A 12-bar blues in the style of Robert Johnson.

Johnson has come to be one of the few Delta blues players to be known for his influential songwriting (Willie Dixon, the bass player and performer is another) and for contributing to the blues repertoire with such standards as "Sweet Home Chicago" and "Crossroads." Besides composing two well-known hits with "Kind Hearted Woman Blues" and "Terraplane Blues," many of Johnson's songs were historically significant.

Table 11-1 shows a list of just some of Robert Johnson's songs. Each song is accompanied by a note on the song's significance and the tuning he used to play that song. You also see the key that the song is in and what fret to place your capo (if you're using one). *Note:* The term *concert key* refers to the actual pitch of the tuning. For example if Johnson were in the key of A, but tuned down a half step, the concert key would be A♭.

Table 11-1	The Songs of Robert Johnson			
Song	**Significance**	**Tuning**	**Key**	**Capo fret**
"Terraplane Blues"	An early popular song, played with a slide and combines shuffle with a 16th-note feel	Open A (E, A, E, A, C♯, E, low to high), down ½ step	A	2nd
"Kind Hearted Woman"	Johnson's only known 12-bar solo	Standard, down ½ step	A	2nd
"Sweet Home Chicago"	Covered by many blues, college, and cover bands, including Magic Sam and the Blues Brothers	Standard, down ½ step	E	2nd
"I Believe I'll Dust My Broom"	A slide anthem, covered by guitarist Elmore James	Aadd9 (E, B, E, A, C, E, low to high) down ½ step	E	—
"Come on in My Kitchen"	Plays the melody in unison with his vocals; a style copied by jazz players and George Benson	Open A (E, A, E, A, C♯, E), down ½ step	A	2nd
"Cross Road Blues" (Crossroads)	An anthem to the myth that Johnson sold his soul to the devil	Open A (E, A, E, A, C♯, E, low to high)	A	2nd

When Johnson sold his soul to the devil (or did he)?

Robert Johnson wasn't always referenced with the devil. The myth only began in 1965 after blues scholar Pete Welding interviewed Son House. House talked about the amazing progress Johnson made on the guitar in such a short time and said, "He must have sold his soul to the devil to play like that."

Eric Clapton and his band Cream perpetuated the myth, perhaps inadvertently, when they changed Johnson's opening lines of "Crossroads Blues" from "I went to the cross road — fell down on my knee. I asked the Lord above, 'Have mercy — Save poor Bob, if you please'" to "'I went down to the cross road, fell down on my knees, saw the devil. I went up and I said, 'Take me if you please.'"

Johnson's command of the blues may have seemed to exceed his command of geography. In "Sweet Home Chicago," he states, "Back to the land of California, Sweet Home Chicago." Many modern performers have changed the words completely by leaving out the California reference or by changing the preposition "to" to "from," which gives an interesting, new meaning to the phrase. In fact, "California" was used from the mid-19th century on after the gold rush to represent the land of golden opportunity — which was Chicago for rural African Americans in the 1930s.

Country Ragtime: The Piedmont Blues

The Piedmont blues feel is achieved by an alternating bass, where the bass plays on every quarter note, with accents and a root-fifth scheme on the first and third beats. This variation lends a two-beat, or *boom-chick,* sound. The sound of Piedmont blues is joyous and happy and is generally played more uptempo than Delta blues. The bouncy ragtime syncopations of ragtime piano — and especially the independence of the bass and treble voices — are often emulated in Piedmont blues, which further enhances its infectious, upbeat sound.

Practitioners of Piedmont picking include Blind Blake, Blind Boy Fuller, Barbecue Bob, Reverend Gary Davis, and Blind Willie McTell.

Blind Willie McTell (1898–1959), one of the most famous early practitioners from the early Piedmont school, was a virtuoso 12-string guitarist. His "Statesboro Blues" from 1928, though neither his best nor most famous song, is a modern classic with the driving, electric shuffle version recorded by the Allman Brothers Band on *Live at the Fillmore East* in 1971.

Distinguishing between Delta and Piedmont

You may be tempted to group the Delta and Piedmont blues under one category. But the Delta blues sound features a persistent bass with a hard-edged blues melody and very often, slide or "bottleneck" guitar. Piedmont blues is more lively and melodic, with a ragtime syncopation and an alternating bass that is more bouncy and less grounded than a Delta blues bass approach.

As students of blues history, consider Delta and Piedmont separately because their stylistic characteristics are so distinct, both from each other, and from the other general categories of country and folk blues (covered in the section "Everything In-Between: Country and Folk Blues") that draw on aspects of these two established styles. As well, each of these styles has important performers and lineage associated with it.

Piedmont is often called *country ragtime* because of its lively, driving flavor. This ragtime is different than the piano ragtime of Scott Joplin that you may be familiar with. Ragtime in Joplin's time was played straight without any bounce or shuffle feel the way country ragtime is.

Geographically, the "Piedmont" in Piedmont blues refers to the area quite a bit east of the Mississippi Delta, between the Appalachian mountains and the Atlantic coastal plain, stretching from Richmond, Virginia, to Atlanta, Georgia.

Figure 11-5 is an example of the driving, two-beat feel, accomplished through an alternating bass. This method is sometimes called *Travis picking,* after country performer Merle Travis, whose alternating thumb technique was widely popular (for more on Travis, check out "Country and Folk Blues Had a Baby; Its Name was Rockabilly," later in the chapter). Note that in this passage, in the key of C, the blue notes E♭ and B♭ figure prominently in the sound.

Track 68

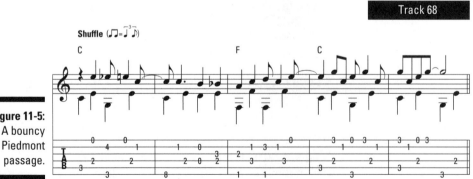

Figure 11-5:
A bouncy Piedmont passage.

After you practice Figure 11-5 a few times, throw in some variety and mute the lower strings to add contrast between the bass and treble voices. This variation is performed on the accompanying CD.

Figure 11-6 shows a Piedmont style ragtime chord progression. This progression is typical from the IV chord (F, in the key of C) that acts as the climax to a song. *Note:* The walking bass runs seem to line up perfectly with the chord progression.

Track 69

Figure 11-6: A ragtime chord progression with bass runs.

Everything In-Between: Country and Folk Blues

For acoustic blues that isn't clearly Delta or Piedmont — or may have elements of both — you can use the adjectives *country* and *folk*. In this case, *country* means old-time country, as in non-urban. It has nothing to do with Nashville, sequins, or Dolly Parton (think mountain hollers and shotgun shacks). Folk blues is more of a labeling convention, where certain performers, like Leadbelly, were considered folk musicians because they sang folk songs. A lot of it is just convention instead of indicating any deeper meaning.

A quick profile of country and folk blues

The repertoire that comprised country and folk blues was often just a loose mix of folk and popular songs that were given a bluesy treatment by blues-influenced performers. These performers often made no distinction between what was blues or not; they just played songs from any genre that suited their performance style. Similarly, audiences didn't notice, either. For example, no one could have led a more emblematic blues life than Leadbelly, yet his best known song was a waltz-time folk ditty called "Irene Goodnight."

Country and folk style blues often included an instrumental melody, usually syncopated on top of an alternating bassline. The guitar imitated the piano-based ragtime style of Scott Joplin's days. The key of C is the favorite key for many country and ragtime blues songs. Ragtime chords in the key of C include E7, A7, and D7, and G7, all of which fall nicely in open position and offer finger-pickers many options for bass runs, open strings, hammer-ons, and pull-offs.

For the audiences that perhaps found the Delta sound a little too dark or stark, country and folk music brought more tuneful melodies with a bluesy treatment that was a more enjoyable mix. People who brought about this mix included Mance Lipscomb, Big Bill Broonzy, Reverend Gary Davis, and Mississippi John Hurt. Like Piedmont blues, these styles feature a lively, relentless bass line in an alternating scheme, and the songs themselves are drawn more from the folk repertoire than from the 12-bar blues arena.

Giving these "in-between blues" a listen

The best way to understand country and folk blues is to listen to these styles. Songsters like Mississippi John Hurt wrote with a bouncy ragtime style, and recorded famous songs such as "Candy Man Blues" (full of double meanings), "My Creole Belle," and "Make Me a Pallet on Your Floor." These lively songs featured Hurt's ingenious ragtime work and had a good blues back story.

In the 1960s a curious sociological phenomenon occurred. Young white blues fans went looking for the forgotten country blues guitarists that they "knew" from their music on old, scratchy 78 rpm records. Mississippi John Hurt was found in Avalon, Mississippi, with the only clue being his "Avalon Blues" record. If this phenomenon hadn't occurred, Hurt's music may have fallen off the musical radar. He had lived in obscurity for 35 years, but his chops were still sharp and he became a favorite of concert goers.

Figure 11-7 is a song that features a melody on top of an alternating bass pattern, similar to Mississippi John Hurt's style. Pay attention to the way his confident, driving bass notes (played with the thumb) contrast the high-note syncopated melodic figures (played with the fingers).

Closing with a lick and some style: Ragtime tags

One of the best parts about country blues and ragtime playing are the tags. *Tags* are closing licks and phrases that are tacked on to the end of songs that provide a little coda — a finale. Tags are melodically unrelated to the song, but they seem to fit because of the key, feel, and mood. The most famous tag is perhaps "Shave and a hair cut, two bits" popularized by bluegrass bands, but ragtime guitar offers an infinite variety of tags, too.

Figure 11-8 shows a single-note tag in C that fits over any song in the style of Blind Blake, Reverend Gary Davis, or Mississippi John Hurt (info on Hurt can be found in the previous section).

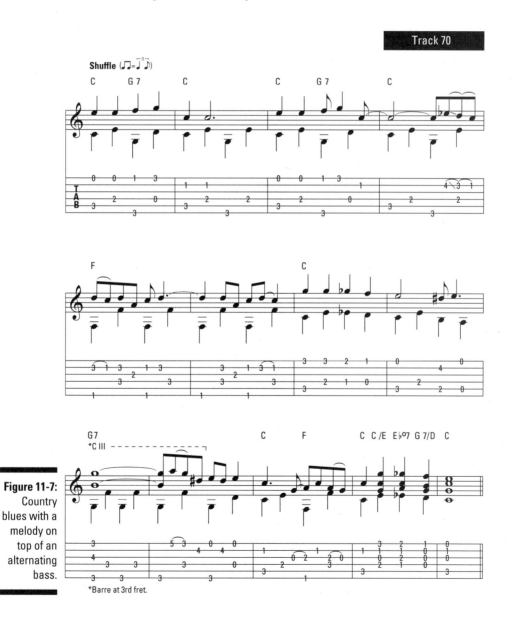

Figure 11-7: Country blues with a melody on top of an alternating bass.

*Barre at 3rd fret.

Figure 11-8:
A single-note ragtime tag in C.

Figure 11-9 shows the deluxe version of a tag, which is a "setup" progression of ragtime chords played in quarter notes and then a descending diminished arpeggio that winds up with a contrary-motion closer. It's a lot easier — and more fun — to play than to describe!

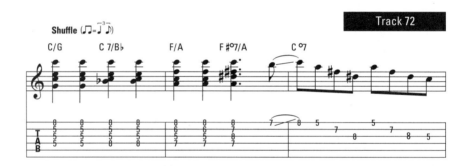

Track 72

Figure 11-9:
A deluxe ragtime tag that uses chords, an arpeggio, and single notes.

Country and Folk Blues Had a Baby; Its Name was Rockabilly

An important offspring of country blues was the hard-driving, alternate-bass sound that came to be known as rockabilly. The style featured blues figures but at a supercharged pace and with a heavy backbeat (provided by a more prominent drum sound) and often a heavy use of effects, such as reverb, slap-back echo, and tremolo. (For more on effects, check out Chapter 18.)

Merle Travis was a rockabilly pioneer (along with Scotty Moore [Elvis's first guitarist] and James Burton [Elvis's second guitarist]) who simplified and adapted for rock 'n' roll. Travis didn't invent the alternating bass sound of rockabilly, but he popularized his own hard-driving approach that featured a I-V-I-V bass motif in an uptempo two-beat feel, and guitar players often call any fingerpicking approach that uses an alternating bass *Travis picking.* Many people call any alternate-bass approach *Travis picking,* while others use the term only for the harder-driving, locomotive style. But Travis and his many followers, including Chet Atkins, Doc Watson, Leo Kottke, and Jerry Reed, have made this a staple sound in acoustic playing, and it works particularly well in an upbeat blues setting.

Figure 11-10 shows an E progression in a rockabilly feel that uses blues-inflected melodic bits.

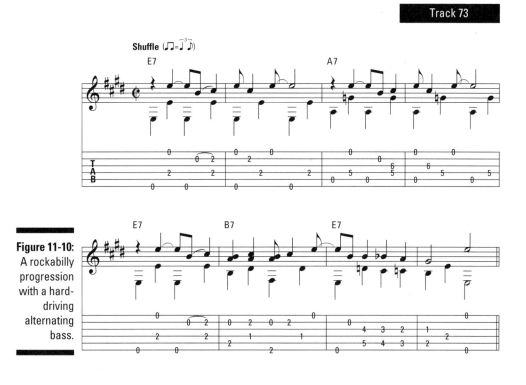

Figure 11-10: A rockabilly progression with a hard-driving alternating bass.

Track 73

Quintessential Blues: Slide Guitar

Slide guitar may have become a stylistic choice over fretted guitar out of necessity by players who didn't have the skills or patience to fret the guitar and found it easy to slide a smooth, rounded object over the strings to achieve a similar effect. But for the greatest practitioners such as Charlie Patton, Sylvester Weaver, Blind Willie Johnson, Son House, and Robert Johnson, slide guitar was an unparalleled mode of expression evocative of the human voice as well as the wail of train whistles — a sound near and dear to country blues guitarists. But whatever its origin, slide guitar is a staple of the acoustic blues guitar sound unlikely to ever be imitated by synthetic, digital means.

The tools that let you slide

Early, rural-dwelling slide players used anything they could find to produce the slide effect. The edge of a pocket knife, a length of pipe, a section of bone from a ham or beef shank, and a medicine bottle were among some of the top "tools" used, but the most popular and effective was a broken bottle neck (which was filed or fired to eliminate the sharp edges). Because the bottle neck was probably the most popular, slide blues guitar is sometimes called *bottleneck guitar.*

These days, you acquire your slippery weapon of choice by going to a music store and selecting from the pre-packaged slides in the display case. Metal and glass tubes are the two most common styles (though prepared bottlenecks are available, too) and come in various diameters to fit different-sized fingers.

- *Metal slides,* especially those made from brass, are heavier (they have more mass), bolder-sounding, and provide better sustain, but they're more difficult to master.
- *Glass slides* are light and have a rounder, mellower tone.

Sliding technique

Many Delta players combined slide technique with fretting, often having the slide play the melodic portions while their fretting fingers played chordal figures or kept the bass line going. This technique dictated the wearing of the slide on the fourth finger (the pinky). Follow the steps below to perfect your slide technique:

1. **Slide an object like a glass or metal tube over a left-hand finger (usually the third or fourth).**

2. **Rest the slide on the strings (not pressed down), directly over the fret wire.**

   Resting the slide on the strings and playing *over* the fret (instead of behind it as you do when fretting) takes a little finesse, but eventually, your intonation (the ability to play pitches in tune) and tone (the right pressure that produces rattle-free sustain) will improve.

3. **Change pitch by gliding the slide along the string.**

   This process produces a smooth, continuous change in pitch (sometimes called a *glissando,* or *portamento,* which is more correct).

   At first, your slide playing may sound clangy and rattly as you move the slide around. You can improve your sound by using one of two techniques:

   - *Dampening* (or muting), which involves placing your unused left-hand fingers lightly on the strings behind the slide (toward the nut)

   - Employing right-hand palm mutes

Slide guitar is physically easy in one sense. You just drag a slide over the strings, and you can instantly hear the effect, right? Well, it can be difficult to get sliding under control to play in tune and keep the accompanying buzzing and rattling artifacts to a minimum. Slide guitar doesn't require left-hand strength the way normal acoustic guitar playing does, but it does require finesse! Focus on intonation first, rhythm second, and dampening third.

Tuning your guitar for slide, a technique all its own

Slide guitar can be played in standard or open tunings, but standard may be easier because your melodic instincts don't have to be translated to the altered tuning of the guitar. However, in standard tuning it's quite a challenge for a beginning slide guitarist to mute the unwanted strings that can create a sour, dissonant sound, as opposed to the chordal harmony of open tunings. So standard tuning presents more of a technical challenge, while open tuning presents a "thinking" challenge as you translate your instincts to fit a different tuning. The solution? Play both ways!

Open tunings favor the technical side of common blues licks. And the main tunings, open E and open A (which are the same, relatively speaking, as open D and open G), each have their specific idiomatic licks. But to get started using the slide, try the passage in Figure 11-11, which is in standard tuning.

Figure 11-11: A slide lick in standard tuning.

Don't press too hard when applying the slide or the strings will buzz against the fret wire and fingerboard. Try to keep the rattle noise to a minimum when going from open strings to slide-stopped strings.

Standard tuning licks

Standard tuning and open E tuning both feature the root of the chord on the top string and an interval of a fourth between the first and second strings. The lower note is the fifth of the chord, and so makes for powerful-sounding licks, as Figure 11-12 shows. The passage isn't that difficult, and the slide doesn't do that much. But what it does is very effective, even in small doses.

The lick in Figure 11-12 is the characteristic sound of one of the most famous slide sounds of all time: "Dust My Broom" — a song originally by Robert Johnson with conventional fretting but covered in the most famous version by electric slide player Elmore James.

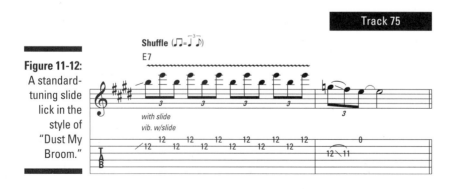

Figure 11-12: A standard-tuning slide lick in the style of "Dust My Broom."

Open E and open D tuning

Open tunings have many technical advantages over standard tuning. The most prevalent is that an open tuning provides a major chord across all six strings, so holding the slide straight across at any fret yields a chord on any set of strings.

Open E (E, B, E, G♯, B, E, low to high) is close to standard tuning because the top two strings are tuned the same, and many blues slide licks lie well in this tuning, because they require only slight movement of a couple of frets above or below to play an entire passage.

Open D is the same as open E but tuned a whole step (two frets) lower (D, A, D, F♯, A, D). Elmore James and Duane Allman (one of the greatest blues-rock slide guitarists and founder of the Allman Brothers Band) played in open E. Figure 11-13 shows a typical lick in open E.

Open A and open G tuning

In open A, the strings are tuned E, A, E, A, C♯, E, low to high. This puts the root of the chord on the fifth string and provides a major chord on the top three strings. Also, having a minor third interval between the top two strings allows for some idiomatic blues moves, especially the chromatic descending lick in thirds.

Track 76

*Open E tuning: E B E G♯ B E, low to high.

Figure 11-13:
A slide lick
in open E.

Open D has the same relationships between the strings as open E but is tuned a whole step (two frets) lower (D, G, D, G, B, D, low to high). Robert Johnson and Bonnie Raitt are two well-known slide guitarists who play in open A. Figure 11-14 shows a typical lick in open G.

*Open G tuning: D G D G B D, low to high.

Figure 11-14:
A slide lick
in open G.

Chapter 12

The Birth and Growth of Classic Electric Blues

*T*o understand electric blues, you must first understand the electric guitar and how it's different from the acoustic guitar. The electric guitar uses a magnetic pickup to capture the sound of the vibrating metal strings instead of a microphone or a *transducer* (a contact microphone that relies on a vibrating surface, such as the guitar's bridge or soundboard).

Early electric guitars, even ones with pickups, weren't much different from acoustic guitars in construction, but gradually the manufacturing approaches to electric and acoustic guitars diverged to produce two entirely different species. And along with the evolution of the electric guitar, so followed the electric blues guitar player's technique.

Today, of course, the electric guitar in blues (as it is in other genres) is far more popular than its older, acoustic counterpart. Think of the biggest blues guitar names playing today — Eric Clapton, B.B. King, Buddy Guy, Bonnie Raitt, Robert Cray. All are electric blues players who rocketed the blues to popularity. The acoustic-blues players of today — Rory Block, John Hammond Jr., Taj Mahal, Keb' Mo', Corey Harris, Roy Book Binder, and Bob Brozman — are no less talented, but don't enjoy the household-name status of, say, a King or a Clapton.

In this chapter, you get to know some of the important blues players who've made lasting contributions to the electrified form of blues guitar.

The Rise of the Electric Guitar in Blues

The electric guitar was invented for *volume*. Unamplified acoustic guitars were hopelessly underpowered to compete with other instruments on the bandstand. Putting a microphone in front of the guitar helped somewhat, but it was awkward — a little clumsy (mic stands and wires everywhere) — and it brought problems of *feedback* (the howling sound you hear when a mic is brought too close to a speaker).

When pickups were developed, performing guitarists lept at the opportunity to have at least a fighting chance to be louder. The new electrified sound allowed guitars to take the spotlight as the featured instrument, and it brought new forms of expression. Searing slide solos, sustained string bends, and a more instrumentally virtuosic approach were the order of the day, fueled by restless musicians anxious to infuse this previously rural sound with urban postwar energy.

The ever-evolving electric body

Very soon after discovering the more sustained, less banjo-like quality of the electronic or electric guitar, guitarists realized that a guitar optimized for acoustic performance actually worked against its qualities as an electric. Big, open bodies, which produced lots of acoustic punch and thumping bass, were a liability in an electric setting, because these larger, more resonant sound chambers just caused feedback. Guitars got thinner and thinner until the 1950s when guitar makers realized you just didn't need a resonating chamber at all and came up with the all-wood-filled guitar — or solidbody. It had virtually no acoustic sound, but it sure rocked the joint when you plugged in! The electric solidbody, which includes the Fender Stratocaster and Gibson Les Paul, is the most popular electric guitar model in the world today.

At first, early electric guitarists simply played the way they always played when playing acoustic and appreciated the benefits of not having to play harder to play louder (instead they just turned up the amp). But as techniques developed, players began to understand that the electric was an entirely different instrument from the traditional acoustic, or "Spanish" guitar. Musicians started adjusting their techniques — and their whole approach to music — accordingly to suit the new medium. With a guitar that could hold its own with other principal instruments on the bandstand, guitarists now focused more on melodic and lead playing.

Although the sounds of electric and acoustic differ, electric guitar is similar to the acoustic in that it has six strings and frets, so any acoustic guitarist can play an electric right off the bat. And if they could afford it, virtually everyone did. Manufacturers like Gibson began selling electric guitars like hotcakes in the mid '30s, and it was soon clear that electric guitars were going to be big. Very big. And sure enough, jazz guitarists snatched them up as fast as Gibson and others could crank them out.

Increased sustain is probably the number-one advantage of electric guitars, allowing long, fluid, horn-like melodic lines. Overdriving an amp into distortion creates the illusion of even longer sustain because the signal is clipped and compressed, which keeps a steady volume level until it abruptly decays.

Other benefits of the electric's sound include

- A smoother tone
- Less drastic *envelope* — a graphic description of the behavior of a plucked note's attack, decay, sustain, and release

When creatively controlled, these effects allowed electric guitars to compete on equal footing with saxes and other horns for solo supremacy.

Giving Props to the Earliest Electric Pioneer

Although electric guitarists became a dime a dozen after electrics became affordable, one name stands alone as the early voice of electric blues guitar: T-Bone Walker.

Aaron Thibeaux Walker is one of the most influential blues guitarists of all time because he bridged the gap from acoustic country blues into the urbanized, electric sound of Memphis, Kansas City, and Chicago. Walker's style and musical sensibilities were sophisticated and jazzy, and he was a versatile and skilled musician who worked a lot. He incorporated jazz-type harmony and phrasing in his playing, using ninth chords in his rhythm playing and crafting lead lines that were melodically and rhythmically complex.

Figure 12-1 shows a passage in the style of Walker's "Call It Stormy Monday" — his own tune and one where he really stretched out, taking the blues to places other melodic players of the day had never been. He achieved this end by throwing in unusual (for the time) string bends, jazzy phrases, and a harmonic sophistication his Delta counterparts would hardly recognize. But it was all grounded in the blues vocabulary.

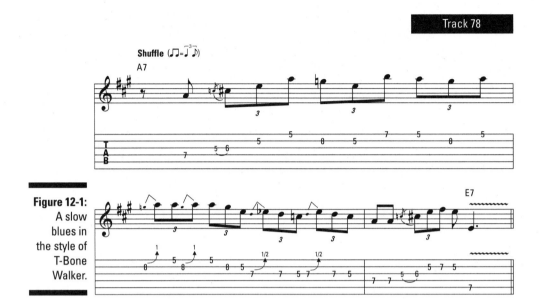

Figure 12-1:
A slow
blues in
the style of
T-Bone
Walker.

Walker influenced countless electric players, including Muddy Waters, Eric Clapton, Otis Rush, Magic Sam, Buddy Guy, Albert King, Albert Collins, Freddie King, and most significantly, B.B. King. The Allman Brothers' cover "Stormy Monday" (from *At Fillmore East*) is a T-Bone Walker composition.

Sweet Home Chicago, Seat of the Electric Blues

Many people *think* they know what Chicago blues is, but the more they discover the diverse influences, overlapping associations, time periods, and even the geography of the city, the more they realize what an open issue the notion of Chicago blues is. Still, if you just try to enjoy the music without engaging in too much analysis, you realize how important the Windy City is to the development of the blues.

The fertile postwar Chicago scene had several players, led primarily by the big wigs I introduce you to in this section.

They called it sweet home: The bluesmen of Chicago

In the period before World War II, important performers included Big Bill Broonzy, Tampa Red, and Memphis Minnie, who played electrically and acoustically. In the postwar period — and after T-Bone's electric influence was felt by all who heard him — the Chicago scene, fueled by an influx of southern talent, took off. The following table shows, in order of birth date, some of the important blues guitarists who all called Chicago home.

Artist	Style	Association
Big Bill Broonzy (1893–1968)	Acoustic folk blues	Friend to Muddy Waters
Tampa Red (1900–81)	Electric, slide, hokum	Influenced Muddy Waters, Elmore James, and Robert Nighthawk
Howlin' Wolf (1910–76)	Electric	Delta influence in the direct lineage back to Charlie Patton ("Founder of Delta Blues"); Muddy Waters's contemporary and sometimes-rival
Muddy Waters (1915–83)	Electric, slide	Delta influence; leader of the first generation of postwar Chicago scene for decades
Robert Nighthawk (1909–67)	Acoustic, electric	Delta influence; the slide link between Tampa Red and Earl Hooker
Elmore James (1918–63)	Electric, slide	Delta influence; the most influential electric slide guitarist of the time, and a contemporary of Robert Johnson
Earl Hooker (1930–70)	Electric lead and slide	Delta influence; followed Tampa Red and Robert Nighthawk; influenced B.B. King, Buddy Guy, Jimmy Page
Otis Rush (b. 1934)	Electric lead	Second generation Chicago; West Side sound; influenced Clapton, Stevie Ray Vaughan, and Peter Green; played "upside-down" guitar
Buddy Guy (b. 1936)	Electric lead	Second generation Chicago; West Side sound; backed Muddy Waters, among others; had a long association with harp man Junior Wells; influenced Jimi Hendrix and Eric Clapton
Magic Sam (1937–69)	Electric, fingerstyle	Second generation Chicago; West Side sound; influenced Robert Cray

Muddy Waters, leader of the pack

Born in Jug's Corner, Mississippi, in 1915, Muddy Waters (birth name McKinley Morganfield) came north to Chicago in 1945 and became the leader of Chicago's South Side blues scene. A large and imposing man, Waters dominated the stage, the scene, and the entire city in all things blues. He had talented contemporaries, like Howlin' Wolf and Sonny Boy Williamson II, but no single person is more associated with the Chicago sound than Muddy.

He had everything:

✔ A guitar style that included both percussive, stinging single-note Delta riffs

✔ An aggressive bone-chilling slide technique

✔ A big raspy singing voice

✔ A commanding stage presence

✔ A long and prolific performing and recording career

Plus, he was one of the very few who played acoustic in Mississippi and electric in Chicago, single-handedly leading the charge to bridge the two styles. Truth is, though, that Muddy was important for his *historical* contributions, being first on the scene, and for bringing his brand of a hopped-up Delta sound into a large-ensemble setting.

Figure 12-2 shows an electric guitar passage in the style of Muddy Waters with both riff playing and straight-picking lines represented.

Track 79

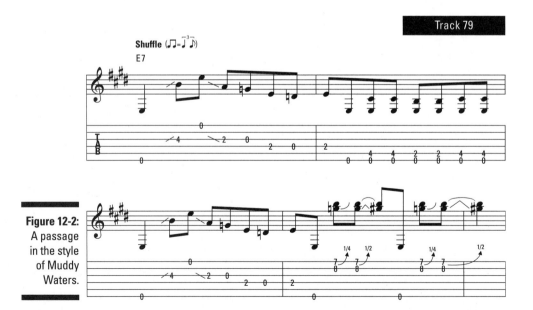

Figure 12-2: A passage in the style of Muddy Waters.

Elmore James, slide guitarist extraordinaire

Elmore James was a Chicago-based blues player known for his electric slide work. His most famous song was actually written and previously played by Delta blues great Robert Johnson (for more on Johnson, see Chapter 11). James recast the signature lick from "Dust My Broom" (James's version is known by the shortened version of the title) from conventional fretted playing to slide and recycled it many times in his other compositions.

James's techniques with an electric guitar and his explosive assault on the strings turned "Dust My Broom" into a piece of blues immortality. James's slide lick is the first lick you need to learn; its importance is matched only by its accessibility, and it's what'll get you kicked out of the South Side if you don't play it correctly.

James's "Dust My Broom" performed in open D tuning (D, A, D, F♯, A, D, low to high) is shown in Figure 12-3. It's a lick that's similar to the one employed by James on this "slide anthem."

Track 80

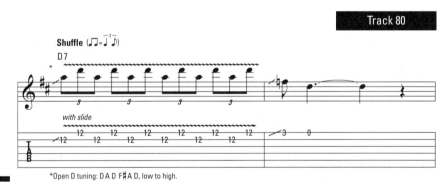

*Open D tuning: D A D F♯ A D, low to high.

Figure 12-3:
A lick in the style of Elmore James's "Dust My Broom."

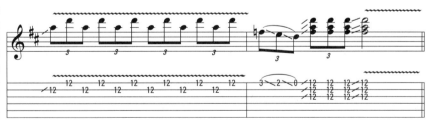

Magic Sam, a man who marched to the pluck of his own pick

Magic Sam (birth name Sam Maghett) was born on February 2, 1937, in Grenada, Mississippi, and was one of the architects of Chicago's West Side sound. Sam played in a unique style, a punctuated fingerpicking approach, dosed with amp tremolo (for more on tremolo, see Chapter 16), exhibited in such tunes as his debut single for Cobra records, "All Your Love." His nickname "Magic" derived from his last name,

Maghett. For many, Sam's one-of-a-kind style, great singing voice, and singular performing persona made him the favorite of the West Side school.

Tragically Sam died young (at age 32) of a heart attack and didn't enjoy the fame and notoriety of some of the other figures of his time such as Buddy Guy and Otis Rush.

Otis Rush: Soulful player with a flair for vibrato

Born in Philadelphia, Mississippi, in 1934 as one of seven children, Otis Rush learned to play the guitar left-handed and upside down, in the same way Albert King did. Rush was exposed to Muddy Waters and Howlin' Wolf, but he also listened to the records of B.B. and Albert King, who deeply influenced his lead approach. His first single, Willie Dixon's "I Can't Quit You Baby," made it to the top-ten on Billboard's R&B chart.

"I Can't Quit You Baby," as well as the rhumba-flavored "All Your Love" and the minor-key songs "Double Trouble" and "My Love Will Never Die," show Rush's smooth, soulful single-string work and stinging vibrato.

Figure 12-4 is a single-note lick in the style of Otis Rush that shows how to play the blues with soul.

Buddy Guy, the father of blues rock

George "Buddy" Guy was born in 1936 in Louisiana and moved to Chicago in 1957 when he was 21, already a seasoned professional. Guy, more than any of his contemporaries, seemed to foreshadow the blues rock movement through his stage show. He played loudly and infused his playing with whammy-bar antics, distortion, and feedback, all of which became a staple in hard rock.

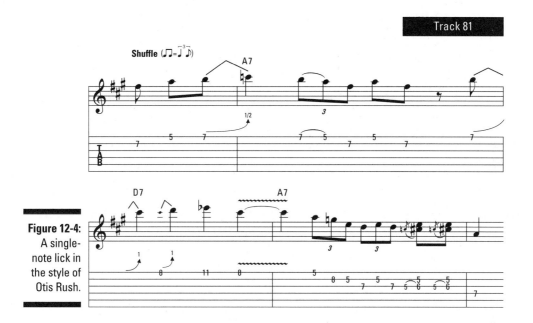

Track 81

Figure 12-4:
A single-note lick in the style of Otis Rush.

Buddy Guy influenced the early British blues rock greats Jeff Beck, Eric Clapton, and the Rolling Stones, and toured the United Kingdom in 1965, sharing a bill with the Yardbirds (for more on the Yardbirds and its members, see Chapter 13). Major rock artists readily acknowledge Guy's influence. Stevie Ray Vaughan said, "Without Buddy Guy, there would be no Stevie Ray Vaughan."

Guy is perhaps the single most important performer (trained by Waters and Howlin' Wolf) to bridge the Chicago sound with blues rock. Through his exceptional talent and longevity, he has become a living legend whose albums have won Grammy Awards, and he's received the praises of later greats such as Eric Clapton, who calls Guy his "favorite blues axe man."

Figure 12-5 is a passage that captures the essence of Buddy Guy's fiery and virtuosic style.

Track 82

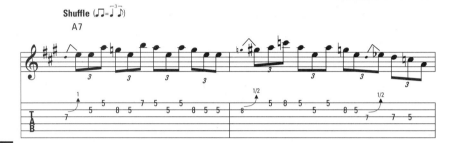

Figure 12-5:
A passage
in the style
of guitar
great
Buddy Guy.

Modern-Day Blues Styles: The Sounds of Texas

As the blues grew up, it developed its own regional flavors beyond the already established locales of the Delta and Piedmont. So of course, Texas, being such a large and diverse state, has a sound and culture all its own when it comes to the blues. Of all the big blues regions, Texas, by virtue of its size (both geographically and in population) and blues hotspots like Austin, Houston, and Dallas, still retain a meaningful connotation in modern-day blues styles.

It's important to distinguish a sound as defined by a region (Texas versus Delta) instead of simply a performer who hailed from that part of the country. For example, T-Bone Walker was from Texas, but he developed his jazzy style when he was living in Los Angeles. His sound isn't so much Texas as it is smooth West-Coast urban.

And speaking of the Lone Star State, when you say "Texas shuffle" to people attuned to the regional dialects of the blues, they instantly think of the many attributes of the shuffle:

- ✔ **Rhythm:** The rhythm section swung harder, influencing the lead guitarists' approach to their solos.

- ✔ **Swing:** The Texas Shuffle has more swing than the slow grind of a Delta blues or the bouncy ragtime of the Piedmont.

> ✔ **Harmonic richness:** This genre also has a wider variety of notes (the major third, the major sixth, and chromatic neighbor tones) than just the minor pentatonic or six-note blues scales favored by Delta players.

Any great blues musician knows a Texas shuffle and can play in that style when asked, so I'm here to help you prepare.

Figure 12-6 is a solo in a Texas shuffle setting. It incorporates a wide vocabulary of notes in the lead part. Note the liberal use of the *sweet notes* — the major third and major sixth of the chords underneath.

Famous early performers to come out of the Lone Star State include Blind Lemon Jefferson, Lightnin' Hopkins, T-Bone Walker, Clarence "Gatemouth" Brown, and Albert Collins. They performed vastly different music from one another, but all are connected through history and influence. Walker's electric playing could hardly be more different from the acoustic playing of Blind Lemon Jefferson, yet both lay claim to the "Texas sound."

A later generation of Texans includes two of the all-time greatest blues players of the post-Chicago heyday: Johnny Winter and Stevie Ray Vaughan. Billy Gibbons and his band ZZ Top achieved huge commercial success with their Texas-based blues-rock sound in the '70s and '80s.

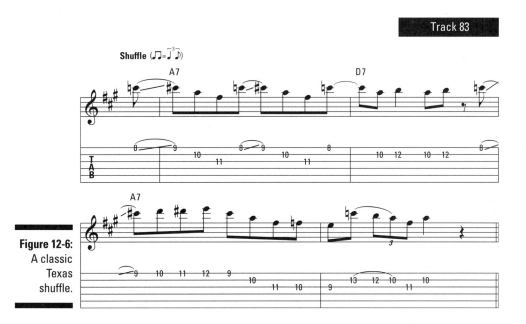

Figure 12-6: A classic Texas shuffle.

Four Blues Giants: Three Kings and a Collins

Beyond the important regions, cultural developments, and trends in blues, individual performers often launch a trend in music. You'd be hard pressed to find any single more influential individual than the four giants of blues guitar covered in the following sections.

Albert King, the upside-down string bender

Mississippi-born, Arkansas-raised Albert King was a big man who squeezed the strings of his guitar into heartfelt submission. Because he played left-handed, upside-down guitar (where the low E string was closest to the floor), Albert's style was unorthodox, especially his approach to bending strings. He pulled the strings of his signature Gibson Flying V down toward the floor, which in part accounted for his unusual, expressive sound.

Figure 12-7 shows a passage that captures Albert's unique string-bending approach and phrasing.

When Albert King was living in St. Louis in the late 1950s and then Memphis, he recorded for Stax Records and enjoyed real success, gaining visibility in both the blues and rock arenas. His soulful sound and R&B arrangements produced his best known songs of the era, including "Laundromat Blues," "Cross Cut Saw," and "Born Under a Bad Sign," all of which placed on the pop charts. Albert King influenced many blues and blues-rock guitarists including Jimi Hendrix, Eric Clapton, Mike Bloomfield, Stevie Ray Vaughan, and Robert Cray.

If you're right-handed and ever want to see "first hand" what it was really like for Albert King and Otis Rush to play guitar, go into a music store and ask to see a left-handed guitar. Hold it "righty-style" with the fretboard in your left hand, and you'll see the low E string is closest to the floor. Then try to play some familiar chords and licks. If you don't get freaked out, or at least a little disoriented by this, either you're an ambidextrous genius, or you're not really trying!

B.B. King, the blues' king of kings

If you know only one name in the blues, it's probably B.B. King. B.B. is the rightly anointed, undisputed king of the blues, and he has a deep historical connection to the Delta performers and trod the early club circuit in the southern United States.

Track 84

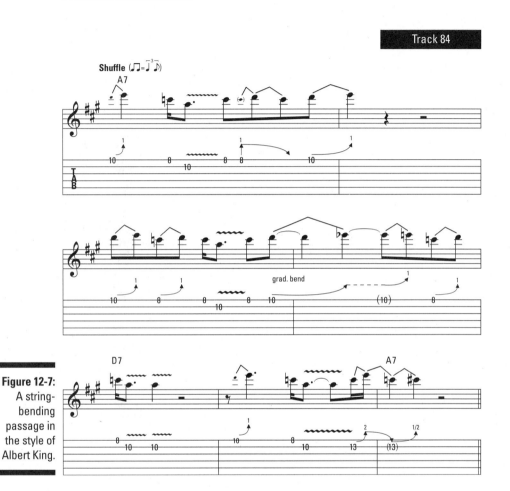

Figure 12-7:
A string-bending passage in the style of Albert King.

Born Riley B. King in 1925 in Indianola, Mississippi, B.B. King began to gain success in his early 20s in his adopted town of Memphis, playing clubs and appearing on radio. His on-air persona was "the Beale Street Blues Boy," eventually foreshortened to "B.B.", and he started recording in earnest in 1949 (only one year after Muddy Waters — who was ten years older — made his first recording in Chicago). B.B. soon had his first national R&B hit with "Three O'clock Blues" in 1951 and was widely recorded in the next decade.

B.B. King has it all: a soulful delivery, chops to burn, a vast vocabulary of blues licks in a variety of genres, and an inexhaustible reservoir of expressive techniques. He's perhaps most often cited for his vibrato, which is effortless and heart rending.

Figure 12-8 shows an example of how B.B. executes his brand of vibrato over a minor blues. To play like B.B. King, work to make every vibrato count, no matter how brief. That means applying a different intensity (rate of bend and depth of bend) to the note at hand, based on the tempo and feel of the groove.

B.B. King has had the best commercial success of any traditional electric blues player, having appeared on *The Ed Sullivan Show* and *American Bandstand,* and enjoying a Top 40 hit with 1969's "The Thrill Is Gone." Today, he may seem like a kindly elder statesman when you see him on TV commercials, but back in the day, B.B. was a formidable force — tearing up stages, clubs, airwaves, and recording studios wherever he went. He was a complete player, who fused his many influences: Delta blues, the jazz of Charlie Christian, R&B, superior guitar technique, and a deep understanding of how to harness the full emotional power of the blues. He remains hardworking, humble, prolific, and his playing hasn't lost one technical step through the years.

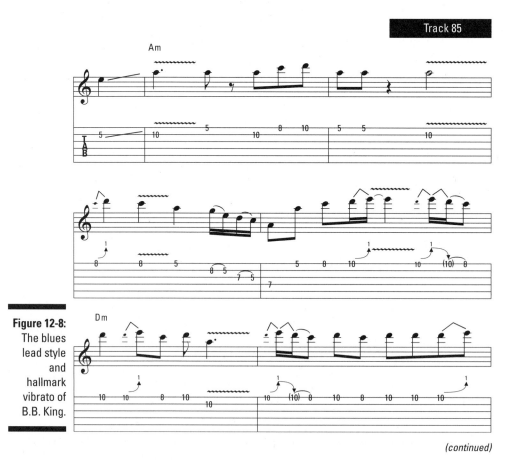

Figure 12-8: The blues lead style and hallmark vibrato of B.B. King.

(continued)

(continued)

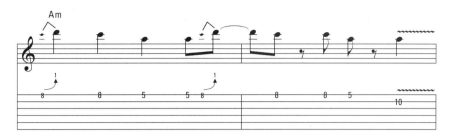

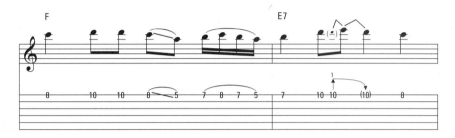

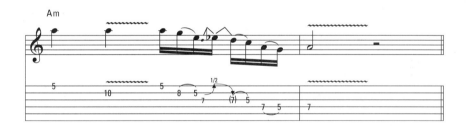

Burning for Lucille

Lucille is the name King gives his main guitar (now a Gibson B.B. King signature edition, modeled after the ES-355). The story goes that King was playing in an Arkansas club when a fight broke out between two men over a woman. During the brawl a pail of kerosene that was being used to heat the club was knocked over, setting fire to the room. After escaping outside, King realized that he had left his guitar inside and rushed back into the burning club, risking his life to retrieve his axe. He later learned that the name of the woman the men had been fighting over was Lucille, and so King named his guitar Lucille and has since named many of his guitars in her honor. (Lucille also reminds King to never do anything so foolish as to run into a burning building again.)

Freddie King, a two-pick man

Freddie King was a Texas-born guitarist who played with a plastic thumbpick and a metal fingerpick, in a two-finger fingerpicking style that he said he learned from Muddy Waters sideman Jimmy Rogers and Jimmy Reed sideman Eddie Taylor. His early influences included Lightnin' Hopkins and saxman/jump blues star Louis Jordan, but he's influenced others, too: Jeff Beck, Keith Richards, Jerry Garcia, Peter Green, Kenny Wayne Shepherd, and John Mayer.

Freddie's family moved from Texas to Chicago in 1950, when he was just 16, and there he sneaked into clubs to hear the greats of that era: Muddy Waters, Howlin' Wolf (who took a liking to the young guitar player), and Elmore James. He began recording as a sideman in the '50s while working in a steel mill.

Freddie King's best-known song is the instrumental "Hide Away," recorded in 1961, which was covered by John Mayall's Bluesbreakers with Eric Clapton, and Stevie Ray Vaughan — and every blues cover band in North America and Europe. Following the success of this tune, which placed on the pop charts as well as the R&B charts, Freddie followed up with more instrumentals, including "San-Ho-Zay," "The Stumble," and "Side Tracked."

Figure 12-9 shows a lick in the style of Freddie King's "Hide Away." Keep the approach light and crisp, as Freddie did, and play "on top of" (or slightly ahead of) the beat to capture his sound.

Albert Collins, master of the Telecaster

Nicknamed the "Master of the Telecaster," Albert Collins was an accomplished showman and a fierce guitarist. Born in 1932, in Leona, Texas, he received his initial musical training on the keyboards, but he soon picked up the guitar and started hanging out in Houston clubs and absorbing the influence of his Texas-based idols, Clarence "Gatemouth" Brown, Lightnin' Hopkins (a distant relative), T-Bone Walker, and John Lee Hooker.

Albert Collins concocted a unique recipe for playing guitar, consisting of a Fender Telecaster, a capo (which was often strapped on at the fifth, seventh, or even ninth frets), unorthodox tunings, and a stinging fingerstyle approach that fairly snapped notes out of the guitar. The essence of Albert Collins's style was his aggressive attack, piercing sound, and staccato phrasing.

Albert Collins had a string of instrumental hits in the late '50s and early '60s whose titles all had a "chilled" theme to them ("The Freeze," "Sno-Cone," "Icy Blue," and "Don't Lose Your Cool"). These songs earned him the nickname "The Iceman." In 1962, he released "Frosty," which became a big hit.

Track 86

Shuffle (♫=♩ ♪)

B7   A7

Figure 12-9:
A lick in the
infectious,
melodic
style of
Freddie
King.

E7   B7

Children of the Post-War Blues Revival

The next generation of blues artists was born after World War II in the 1950s. If you were a student of the blues growing up in an ever-growing media-savvy society, you could hitch your wagon to any style or personality and immerse yourself in study. A Californian could play Delta blues just as well as someone from Mississippi, because chances are, he'd be drawing from the same sources: many available records and tapes.

In the rock world, the guitarists who seemed to be capitalizing most success-fully on the early electric blues weren't even American, they were British. (See Chapter 13 for the influence of British guitarists on blues rock.) But it meant that the blues was undergoing a democratization. You could be from anywhere, with any background, and learn to play the blues.

Son Seals, Chicago's favorite son

Born in 1942, in Osceola, Arkansas, Son Seals grew up watching established performers Robert Nighthawk and Albert King from backstage at his father's club when he was a little kid. At age 13, Seals was playing drums profession-ally, even backing up Nighthawk. In the 1960s, having switched to guitar and then moving to Chicago, Seals played guitar with Earl Hooker and drums with Albert King. He was hanging with the real deal.

Seals was a fixture on the Chicago blues scene during the late '60s and early '70s. He had a raw vocal quality and muscular approach to guitar playing and was the true link between the old school and the new. His traditional approach derived from the leaders of the West Side school but helped keep alive the 1970s Chicago blues scene.

Robert Cray, smooth persuader

Robert Cray took the pop charts by storm in the 1980s with his soul and R&B-based blues, but he wasn't exactly an overnight sensation, having been around long enough to see Albert Collins, Freddie King, and Muddy Waters play in concert, and to join Collins on the stage before the elder blues man passed. Cray, who was born in 1953, was largely influenced by Albert King and was the leading blues guitar personality of the '80s, along with Stevie Ray Vaughan (covered in Chapter 13).

Cray demonstrated a complete package: great singing, songwriting, showmanship, and guitar playing. He won a Grammy for his album *Strong Persuader* in 1986, featuring the song "Smokin' Gun." He also has a close association with Eric Clapton (often appearing with him in concert) and continues to be a major influence in the modern movement of electric blues players today.

Figure 12-10 shows a lick in the style of Cray's smooth, economical, and tasteful approach to lead guitar. To achieve a similar sound, work to make your lines forceful (with plenty of attack) but *legato* (that is, hold them for their full value), and apply some high-quality effects to the guitar sound (digital reverb). And don't play too busily, either. Cray makes every note count.

Bonnie Raitt, stellar lyrical slides artiste

Bonnie Raitt was born to a musical family (her father was a Broadway star), and Raitt split her time between music, political activism, and academic pursuits. Performing kept pulling her away from her academic studies at Radcliffe, but those performances turned her into a seasoned performer who appeared in Boston clubs with blues legends such as Howlin' Wolf and Mississippi Fred McDowell. At age 20, in 1970, she was offered a spot touring with the Rolling Stones.

Raitt was a hard-working blues player for many years before commercial success finally found her in the 1980s. When her two expertly produced albums appeared in close succession — 1989's *Nick of Time* and 1991's *Luck of the Draw* — mass audiences finally appreciated what discerning blues listeners had known for a long time: Raitt possessed a talent for playing melodically lyrical slide lines, which she does in open A tuning.

Figure 12-11 shows an open A (E, A, E, A, C♯, E, low to high) slide solo in the accessible style of Bonnie Raitt. To capture Raitt's quality, play your slide melody lines as if they were beautiful vocal melodies — taking to let each note ring for its full duration and applying judicious use of scoops and fall-offs the way a torch-singing balladeer would.

Figure 12-10: Robert Cray's tasteful and economical lead approach.

Figure 12-11:
An open-A
slide solo in
the style of
Bonnie
Raitt.

Chapter 13

Blues Rock: The Infusion of Ol' Rock 'n' Roll

*T*he year 1965 was one of the most important years in popular music history. It was the year of Bob Dylan's "Like a Rolling Stone," and the Rolling Stones' "Satisfaction." For guitarists, it was also the beginning of a vast blues revival. Suddenly, mid-'60s electric guitarists on both sides of the Atlantic began re-exploring the blues and the roots of rock 'n' roll, along the way inventing an exciting, influential genre called "blues rock."

What traditional electric blues gave to the emerging style of blues rock was widespread use of string bends and finger vibrato in composed melodic lines and improvised solos. Before the influence of blues, rockers in the '50s could buy only heavy-gauge guitar strings, but '60s blues rockers learned how to bend new, lighter-gauge strings, develop a strong vibrato, and hold long, sustained notes for many beats. These blues techniques gave rock guitar leads a more human, vocal-like quality.

This new level of expression also gave birth to the "guitar hero." By the end of the 1960s, guitar gods like Eric Clapton, Michael Bloomfield, Jimi Hendrix, Jeff Beck, and Jimmy Page had become the gold standard of blues-rock currency. But these guitarists went beyond just bending strings — they also employed high-powered amplifiers, such as the fabled Marshall stack, to play blues guitar at previously unheard of volumes, and infused their tone with tube overdrive, fuzzbox distortion, and the deep funk of wah-wah pedals. (For more on these effects, see Chapter 15.)

In this chapter, I show you how to transform your playing to this new realm, highlighting the great blues-rock guitarists of this era and bringing bend as well as the effects of overdrive and wah to the forefront, so you can impress all your friends with your screamin' tricks.

The Blues Had a Baby, and They Called It Rock 'n' Roll

When rock 'n' roll began in the mid 1950s, it was essentially a blend of rhythm-and-blues and jazz chord changes with country rhythms. Later, pop entered the genre via catchy tunes and more sophisticated lyrics. But the blues had only a negligible influence in a world of sweet and boppy melodies of the day, until one very stylish, duck-walking performer burst onto the scene — Chuck Berry. And following Berry was a whole movement of first British and later American artists who brought the blues to the world's screaming teens. The sections that follow trace that progression and show how the blues was instrumental in shaping this new sound.

Chuck Berry, blues rock's first superstar

Chuck Berry is both rock's first guitar star and a subtle champion of the blues. Berry played in a raw, aggressive straight-eighth style, but used many of the repeated-note motifs of blues players, especially in his syncopated bends.

Berry's classic hits from the late 1950s, such as "Johnny B. Goode," "Roll Over Beethoven," and "Back in the USA," were powered by a new spin on the I-IV-V blues progression (covered in Chapter 6) to which Berry added a straight-ahead drum beat. It became such a standard that even 15 to 20 years later, big-ticket rock bands would close their shows with a Berry-styled jam. You can hear a classic example of Berry's lead style in Figure 13-1.

Beyond just strumming a simple I-IV-V progression, try these variations that make the 12-bar pattern more interesting:

1. **Start on the I (tonic) chord.**

2. **Strum a steady G5 chord (G on the sixth string, and D on the fifth string), and use your pinky finger to alternate an E note (on the fifth string) with the D.**

   This motion creates a *boogie* sound, popularized by blues guitarist Jimmy Reed (covered in Chapter 6) and R&B pianists of the pre-rock 'n' roll era.

3. **Duplicate this pattern on the IV chord and the V chord.**

4. **Take it one step further by adding an F note on the G chord. (So while you're strumming the G bass note, play in succession the D, E, and F notes with your ring and pinky fingers.)**

   This variation is classic boogie used by Chuck Berry and other early rock 'n' roll guitarists.

Track 89

Figure 13-1:
A I-IV-V
progression
in the Chuck
Berry style.

Bo Diddley, king of the jungle beat

Guitarist Bo Diddley, meanwhile, picked up a rectangular Gretsch electric and strummed a syncopated chord rhythm, later known as the *Bo Diddley beat*. This jungle beat (along with a heavy, throbbing drum sound), also known as the "Burundi beat," became another '50s guitar staple, turning up in hits like "Hey Bo Diddley" and Diddley's eponymous hit, "Bo Diddley."

Other '50s and early '60s rockers who mixed blues into their rock stew included bass-string riffer Link Wray (sometimes called the Godfather of Heavy Metal, for his aggressive style) and Lonnie Mack. On Mack's legendary 1963 album, *The Wham of That Memphis Man,* you can hear one of the earliest examples of Chicago-style blues bends in a rock context. Listen to his hit singles "Wham" and his cover of Chuck Berry's "Memphis" for proof.

The Brits Invade the Blues

Blues rock took a huge leap forward in the mid-'60s, thanks to a few key bands from England: The Yardbirds, John Mayall's Bluesbreakers, and Fleetwood Mac, all of whom brought Chicago-style blues into the distorted and high energy world of 1960s rock 'n' roll. At the time, Britain's *skiffle* fad — a type of folk music with jazz and blues influence that used instruments such as washboards, kazoos, combs, paper, and so on to make music — triggered fresh interest in black American music, such as ragtime, Dixieland jazz, and especially the blues.

These distant sounds appealed to young Brits and that generation became passionate lovers of traditional American blues music, both acoustic and electric. These young artists are covered in the following sections.

Clapton and Green, early blues icons

After a stint with the Yardbirds, Eric "Slowhand" Clapton joined John Mayall's Bluesbreakers later in 1965 and started gigging all over London. His fiery playing was such a sensation that the phrase "Clapton is God" was scrawled all over London's subway walls. As if to prove it, the 21-year-old guitarist displayed a mastery of electric blues styles well beyond his years. He had a deep knowledge of traditional blues licks; he had an evolved vibrato; he paid respectful homage to the blues greats — all showcased on the following year's *Bluesbreakers with Eric Clapton* album.

On key cuts like "Hide Away" (made famous by Freddie King six years before), "Steppin' Out," and the epic slow blues "Have You Heard," Clapton can be heard literally inventing the modern rock-guitar solo.

However, another Clapton vacancy occurred when the guitar hero left Mayall's band to form the supergroup Cream. He was replaced by another British blues whiz, Peter Green. Green's claim to fame was the minor blues — a sad, haunting sound that became his trademark. It's still a I-IV-V 12-bar blues progression, but with minor chords. On top, "Greenie," as he was popularly known, soloed by using the six-note blues scale (in A: A, C, D, E♭, E, G — for more on the blues scale, see Chapter 8).

In 1966, Peter Green left Mayall's band and formed the legendary Fleetwood Mac, which later transformed into a pop supergroup without him. But originally, Fleetwood Mac was known as one of the best British blues bands of its day.

Jeff Beck, blues-rock's mad scientist

When Eric Clapton left the Yardbirds in early 1965, his spot went to a relative newcomer named Jeff Beck. Beck was a constant innovator and experimenter, and he added the fuzz box — an effect that gave his guitar a raspy, sustaining tone, and further pioneered the use of electronic feedback.

To create controlled feedback, follow Beck's lead:

1. **Apply a high amount of distortion to your guitar and amp setup.**

   To create this distortion, turn up the gain knob on a fuzz/overdrive box or on the lead channel of your amp.

2. **Turn up your amplifier to a loud but safe level.**

3. **Aim your guitar at the amp, with your guitar's pickups facing the speaker, and aggressively bend a note between the 5th and 12th frets and hold it, applying a little finger vibrato (bending and vibrato are covered Chapter 10.)**

   You should hear a second, ghostly note emanating from the amp — this is feedback. With practice, you can control this feedback and use it to enhance your blues-rock solos.

These tools and techniques led to the revolutionary work on the Yardbirds' single "Heart Full of Soul." Subsequent hits, such as "I'm Not Talking," "Over Under Sideways Down," "Jeff's Boogie" (that quotes from Les Paul) and "Shapes of Things" all cemented Beck's genius as one of the first authentic blues-rock guitarists.

If you're a fan of Jimi Hendrix and Eddie Van Halen, you can control the feedback the way they did by using the whammy bar on your guitar (if you have one). The bar creates thrilling "divebomb" effects. Dampen the strings you don't want to sound, and the feedback actually causes open strings to vibrate, which then creates more howling tones, creating an endless cycle of runaway sound in what's known as a *feedback loop*.

Trippin' the Blues

Peace, love, and screaming guitar solos became part of the genre-stretching late-'60s sound. These so-called "psychedelic" guitarists were deeply interested in mixing vintage blues licks with modern effects. By 1967, the guitar was king in rock 'n' roll because the blues renaissance was fueling the music.

Among the key players at this time were Chicago-born Mike Bloomfield, whose clean electric-blues solos highlighted recordings by the Paul Butterfield Blues Band and the Electric Flag, and Dave Mason, who added Clapton- and Hendrix-influenced solos to the music of England's Traffic ("Paper Sun" and "Pearly Queen").

One later but still important psychedelic band was Santana. Taking influence from "the three Kings" of blues guitar (Albert, Freddie, and B.B.), guitarist Carlos Santana laid his soulful guitar breaks over hot Latin and rock rhythms, as heard in hits like "Evil Ways" and Peter Green's "Black Magic Woman." The band's groove might have been Latin-based, but Carlos's soloing was pure pentatonic-blues rock.

Among the top psychedelic blues-rockers, two names tower over the rest: Eric Clapton and Jimi Hendrix.

Eric Clapton, the original guitar god

Eric Clapton formed the power trio Cream in 1966 and they quickly became a focal point in the blues revival. The guitarist's articulate, overdriven guitar solos were a sensation, incorporating powerful bends, vibrato, and blues-scale licks by the score. By 1968, he was the most famous rock guitarist in the world and demonstrated his expertise on the live cut of the Robert Johnson tune "Crossroads" from *Wheels of Fire*. As heard in Figure 13-2, Clapton pushed the tempo and technique for playing pentatonic-blues-box solos — he was making blues-rock history in real time.

To play fast blues scales like Eric Clapton, you must practice! What differentiated Clapton, for example, from other '60s guitarists was his *clean* technique — you won't find any sloppy or flubbed notes in his famous "Crossroads" solo. In order for you to get to that level, you must practice your blues licks slowly at first, and then gradually increase the tempo over the course of a few days or weeks. You can use a metronome to help slow their playing down and then help speed it up.

Figure 13-2: Fiery string bends and flawless technique are hallmarks of Eric Clapton's style.

Jimi Hendrix takes the blues psychedelic

Jimi Hendrix, meanwhile, was carving out new sonic territory of his own. A true musical genius, Hendrix — who paid his dues in the R&B circuit by playing with the Isley Brothers and Little Richard — fused blues, rock, R&B, and funk style into a true psychedelic soup, blowing guitarists' minds with legendary tracks like "Purple Haze," "Foxy Lady," "Little Wing," and "Voodoo Child (Slight Return)."

Hendrix's innovative use of fuzz, wah, Octavia (which adds a note one octave above the one being picked), and UniVibe (a swirling modulation effect) expanded the guitar's repertoire and took his bluesy guitar solos to all-time highs.

Figure 13-3 shows his radical approach to both blues style and, more specifically, blues tone by taking a standard blues-based passage and adding — horror of horrors! — a wah-wah pedal. When Jimi played traditional, slow blues, as he did in his extended jam "Red House," he showed the world the depth of his blues roots.

To emulate Jimi (as if anyone would dare!), play your instrument over your head, behind your back, in a sexually suggestive position, and douse the sound with wah, distortion, and flanger. (For information on these effects, see Chapter 15. For the other stuff, check out Jimi's live performances on video.) Bend strings at unusual times and to unusual intervals and make it all work. Good luck!

Figure 13-3: Hendrix's brand of "psychedelic blues."

Heavy "Blooze": The Infusion of Hard Rock

Beginning in 1968, blues rock took a *huge* leap forward with the arrival of early hard rock and metal bands like the Jeff Beck Group, Led Zeppelin, Deep Purple, Black Sabbath, Ten Years After, Grand Funk Railroad, and Mountain. Within a few years, hard rock guitarists in both the United States and the United Kingdom were turning vintage blues licks into liquid metal with screaming string bends, power chords, and heavy distortion from their stacks of high-wattage tube amps.

In this section, I cover the hard rock blues guitar greats: Jimmy Page, Leslie West, and Ritchie Blackmore of Deep Purple.

Jimmy Page, frontrunner of the metal blues

The quintessential group from this heavy era was Led Zeppelin, led by ex-Yardbirds guitarist Jimmy Page. A former London session guitarist, Page was a jack of all trades: He played everything from speedy blues-box leads ("Good Times, Bad Times"), country- and rockabilly-inspired breaks ("The Song Remains the Same"), bottleneck slides ("You Shook Me"), and excellent acoustic fingerstyles ("Bron-Yr-Aur"). The melodic jazz-pop of '50s guitarist Les Paul was also a major influence.

Page's finest blues playing, however, may be on the epic minor key ballad "Since I've Been Loving You" from *Led Zeppelin III*, a masterful mix of soul-stirring bends and heavy metal pyrotechnics. Later, Page's playing moved in a more progressive direction (with sophisticated studio-production techniques — including an evolved use of effects — and a grand, orchestral arranging approach to guitar-based rock), but his guitar work on the first four Led Zeppelin albums was lovingly steeped in the electric-blues tradition.

Figure 13-4 shows how Page took the minor pentatonic scale and revved it up to overdrive. To emulate Page's playing, play largely in the minor pentatonic scale, give your guitar plenty of amp distortion (more on that in Chapter 15), don a Les Paul, bend with soul, and apply some tasty studio manipulation to your recorded sound.

Figure 13-4:
A solo in the style of Jimmy Page.

Leslie West, big man with a big sound

Another influential heavy rocker from this period was Mountain's Leslie West, a Clapton-loving player with a gorgeous tone and a finger vibrato as wide as the Grand Canyon. West wasn't a speed demon like Page, but his expressive bluesy bends and huge vibrato, as evidenced on his work in "Mississippi Queen," had few rivals. Another Leslie West guitar classic worth checking out is Mountain's power ballad, "Theme from an Imaginary Western."

Blackmore and beyond, where blues gets scary

One of the true hard rock masters was Ritchie Blackmore of Deep Purple. This aggressive, high-volume player freely fused blues and classical ideas into a startlingly new — and highly influential — style. This sound can be heard in "Smoke on the Water," "Child in Time," "Lazy," "Mistreated," and "Highway Star."

Other key players of the period included:

- ✔ Black Sabbath's Tony Iommi ("Iron Man")
- ✔ Irish superpicker Rory Gallagher ("Calling Card")
- ✔ Robin Trower ("Too Rolling Stoned," "Bridge of Sighs")
- ✔ AC/DC's Angus Young ("Back in Black," "You Shook Me All Night Long")
- ✔ Pink Floyd's David Gilmour ("Comfortably Numb")

Southern Comfort

Like the blues itself, there are few forms of popular music as quintessentially American as southern rock, which hails largely from the southeastern corner of the United States (notably Georgia and North Florida). Launched by the Allman Brothers Band, southern rock was the purest blues-rock sound ever created. The genre melded blues, country, gospel, and heavy rock.

In all, the '70s southern rock sound had dozens of hot blues-rock players: The Outlaws ("Green Grass and High Tides"); The Marshall Tucker Band ("Can't You See"); and the fusion-fueled Dixie Dregs, featuring bluesy guitar virtuoso Steve Morse ("Take It Off The Top").

The Allmans, especially brother Duane

The original Allmans featured two excellent guitarists, Duane Allman and Dickey Betts. Both men could play the heck out of a 12-bar blues, but in Duane's brief career, he shined most on slide guitar (see Figure 13-5 for a slide solo, Allman-style). Allman's stylistic hallmarks were rapid up-and-down slides into and out of eighth notes, plus a penchant for throwing in large, unexpected melodic leaps to keep listeners on their toes. His exceptional slide work can be heard all over the famous *At Fillmore East* live album from 1971, especially on the blues masterpiece "Statesboro Blues." He died shortly thereafter, but his slide work was so ahead of its time that he set the bottleneck standard for the next 25 years.

Track 93

*Open E tuning: E B E G♯ B E, low to high.

Figure 13-5:
A slide riff in the style of the great Duane Allman.

Lynyrd Skynyrd

Lynyrd Skynyrd became the next southern supergroup, thanks to the 1974 smash, "Sweet Home Alabama." Skynyrd had three fine guitarists: Ed King, Gary Rossington, and Allen Collins. Rossington and Collins can be heard tearing up the concert favorite "Freebird."

Skynyrd guitarist Ed King is notable for a squealing, edgy tone (thanks to an electronic compressor), and for punching up the blues bends dramatically. King's solo in this song is inspired, yet controversial, because many claim that it's "in the wrong key." The song (whose first chord is D) is actually in the key of D. King himself admitted that he approached the solo as if it were in G, but most people agree the song is in D. Yet the solo seems to work anyway, and the song and King's solo both go down in history as one of the great events for guitar.

Hot Barbecue Blues, Texas Style

Head due west to land smack in the middle of the musical hotbed of Texas. The Lone Star State has a long history of acclaimed blues artists (T-Bone Walker) and country-jazzers (Bob Wills and His Texas Playboys). Not surprisingly, there are also a zillion great rock guitarists from the great state of Texas:

- ✔ Eric Johnson ("Cliffs of Dover")
- ✔ Jimmie Vaughan (heard on the Fabulous Thunderbirds hit "Wrap It Up" and "Tuff Enuff")
- ✔ David Grissom (with John Mellencamp, Joe Ely, Storyville, Dixie Chicks)

But the artists in the next sections have made significant contributions to the blues through their efforts in the blues rock arena.

Johnny Winter, Texas blues-rock titan

Blues-rock guitarist Johnny Winter exploded out of Texas in 1968 and proceeded to become one of the top concert draws of the early '70s. Winter was a virtuosic soloist who played with a thumbpick, and his speedy leads lit up a number of gold albums.

TIP

You can hear him trade red-hot blues leads with co-guitarist Rick Derringer on the 1971 cover of B.B. King's "It's My Own Fault" (from *Johnny Winter AndLive*).

Figure 13-6 is an example of a typical blues line as Winter played it — aggressive and authoritative, but just as much of a blues figure as a rock one. To play like Winter, develop the best blues vocabulary you can and work on making any phrase fit in any groove — straight, shuffle, or 16th-based, fast and slow.

Billy Gibbons and ZZ Top, giving rock some soul

The power trio ZZ Top is a powerful mix of Texan music and the blues. Guitarist Billy Gibbons wasn't a high-speed player like Johnny Winter (see the following section), but his slow, smoldering solos helped set the standard for "soulfulness" in the rock guitar world.

Track 94

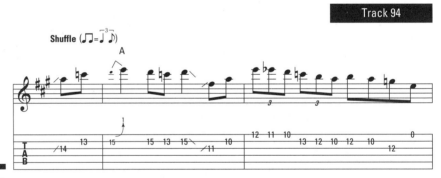

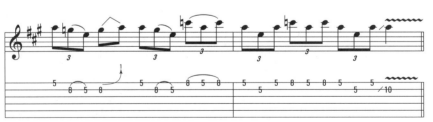

Figure 13-6: A line similar to Johnny Winter's classic approach to a blues solo.

Gibbons was a masterful blues player with a well-rounded playing approach, but he's best known for his edge-of-the-pick (also known as *pinch*) harmonics. To play a pinch harmonic, follow these steps:

1. **Grasp your pick so that only a small piece of the tip can be seen from between your thumb and index finger.**

2. **Just as you strike the string, give the pick a little forward twist, almost digging into the string and touching the flesh of your finger to the string, to stop or mute it slightly.**

   This technique is going to take some practice and getting use to, but the resulting note should have a *harmonic* (a high, bell-like sound resulting from the string being partially stopped) in it.

3. **Add plenty of distortion to help the effect "read" better.**

   You can hear this distortion in many of Gibbons's solos. See Chapter 15 for the how-to on adding distortion.

Among Gibbons's best guitar tracks were "La Grange," "Tush," "Cheap Sunglasses," "Blue Jean Blues," and "My Head's in Mississippi." Figure 13-7 shows two of Gibbons's hallmarks — his dark, Texas-style riffing and a blues line that closes off with his patented pinch harmonics.

Gibbons's fat lead tone is legendary among rock players. He's particularly famous for using a flametop 1959 Gibson Les Paul Standard lovingly named "Pearly Gates," as well as a pink late-1950s Strat given to him by Jimi Hendrix, which greatly contribute to that tone. But did you know that he doesn't pick with a plastic piece, but with a real Mexican *peso?* Just a cool fact to know.

Stevie Ray Vaughan, the greatest modern bluesman of them all

Austin's legendary Stevie Ray Vaughan burst into the spotlight in 1983, first on David Bowie's *Let's Dance* album, and then on his solo debut, *Texas Flood*. Aside from the fact that Stevie Ray could channel Jimi Hendrix's Strat attack (he would often perform "Voodoo Child [Slight Return]" and "Little Wing" as a tribute), he developed his own style that put the Fender Stratocaster back on the map as the definitive blues rock instrument.

Throughout the '80s, Vaughan blew minds with both a blistering blues technique as well as the fattest guitar tone imaginable. He achieved his tone by using a combination of classic Fender, Marshall, and Dumble tube amps, pumped up with an Ibanez Tube Screamer TS-808 overdrive pedal, as well as a vintage Strat set up with heavy-gauge strings. He also tuned down a half-step, which contributed to his sound's girth.

Track 95

Figure 13-7:
Smoldering
riffs and
edge-of-
the-pick
harmonics
equal a
classic
Gibbons
tribute.

Stevie Ray died in a helicopter crash in 1990, just after performing a concert with Eric Clapton, but over 15 years later, young guitarists are still mystified at how he achieved his one-and-only Strat sound, heard in such classics as "Pride and Joy," "Crossfire," and "The Sky Is Crying."

Vaughan's playing style was unique, evolved, and identifiable, with an integrated chord-and-single-note approach for rhythm as well as over-the-top lead playing that sounded on the verge of losing control (which he never did). To emulate the style of Vaughan, put heavy strings on your guitar, build up your arm strength, and combine melodic licks and riffs with open-position, jazz, and barre chords. (Listen to Figure 13-8 to hear how Stevie also threw tasty little chordal riffs into his solos — a hallmark of Texas blues guitar.) You must also play with complete authority, whipping off rhythm figures and lead lines with equal abandon.

Figure 13-8: Stevie Ray Vaughan often combined chord vamps with his leads.

Blues on Steroids

By the late 1970s, blues-rock was beginning to change. Thanks to influences from jazz-fusion (Mahavishnu Orchestra, Return to Forever) and progressive bands (Yes, Jethro Tull, Emerson, Lake & Palmer), rock guitarists began speeding up pentatonic "blues box" scales to previously unheard of tempos. Eventually, it launched the "hair bands" of the '80s, which were characterized by virtuosic pyrotechnics known variously as "speed metal" "neo-classical," and "shred." But it started out with the blues.

Eddie Van Halen takes the blues to '80s metal

When Van Halen burst on to the heavy metal scene in 1978, guitarists all over the world took immediate notice. Guitarist Eddie Van Halen steered away from the standard blues box, instead employing fast modal runs, classical-sounding tapping arpeggio licks, and crazy whammy bar dives to his solos. The California guitarist was primarily influenced by Eric Clapton's group, Cream, and had a real blues-rock base to his playing, especially in his screaming string bends. Van Halen often cites how important Clapton's "Crossroads" solo was in his early development as a guitarist, and how he learned it note for note. He played it in concert, too, in tribute.

Listen to "You Really Got Me" from *Van Halen* (Warner Bros/WEA) or "Somebody Get Me a Doctor" from *Van Halen II* (Warner Bros/WEA) to hear how Van Halen took old-school blues and blasted it to smithereens.

Euro-Metal brings virtuosity and precision to the blues

Across the ocean, new Euro-metal guitarists were also beginning to deconstruct the blues scale. Michael Schenker played blues scales for the band UFO, and his techniques were polished and classic. His warp-speed leads on "Lights Out" and "Rock Bottom" (from 1979's *Strangers in Night*) were hugely influential on '80s shred guitarists like Yngwie Malmsteen and Joe Satriani.

Ireland's Thin Lizzy was also pushing the limits of the blues scale, notably in the blitzkrieg leads of guitarists Scott Gorham, Brian Robertson, and Gary Moore. Later, Moore went on to a successful career as a solo artist, culminating in a 1990 return to his roots with the hit album *Still Got the Blues*. His blues leads on the uptempo "Oh Pretty Woman" are simply jaw-dropping.

21st-Century Soul

Today's music scene may be dominated by computers and digital downloads, but happily, blues rock, like traditional electric blues, has carved out a path and proceeds on its journey into the 21st century.

In addition to the guys I highlight in this section, a few other young guns of modern blues worth checking out include the hot-pickin' Joe Bonamassa ("Travelin' South"), Kenny Wayne Shepherd ("Blue on Black"), and Henry Garza of Los Lonely Boys ("Heaven"). Coincidentally, or not, all of them play Fender Stratocasters, just like their blues-rock idols, Jimi Hendrix, Eric Clapton, and Stevie Ray Vaughan.

To make your Strat-style guitar sound extra soulful and get that funky "out-of-phase" tone, put your five-way pickup selector in the second or fourth positions, which combines the middle pickup with either the neck or bridge pickups. This sound is especially good for funk-styled chord grooves.

John Mayer, new kid on the blues block

Among the brightest lights of the new millennium is singer-songwriter John Mayer, who fuses the best of Hendrix and Stevie Ray Vaughan into a stunning Strat style.

Listen to "Route 66" from the *Cars* soundtrack to hear this young picker play a joyous blues solo and throw down a wad of chunky chord work.

Allmans Redux: Warren Haynes and Derek Trucks, keepers of the flame

Over 35 years after their debut, the Allman Brothers are still a top concert highlight, and the band's guitarists — Warren Haynes and Derek Trucks — have a huge part in the group's success.

- *Haynes,* who's been in the band longer than Duane, is a wizard at both straight soloing and the Duane Allman-style slide. To play slide like Haynes, keep your guitar in standard tuning and transcribe all Duane's moves (who played in open E) into standard tuning.

- *Trucks,* meanwhile, has taken bottleneck to a whole new dimension, infusing it with bebop jazz influences from sax legend John Coltrane and trumpeter Miles Davis. You can hear both Derek and Warren just tearin' it up on "Firing Line" from the Allman Brothers album *Hittin' the Note.* To play like Trucks, you need to wear a slide and brush up on your bebop vocabulary.

If you want to check out some info on Coltrane and Davis, get a copy of *Jazz For Dummies,* 2nd Edition, by Dirk Sutro (Wiley).

Part V
Gearing Up: Outfitting Your Arsenal

The 5th Wave   By Rich Tennant

"Gee thanks, but I don't think a gingham neck cozy and peg board bonnet really goes with the rest of my guitar."

In this part . . .

There's more to your guitar than just the guitar itself. In this part, you discover all the gear that comes with playing the guitar. You evaluate which gear is for you and then go shopping for it. I even give you some advice on how to haggle for the best price when the time comes to shell out your hard-earned money. To break it down even further, Chapter 14 explores the many different aspects of guitars and what to look for in a quality instrument. And you can't make music with an electric guitar without an amp, so Chapter 15 shows you what you need to know about amps. Chapter 16 highlights the effects — those magic little gizmos that create even more sonic possibilities for your guitar and amp and give you a polished, professional sound. Chapter 17 covers changing strings for both acoustic and electric guitar, and Chapter 18 covers basic maintenance and repairs.

Chapter 14

Shop Till You Drop: Buying the Right Guitar for You

In This Chapter

▶ Defining your guitar needs

▶ Pricing guitars

▶ Shopping strategies

▶ Bringing along an expert

*T*he good news about shopping for a guitar is that unlike high-performance auto or horse racing, you don't have to spend hundreds of thousands of dollars to get in the game. If you're smart, and you shop carefully, you can end up with the same model guitar that the most famous players in history played — for just a few hundred dollars. The other bit of encouraging news is that there are no wrong choices. You can create the blues on *any* electric or acoustic guitar, and even the best players — Jimi Hendrix and Eric Clapton, to name two — have famously switched guitars midway in their careers, and it didn't seem to hurt their playing one bit.

Shopping for a guitar gives you the excuse to go out and audition the instrument of your dreams, but eventually your dreams have to reconcile with your wallet. But for a blues guitar, reality isn't that harsh. Even a cheaper guitar was played by the Delta blues players from the '20s and '30s. If you look at old photos, you can see that even these players all had cheap guitars, and the music is immortal.

So don't fear. In the sections of this chapter, I give you some guidance on picking out the guitar that best suits you and your budget.

Before You Begin Shopping

You need to have a clear head if you're going out to spend a few hundred dollars (or more) on your new guitar. Luckily, I give you a few things to think about in the following list, before you take the leap and buy your instrument:

✔ **Your level of commitment:** Are you just exploring the blues to see if it sticks with you or grows on you? Are you just trying to figure out if you even have the aptitude for playing? Or are you bursting with passion and want to devote long periods of your life to the pursuit of blues excellence? It's okay to be unsure about any new endeavor, but you should invest appropriately. There's nothing like having a state-of-the-art instrument to inspire you, and to help keep you inspired during the lulls that accompany any long-term study, but figure out where your passion lies and if you're willing to commit after you shell out the big bucks.

✔ **Your spending limit:** Set your budget without ever looking at an instrument, and then try for the best guitar your money will buy. You don't have to spend your entire proposed budget, but money is meant to be spent (just ask Congress). So aim as high as you're comfortable with without making your wallet scream, and don't be afraid to follow through if the right opportunity presents itself. Just remember, there is no ideal guitar for the blues. The music comes from the artists holding the instrument, not the instrument itself. You might think that that's true of any type of music, and it is certainly true of rock, but blues seems even more inclusive for instrument choice. You don't want to be close-minded about a guitar, just because it wasn't what you initially had in mind — especially if a super deal is staring you in the face. You can always write "Buyers' Remorse Blues" on your new instrument.

✔ **The type of guitar you want:** Do you know whether you're looking for a flattop acoustic or a steel guitar; a Strat-type or a Les Paul-type solid-body; or a semi-hollowbody electric or an archtop? You also must decide whether you're buying a new or used guitar, and whether you want to settle for an imitation of a classic model or the real deal.

If the types of guitars in the previous bullet have you thinking "huh?" — don't give up! Read on! This chapter helps you decide what type of guitar you want by explaining the differences between guitar models. As far as the budget issue, well, that's none of my business. It's strictly up to you (and your significant other, if your situation is anything like mine). But expect to spend no less than $200 on a new electric and $300 for a new acoustic.

Deciding On a Make and Model

Deciding on the basic format is at once the hardest and easiest decision in buying a guitar, and it comes at the very beginning of the buying process. It could be a hard decision if you have no idea what you want in a guitar. Then all the different makes and models and price ranges create a confusing, noisy blur. However, if you know exactly what you want — down to the color of the finish and whether you want black matte or gold hardware, the decision is easy. You just then have to shop for the best price.

Most people don't have it so hard or as easy as the preceding scenarios describe. Certainly if you have no idea what you want, you should do more research — read articles in magazines and online, visit discussion boards, and gaze at the guitars on the wall in the music shops. But even if you *think* you know the exact specs of your desired guitar, you'll find that living in the real world forces you to adjust your expectations on some aspect — unless you're willing to wait until you find exactly what you want and money is no object. Most experienced guitar shoppers learn to accept substitutions and variations when they occur.

The more you know about guitars, the more accommodating you become to the many variations and different forms guitars appear in.

Evaluating a Guitar

This section helps to show you what to look for after you've narrowed down your choice to a particular make and model — or the best deal between a couple of different types. It may not change your mind about the guitar you've set your sights on, but you can gain perspective into how two similar guitars (except for, perhaps, the color) can be so different with respect to materials, workmanship, and options.

You don't have to have the eye of a jeweler (and sport one of those weird loupe thingies around your neck) to be a good judge of quality. If you have a little experience, you can tell just about all you need to know by playing a guitar for a while. A quality guitar looks good, plays in tune, frets easily, and holds up under abuse (the musical kind, anyway). What you're actually responding to — if a guitar stands up to this scrutiny — are the following four categories in quality:

- ✔ **Construction:** The design and physical components of the system
- ✔ **Materials:** The type of wood, hardware, pickups, electronics, and other substances used
- ✔ **Workmanship:** The execution or quality of the building and construction
- ✔ **Appointments:** The non-functional parts that add to the look of the guitar, such as the fretboard inlay, binding (edging around the body and neck of the guitar), and decorative elements on the knobs and tuning keys

Each category is explored in more detail in the following sections.

Construction

A guitar's construction determines whether it's an electric solidbody guitar or an acoustic archtop. Different construction methods use different materials and require a different build approach. So you wouldn't evaluate a solidbody the same way you would an archtop, even though both may exhibit excellent workmanship.

In the following sections, I show you some characteristics to look for in your guitar and what those mean.

Solid and laminated wood (acoustic guitars only)

Acoustic guitars are made of wood, but that wood varies in construction:

- *Solid-wood construction* means that one piece of thicker, high-quality wood is used, instead of laminated wood. Solid-wood guitars sound better but are more expensive — upwards of $1,000.

- With *laminated wood,* you get thinner pieces of lower-quality wood, which are glued together and then covered with a thin veneer of higher-quality wood. Laminated wood instruments are cheaper, but you sacrifice a little sound quality.

In an acoustic guitar, the top is the most important factor in producing sound, so if you're trying to save some money, buy a solid-wood top guitar — the top is solid and the back and sides are laminated. You can find a wide variety of acoustics constructed this way at around the $350 mark and even slightly less.

Unless you really know where to look, it can be difficult to tell whether the guitar uses solid or laminated wood. Always check with the salesperson or consult the manufacturer as to the guitar's specific configuration.

Tops and body caps (electric guitars only)

With electric guitars, the top is less critical to the sound but can add to the expense if a cap is used. A *cap* is a thin layer of fine, decorative wood with an attractive grain pattern. Popular cap woods include flame maple and quilted maple. Fine-quality wood tops usually come with clear, or see-through, finishes to show off the wood's attractive grain pattern. Solid, opaque colors don't have that natural-wood look to them but can be cheaper. A guitar with a cap, especially one of fancy wood, will cost more than a guitar without a cap. And the cap doesn't contribute to the guitar's tone, so it's just an aesthetic consideration (which doesn't mean it's not important).

Neck construction

Electric guitar necks are defined by how they connect to the body (acoustic guitars are all the same with regard to the way their necks attach). Below are the three types of necks:

- ✔ **Bolt-on:** The neck attaches to the back of the guitar at the *heel* (the part of the neck that sticks out where the neck joins the body) with four or five bolts (a *heel plate* sometimes covers the bolt holes). Fender Stratocasters and Telecasters have bolt-on necks.

- ✔ **Set in (or glued in):** In this type of construction, the neck joins the body in a connected way with an unbroken finish covering the connection. The connection can't be unbolted, because it's glued in, and then finished over. The Gibson Les Paul and Paul Reed Smith models have set-in necks.

- ✔ **Neck through body:** This high-end construction has the neck in one long unit (although usually consisting of several pieces of wood glued together) that doesn't stop at the body but continues all the way through to the tail of the guitar. This isn't typically used for blues guitars but is a favorite for high-end rockers.

Guitars with bolt-on necks are easier to produce than models with set-in necks and are therefore less expensive. But most people don't base their guitar-purchasing decisions on how the neck attaches to the body. Just because one construction process is more advanced or expensive than another doesn't mean that it's necessarily better than other techniques.

Materials

One way to tell why a guitar is expensive or inexpensive is to simply look at the materials used. If the wood is rare or beautiful, or the fret inlays are abalone instead of plastic, chances are it's an expensive, well-made guitar. It's not that badly built guitars don't use quality materials; it's just that in reality you won't see them.

So while you shouldn't judge a guitar *only* by its materials, it's a good bet that the better materials (abalone inlays as opposed to plastic ones) wind up on better guitars — ones with construction methods and workmanship to match.

Woods

Guitar makers break woods down into categories, and the categories determine the wood's quality and expense:

✔ **Type:** Type indicates whether the wood is alder, ash, mahogany, maple, rosewood, and so on. In acoustics, rosewood is the most expensive wood used for the back and sides, followed by maple, and then mahogany.

✔ **Style:** Style shows where the wood came from or its grain style. Brazilian rosewood is redder and wavier than East Indian rosewood and is also more expensive. Figured maple, such as quilted and flame, is more expensive than rock or bird's-eye maple.

✔ **Grade:** Guitar makers use a grading system, from A to AAA (the highest), to evaluate woods based on grain, color, and consistency. The highest-grade wood goes on the most expensive models in a line.

Exotic or rare woods — such as walnut or Brazilian rosewood — drive the price of a guitar up significantly. If money is no object, you can get the rarest, prettiest, most highly figured wood available. If you're on a budget, don't worry so much about the type of wood, because guitar makers use some unusual varieties, and you may not even recognize the wood's name. But you can be assured that all established and reputable guitar makers choose their woods carefully for structural integrity.

Hardware

Hardware, or the metal parts of the guitar, is a common area where makers upgrade the quality for higher-priced instruments. Cheaper guitars use chrome-plated or chrome-dipped hardware, so expect to see gold-plated and black-matte-finished knobs, switches, and tuning machines on more expensive guitars, instead of chrome-colored ones. The better the hardware, the longer it lasts and the more reliably it operates.

Hardware is often made by third-party companies (not the same people who make the guitars), so on more expensive instruments you start to see name-brand hardware components replacing generic or less prestigious brands of hardware. For example, manufacturers may use higher-grade tuners — such as *locking Sperzels* (a popular third-party tuner type and brand, shown in Figure 14-1), which lock the string at the tuning post and are a popular choice among professionals.

Figure 14-1:
Sperzel's
high-quality
tuning
machines.

The bridge is a critical hardware component on an electric guitar. The *floating bridge* (so designated because you can move it up and down by means of the whammy bar) is a complicated system of springs, fine-tuning knobs, and anchors. The better floating assemblies, such as the Wilkinson system (shown in Figure 14-2), provide smoother operation than some generics found on low-cost guitars.

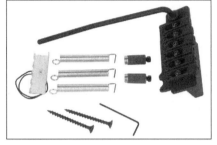

Figure 14-2:
The Wilkinson bridge.

Pickups and electronics (electrics only)

Companies specializing in making pickups are commonly found on high-quality guitars. Seymour Duncan (shown in Figure 14-3), DiMarzio, Bartolini, Bill Lawrence, Lace, and EMG are examples of high-quality pickup brands that guitar makers install into their instruments. These brands are sometimes referred to as *replacement* pickups.

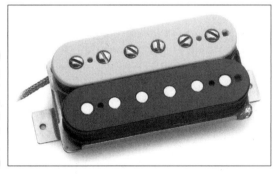

Figure 14-3:
Seymour Duncan's high-quality third-party pickups.

Higher-quality guitars tend to offer more-advanced circuitry that changes double-coil, or humbucker, pickups into single-coils, enabling them to simulate the behavior of Stratlike pickups. Having one guitar with the flexibility to emulate the pickup behavior of other guitar types provides you with a range of tonal options from a single instrument. You also see more manipulation in wiring schemes. For example, guitar makers may reverse a pickup's *polarity* — the direction the signal flows — to make the guitar sound softer and more swirly when played against another pickup with the opposite polarity.

When you encounter a guitar that has several switches (and not just one, as in the standard pickup selector switch in a Les Paul and a Strat), make sure that you know the wiring scheme before you start playing. Ask the salesperson, if you have to, but be sure that you know that you're listening to the expected pickup configuration (double-coil versus tapped coil) and combination (bridge only or bridge plus middle) before you make any serious judgments about the guitar's tone.

Workmanship

Most guitars these days exhibit excellent workmanship, or they don't make it off the factory floor. Still, mistakes slip through, and sometimes even escape the sales staff at the store, too. So you do have to inspect any instrument you play for obvious defects, like cracks, bad joints (with gaps or bad fits), scratches, rough-sanded or unfinished areas, and glue spots.

For acoustic guitars that cost more than $600, you should expect to find certain criteria:

- *Gapless joints* — solid wood-to-wood connections between components, especially where the neck meets the body
- Clean and glob-free gluing (in the top and back bracing)
- A smooth and even finish application
- A good setup: the strings at the right height with no buzzing, the neck warp- and twist-free, and the intonation true

For electrics, most of the above requirements apply to the wood parts, but electrics have many more metal parts, so you need to check a few items:

- Check that the metal parts are tight and rattle-free.
- Check that tuning machines turn easily and that there's no slop or play in the gears.
- The metal should be smooth.
- Make sure that the paint or coating over any hardware isn't masking any rough spots.
- The frets should feel smooth as you run your fingers along both sides of the neck.
- No single fret should stick out enough to grab or catch the skin of your fingers.

In either case, acoustic or electric, if it's built well, it plays well, and you can tell if the instrument is in harmony with nature — even if you're having trouble playing your own brand of harmony on the guitar.

Appointments (aesthetic options)

Appointments are decorative elements that enhance a guitar's appearance but don't contribute to its sound or playability. They include

- **Inlay:** The designs and shapes in the fretboard and headstock
- **Binding:** The edging strip around the sides of the guitar
- **Soundhole rosette or marquetry:** The ring of decorative wood, often inlaid with multiple pieces, that encircles the soundhole

Some people feel that highly ornate appointments are too showy, but others feel that those same inlays add to the guitar's visual splendor. It's all in the eye of the beholder.

Because the blues is about hardship, loss, and love interests doing you wrong, your credibility might be served better with a guitar with only modest appointments. Leave the superfancy stuff to teen idols and country performers.

Welcome to the Jungle: Shopping

When you go on your shopping adventure, you should be prepared. Buying a new instrument is exciting and fun, but you must still exercise caution and not exhibit so much enthusiasm that you look like a kid in a candy store to the salesperson. Before you seek the salesperson's assistance, try to formulate some questions that you can ask the salesperson:

- Are there other models in different color schemes or slightly different configurations that you can compare to the current model in your hands?
- What is the closest instrument, in price and quality, to your selection that the salesperson recommends?
- What make and model would be one step up from this one, what makes it better and why, and what is the price difference?

Bringing a friend

For really important purchases, especially when you're entertaining several possible options, bring along a friend. A second opinion always helps and keeps you from making rash decisions. Also try to bring a buddy who knows as much or more about guitars than you do. If he's a friend, he not only knows about guitars, but also he knows *you* and has your best interests at heart.

Another excellent choice for a buddy is your guitar teacher (if you have one). This person can help you navigate through the guitar buyer's jungle, especially if he's been with you a while and knows your tastes and playing style. Your teacher may know things about you that you may not even realize about yourself — for example, that you've gotten sidetracked playing Les Pauls, even though your stated mission in life was to emulate Albert Collins (who played a Telecaster). A good teacher asks questions, listens to your answers, and gently guides you to where *you* want to go, not where the salesperson does.

It's always good to have a sounding board for your own opinions. Make sure that the person you take with you stands back and listens to you play the instrument you want to purchase. Sometimes you can lose "listening objectivity" because you're wrapped up in the playing — and a good-playing guitar might influence your listening. Having another person do the listening helps ensure that the guitar sounds good as well as feels good.

Money matters: Deal . . . or no deal

An instrument is priced by its *list* or *manufacturer's suggested retail price* (sometimes abbreviated in catalogs as MSRP), which, as the name implies, is given to the retailer by the manufacturer. You can find out the MSRP of an instrument online or from the manufacturers. As of this writing, a Gibson Les Paul Standard *lists* for $3,248, and a Fender American Standard Stratocaster *lists* for $1,327.99. Figure 14-4 shows these two industry favorites.

Figure 14-4:
The Gibson Les Paul (left) and Fender Stratocaster (right).

a

b

Face time makes all the difference

You may wonder why everyone doesn't buy online. Purchasing a guitar is a highly personal endeavor, and music stores are in a better position to offer you a hands-on experience with an instrument, and to devote close, personal service to a new guitar customer. Many stores have increased their customer service to compete with the online menace (as the salespeople at my local store call it). Customer service includes anything from giving advice to fixing minor problems to providing periodic _setups_ — making the necessary adjustments to improve the action and intonation of your guitar. A music store can be a great place to just hang out and talk guitars, and you can learn a lot from knowledgeable salespeople and a good guitar tech.

From the list price, music stores discount the guitar between 10 and 40 percent — sometimes even more. Large retailers usually offer greater discounts than smaller (mom-and-pop) stores. Online and mail-order retailers can often match and even beat these prices, because they don't have the overhead of maintaining a storefront or showroom facility.

Protecting Your Guitar

For all the excitement that exists in choosing among all the brightly colored toys hanging on the wall in front of you, don't forget a vital element for your guitar that rarely sees the light of the showroom floor: the case. For most new guitars, a case is included with the purchase price. Always verify this to be the, uh, case, when considering your purchase. If the price doesn't include a case, you have to add that on top of the guitar's price. Don't think for a second that you can scrimp on this vital piece of guitar equipment. If you spend hundreds of dollars on a guitar, you want to protect it! In the following sections are the three types of cases for your guitar, listed in order of best protection, that shield your prized possession from the elements.

Hard cases

The best protection for your guitar is a hard case, sometimes referred to as a hardshell case. This enclosure is made of a stiff plastic that you can step on with your full weight and your guitar will still be protected.

Whenever you put your guitar in the case, either leave the lid open or shut it and fasten at least one of the latches. Don't ever simply lower the lid without latching it. This precaution prevents someone (even you) from grabbing the closed case by the handle to move it and the guitar falling out.

Compromising and accepting change

You may find yourself in a situation where you can't get exactly what you want in a guitar. The more research you do, the more you know what your ideal guitar is — and not just the guitar's make and model but everything about it: its condition, its color, the hardware it sports, and the selling price. When you venture out into the real world, though, the reality doesn't always live up to the vision.

When that happens, be prepared to compromise. You may want to spend $500, and the store you visit charges $600. Or the price isn't an issue, but you want a blue guitar, and the only available models are in black and red. Keep in mind that if either of these scenarios occurs, neither one affects the sound or playability of the guitar. But it's a setback. You can either

adjust your thinking or walk away and wait until the right deal comes along. Maybe you can solve the problem by ordering online and waiting a week or two. But then you won't have a guitar in hand. And you won't be able to evaluate it before purchasing it. No one said this would be easy.

That's when you have to accept the detours in the journey and just go with it. But shopping is fun, and coming to terms with the models that are there in the flesh is part of the process. Research has a way of making you build up your expectations — sort of like creating the perfect mate on paper. It may not work out the way you planned (except of course in my case), but it works out, and you wouldn't have it any other way.

Soft cases

A soft case isn't really soft; it's firm — like the way a shoebox is firm. And that's because it's made of stuff not much stronger than a shoebox. In very predictable, controlled situations you can transport your guitar from one place to another, and a soft case is fine, but it's no substitute for a hard case. You can rest a notebook on top of your soft case, but a foot can go right through it!

Gig bags

Gig bags are convenient because they allow you to sling your guitar over your shoulder, leaving your hands free to carry something else or to hold on to a handrail. The bags are made of padded nylon or leather and offer minimal protection from scratches, but can't fend off a major impact, like being stepped on or banging into a wall. Gig bags are essential for urban musicians who take taxis, subways, and buses and must park in lots blocks from their gigs. And they look really cool, too.

Chapter 15

Choosing Your Amp and Effects

● ●

In This Chapter

▶ Starting out slow: Looking at practice amps

▶ Checking under the hood: The parts of the amplifier

▶ Deciding on the amp for you

▶ Plugging in your guitar for good sound

▶ Touring classic amps through history

▶ Discovering the world of effects

● ●

*T*he guitar may be the single most important piece of hardware in creating your sound, but it's still part of a system, or what musicians like to call a *signal chain*. Because any chain is only as strong as its weakest link, I need to explore the two other links in the chain: the amplifier and the effects processors.

You can play through *any* amplifier designed for an electric guitar and your guitar is better heard, and it may even sound pretty good. But eventually you should own an amp that's specially designed for the type of music you want to play: blues.

A good blues amp produces clear, full tones for rhythm, and a versatile lead sound that can go from warm and smooth to biting and edgy. If you listen to the great electric blues artists from B.B. King to Stevie Ray Vaughan, you hear a rainbow of tonal colors coming from their guitars. Much of that variety is the result of the amp — and the artists' ability to manipulate it.

A good way to get a handle on blues amps is to explore the amps that throughout history, either by design or happy accident, have established themselves as classic choices. Some of these include models by Pignose, Fender, Vox, Marshall, Laney, and Mesa/Boogie. This chapter deals with different types of amps, from the practical to the ideal, what to do with them after you have one connected to your guitar, and how to get certain effects.

Getting Started with a Practice Amp

If you don't have an amp — any amp at all — you won't even be able to hear your electric guitar properly. So the absolute first step before you walk out of the music store or close that online-shopping window on your computer is to make sure that you have some kind of amp to play your guitar through. If you're trying to save money — or to use whatever money you have to buy the best guitar possible — you still have to set aside a chunk of change for an amp. If you're not yet ready to spend the dough for the amp of your dreams, perhaps the amp for you at this point is what's known as a practice amp.

A *practice amp* is a small, low-powered *combo amp* (with all the components contained in one box). A practice amp is just loud enough to be heard in a room in your house, but isn't powerful enough to cut through a band or to reach an audience from a stage. If you turn a practice amp up to ten — the highest sound level — it distorts unpleasantly, but the sound still won't be all that loud. But the benefit of a practice amp is that it gives your guitar good amp tone at low volumes and serves you well in practice or when rehearsing with one other musician, if he's also playing quietly.

Just because a practice amp is small doesn't mean its sound should be minuscule. Look for an amp where you can turn up the volume and still get a full, clean sound. The amp should be loud enough for you to play in a room by yourself or with another instrument (albeit at more subdued, practice volumes). All practice amps distort the more you push them, but you want to find a sound you can live with at a decent volume.

Shopping for a practice amp

A practice amp for blues is no different than one for any other type of music. (When you decide to move up, you may want to choose a different path on your quest for the tonal utopia.) When choosing your amp, base your decision on a few different factors:

- ✔ Good clean tone
- ✔ A serviceable distorted sound
- ✔ Flexible features
- ✔ Personal taste
- ✔ Budget

Run a volume check on any practice amp. With that thought in mind, I suggest that you inform the salesperson at your local music store that you intend to try the amp *before* you buy it. He should understand, and may appreciate the warning. He may even take preparations for the impending loudness. (Many music stores have a separate room for just such high-volume noise-making.) Try to keep the time where you're cranking out maximum decibels short, but you do need to perform this loudness check to evaluate and compare amps.

After you determine the loudness factor, consider the amp's features. These features include

- How many knobs and switches it has
- How extensive the effects section is
- How many sockets, or jacks, it sports

One very handy jack is a headphone output, which allows you to practice in silence, but still enjoy all the tonal-shaping properties of the amp.

But you have to decide if having an extensive effects section (reverb, delay, chorus) is important to you or if you'd rather see more control in the tone section (bass, midrange, treble) of the amp. Some amps are designed to accept more than one instrument simultaneously and may not have as many controls over, say, the tone, but allow you to plug in both your acoustic and electric guitar simultaneously (handy for quick changes in a performance setting).

Even though all practice amps are low-powered, many are endowed with fairly sophisticated electronic circuitry that still makes them sound good. In fact, you can often find a practice amp that has almost the same features and tonal flexibility as larger amps. But in amplifier design, power equals cost, so if you stay in the low-power arena, you'll have more money left in your pocket.

Playing with a practice amp

The advantage of a practice amp is that it gets you familiar with amps in general, which includes plugging in and out, adjusting controls, and hearing your sound through a speaker. (You make the same adjustments when you move up to a larger amp — only the sound is better and louder, and you have greater control.) They're good for practicing by yourself, or with one other person. But if you want to play with a group of musicians, or you want to project your sound in a space larger than a bedroom, you should get a larger amp.

The amp has a set of controls, called the *front panel,* where you make all your adjustments. Figure 15-1 shows a typical practice amp. This one is small, although amps can be larger or smaller.

Figure 15-1:
A typical
practice
amp.

If you're planning on picking out an amp at the store and playing it there, check out the following steps for correctly plugging in and getting ready to play:

1. **Check that the amp is plugged into the wall or into a power strip and that the outlet is live.**

   Outlet issues can sometimes be an obstacle in places where the outlets are controlled with a switch.

2. **Find the volume knob(s) (some amps have more than one) and turn them all the way down — usually fully counterclockwise.**

   This adjustment ensures that you don't produce any sudden loud noises, which can, at the very least, scare and disturb people around you and, at worst, blow a fuse or damage the speaker.

3. **Turn the amp on with the power switch.**

   Many amps have a lamp or LED (light-emitting diode) that shows that electrical power is flowing successfully and that the amp is on.

4. **Turn the tone controls — bass, middle, and treble — to their midway point (about 12:00 if you picture the dial as a clock).**

   This ensures that you get a neutral, uncolored sound from the amp.

Observing the above steps not only ensures that you don't create an unexpected loud burst of sound from your amp, but also it exhibits professional behavior. If you're in a music store, and you show proper volume-tweaking etiquette, you may impress the sales staff and get them to take you seriously.

Powering Up to a Larger Amp

After you have enough money and inclination — and the smallish sound of your practice amp isn't cutting it anymore — you may want to invest in a larger amp, suitable for playing out on the town and taking your blues guitar-playing career to the next level. Acquiring a more-powerful, performance-level amp is important for two reasons:

✔ You can be heard in a public performance or jam session with other musicians.

✔ Your guitar sounds better. Practice amps are nice, but they don't do the blues justice. The best amps are of the non-practice variety — the big amps that make your sound soar and wail.

When shopping for a serious amp, bring your own guitar. If you play with a favorite effect all the time (such as a distortion pedal), bring that along, too. And even if you don't like to change strings that often, always have a new set on your guitar when you venture out to audition amplifiers. Having fresh, new parts ensure the fairest and most controlled tonal conditions, and show amps in their best light. And remember to advise the salesperson that you want to "move some big air," so that he or she can make the necessary arrangements.

In the following sections, I describe the different configurations of amps available. An amp's format doesn't necessarily affect the quality or loudness of its sound but often affects how and where you would use it.

Choosing among different amp formats

When choosing a larger amp, you have choices. Each selection depends on your intentions for using it and in what environment you and your amp operate. An amp comes in three configurations, or physical housings.

Combo amp

A *combo amp* consists of an amplifier circuitry and speaker that are contained in the same box. Combo amps can come with one to four built-in speakers, so you must decide between convenience and power when choosing the one-box-fits-all approach.

Most blues players opt for the combo type of amp (shown in Figure 15-2). If you need more power than your combo amp delivers, you have three choices:

✔ Mic the speaker and run the sound through your band's (or the venue's) public-address (PA) system.

✔ Hook up an extension speaker (if your amp has that feature).

✔ Switch to a head and cabinet (stack) setup (covered in the next section).

Figure 15-2:
The Fender
Twin amp.

Head and cabinet amp

In a head and cabinet amp setup, the amp is separate from the speaker cabinet. This arrangement is more flexible than the combo amp because it allows you to mix and match speaker cabinets with the amp. If you play in a small space, you can use a smaller speaker or cabinet than you would for playing in a larger area. But you can still use the same head and get a consistent sound and the features familiar to you.

Many people refer to a head and cabinet configuration as a *stack,* because the head stacks on top of the speaker cabinet. But some purists, especially when discussing Marshall amplifiers (shown in Figure 15-3), argue that a stack is two speaker cabinets with a head on top, and that one speaker cabinet with an amp head is really a *half stack.* So if you really want to use the term "Marshall stack" correctly, make sure you see three boxes on top of each other.

The Fender Bandmaster, Fender Bassman, and Marshall stacks are famous examples of the head and cabinet configurations. Figure 15-3 shows a head and cabinet configuration.

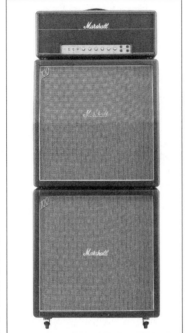

Figure 15-3:
The
Marshall
Super Lead
100 amp.

Rack mount amp

A rack mount amp includes both an amp and a *preamp* (circuitry that boosts the relatively weak signal coming straight from the guitar and prepares it for the power amplifier section). Blues players rarely use this type of amp because it's complex and logistically more involved because of the separate parts, which must be connected with extra cables. Mostly studio players and performers with high-end stage gear use the rack mount system to hold the electronic gear.

Figure 15-4 shows a rack mount preamp and power amp as separate components.

Figure 15-4:
Studio
players
sometimes
use a rack
system like
this one.

Feeling the power

If you've chosen your configuration for your amp (covered in the previous section), then decide on the appropriate power rating. Power — measured in output watts — determines the size, weight, and expense of your purchase, so you need to have a concept of how power affects your music before you shop.

Power in amplifiers is like money: You can never have too much. So a 100-watt amp is better than a 60-watt amp. But don't forget that the more powerful amp is both pricier and heavier. If you're in a band and performing in medium-sized clubs, you may only need 50 watts for a good performance.

Dissecting the Amplifier

To help you better understand the makeup of an amp, you must explore the five basic sections of an amp. If you know the parts of an amp, you can relate better to it, and you know how to tweak the controls and manipulate the sound when you're in the music store (and, of course, at home and in performance).

An amp can be an acquired taste because people don't often connect with amps like they do guitars. You rarely hear people say, "Wow, that's a sweet looking amp you have." What's important about an amp is that you know the different parts, so you understand what you're getting and how to work it.

Input jack

The amp's input jack is where you plug your guitar in. Several amps offer jack options right off the bat:

- ✔ Jacks for independent operation of more than one instrument
- ✔ Jacks rated at different levels for high- and normal-gain guitars
- ✔ Jacks for a channel without effects or extensive tone-shaping and the other for more precise control over effects and tone

Multiple jack choices give you an indication of the amp's versatility. Versatility allows you to use the amp in different settings (with or without your own effects, or in different-sized spaces) or to provide completely different sounds (for an acoustic guitar and an electric guitar, for example). An amp may have separate channels, or it may have one jack for high-gain and one for low-gain, but the more inputs the better.

Preamp

The preamp section of the amp takes the rather puny (electronically speaking) guitar signal and boosts it to a level that the rest of the amp likes to see. The preamp circuitry is important to an amp's tone because it's the first stage in the amp's chain and deals with the guitar signal in its purest form. So the preamp must be sensitive and respectful of the signal it sees from the guitar. The circuitry also often features a separate volume control called *gain*, *level*, or *volume*. The preamp provides the most influence on the guitar's character and prominently forms the guitar's distorted sound.

Figure 15-5 shows the preamp section on an amp.

Figure 15-5:
The preamp
section of
an amp.

Tone

The tone section of the amp allows you to shape your sound by using the
bass and treble controls (like those found on a stereo) as well as an in-between
control called midrange (or middle). The *treble* provides brightness and edge
to a sound; the *midrange* gives the sound fullness; and the *bass* provides girth
and boom. These controls are shown in Figure 15-6.

Figure 15-6:
The tone
section of
an amp.

Some amps feature more than one knob to control a given range of frequencies. For example, the midrange may have two controls — one for the frequency range covered (the high, middle, and low area of tone) and the other to boost or cut the level of that frequency range (to emphasize or de-emphasize).

Effects

An amp's effects section is where the reverb, chorus, and other effects reside. The signal travels from the tone controls (covered in the previous section) to the effects section, shown in Figure 15-7. On some amps, this part can be just a reverb, but many amps feature an entire digital effects section with reverb, delay, chorus, vibrato, and so on. (For more about effects, see "Messing Around with Your Sound: Effects," later in this chapter.)

Figure 15-7:
An amp's
effects
section.

An amp with built-in, or *onboard*, effects is very convenient. But even with the handiness of onboard effects, most guitarists opt to create effects with signal processors or stompboxes placed between the guitar and amp (called *outboard effects*) because you can get more of a selection by choosing external effects and because they offer a wider range of tonal variation.

Power amp

The power amp is the heart of an amplifier. It takes your guitar signal and beefs it up to the point where it can get the speakers moving and push the air around that your ears perceive as sound. Power amps are made of heavy components, including transformers — which harness the electricity coming out of the wall socket into current that the amp can operate safely and optimally at.

Most amps are defined by their power-amp rating (express in output watts). An amp with a high power rating (over about 40 watts) is heavier, more expensive, and professionally oriented. You access this power with the master volume. The master volume determines the overall loudness the listener hears.

You can increase your loudness of your amp in one of two ways: increasing the input gain or increasing the master volume (which controls the power amp). But to achieve a distorted sound at a low volume, you turn the gain way up but keep the master volume down. This balance ensures that the signal gets distorted in the preamp stage, but stays below deafening levels as it goes through the power amp and out to the speakers.

Speakers

Speakers are the last in the amp's signal chain and turn the electrical signal of the amp into actual sound. A speaker is a surprisingly simple system, which uses a vibrating wire coil, magnets, and paper. You control the speakers by turning the volume knob up or down, which regulates the amount of level — or electrical current — the speaker receives. More current equals louder sound!

When considering an amp, always know the brand of speakers that it uses, because certain speakers have their own individual sound, like being brittle or clean or warm, and so on. For the best quality amp speakers check out Celestion, ElectroVoice, Eminence, Fane, JBL, Jensen, and Vox — a few brand names known for their guitar-amp speakers.

The flexibility of having separate channels

An amp may have separate paths, or channels, capable of producing two independent sounds. Using separate channels, you can set up one sound for rhythm playing (chords, riffs) and one for lead (melodies, waling solos), and then switch instantly between them by using a footswitch, which leaves your hands free to keep playing the guitar, for a seamless transition from rhythm to lead. On some amps, you don't have two entirely separate paths but instead a footswitch-activated boost (for increased volume and distortion). (See Figure 15-8 for an example of an amp with one channel and a footswitch-activated boost.)

What's That Sound? Checking Out Your Amp Choices

When shopping for an amp, you should be aware of what's under the hood, as far as the amp's sound-producing engine is concerned. The type of amp is defined by the sound-producing technology it uses, and the following sections outline the different types of amps.

Tube amps

At some point in your blues-playing career, you may own a tube amp. *Vacuum tubes* are the big, glass cylinders in amps that glow orange and get hot the more they're used. Playing through tubes makes you believe the amp is playing along with you — that it feels your notes as you do.

Valve is the British word for *tube*. If you're talking to Pete Townshend and Eric Clapton about amps, don't be confused if they use the term *valve* when discussing simply brilliant amps.

Tube technology is old, electronically speaking, and virtually obsolete, except in amp design. But you simply can't beat a tube for producing warm, dynamic, musically responsive tone. You sometimes have to hunt far and wide to find replacement components for tube amps, but it's worth it for the vintage and classic tone they produce.

Some potential drawbacks of tube amps include

- ✔ **Cost:** Tube amps tend to be more expensive than other amps.

- ✔ **Weight:** These amps are heavy, often weighing 60 pounds or more.

- ✔ **Burn out:** Tube amps are more finicky — the tubes get old, and they burn out more often than the circuitry in other types of amps, which means tube amps require more maintenance.

When considering the above drawbacks of tube amps, you may need to go with an alternative technology for practicality's sake. (These alternatives are covered in the next few sections.) But tubes are considered desirable for all types of electric guitar sound — especially blues and rock. The Fender Twin Reverb, shown in Figure 15-9, is an example of a classic tube amp.

Figure 15-9:
A tube amp.

Solid-state amps

One alternative to the tube amp for a budget-conscious guitarist is the *solid-state amp.* This amp style uses transistors and printed circuit boards in its technology. Solid-state amps are the most popular types of amps available, and many performers actually prefer their tone — including the distorted sound — to tube amps. But tone quality aside, solid-state amps are light, reliable, consistent, inexpensive, and provide a wide range of tonal and effects possibilities.

Hybrid amps

If you can't afford a tube amp right away, look into a *hybrid amp,* which combines both tube and solid-state circuitry. In a hybrid amp, the preamp uses a tube to create the initial sound, and the power amp uses solid-state circuitry to drive the speakers. This method puts the tube circuitry at the front of the chain, where it has the most effect on the sound. Using solid-state circuitry for the power amp keeps the cost and the weight of the amp down, which is great for both your wallet and your biceps!

The Marshall Valvestate series, as shown in Figure 15-10, uses hybrid technology.

Figure 15-10:
A hybrid amp.

Digital-modeling amps

For tubeless amps, which are cheaper and often lighter, you can also choose *digital-modeling* amps, which use computer modeling to create their sounds. Digital amps tend to be more expensive, but they have a wealth of effects and flexibility associated with them. Modeling technology has the advantage of being able to imitate sounds, so modeling amps can emulate a tube-amp sound quite convincingly.

Line 6 is an amp manufacturer that led the market in modeling technology with their Flextone series of amps, shown in Figure 15-11.

Figure 15-11: The Line 6 Flextone series of amps uses digital-modeling technology.

Remembering the Good Old Days

If you decide you like the amps of yore, you still have a choice in buying an actual vintage amp or one that's designed to be exactly like an older amp. The advantage here is that modern manufacturing methods use high-quality electrical components and a quality control standard that guarantees your amp works hassle free.

Many established companies, such as Fender and Marshall, make new versions of the classic amps that made the sounds that put Jimi Hendrix, Pete Townshend, and Eric Clapton on the map back in the day.

The following categories present the two choices you have if you want to sound like they did back in the day.

Vintage amps

As with guitars, many musicians argue that the classic amps of yore have never been equaled by modern attempts as far as sound quality and workmanship. The best vintage amps are hard to beat. Some of these include the Marshall "plexi" series (for the Plexiglas faceplate that appeared on the control panel) and the Fender Bassman, Twin, and Deluxe Reverb amps.

Although vintage amps are often best used in recording, where the environment is controlled, when you play a live gig, newer technology is generally more robust than vintage technology.

Reissue amps

Amp manufacturers, recognizing the appeal of vintage amps, often create *reissues* — amps that in many ways resemble their original, vintage counterparts from previous decades. If this interests you, look for amps that have "reissue" in the title or somewhere in the amp's description. Often these are quite faithful to the original specs, but do use a rubber coated power cord instead of a cloth-insulated one. Trust me — this is a good thing.

The Fender Vibrolux is an example of a reissue amp. It's made with modern materials and current manufacturing standards, but it's faithful to the look and feel of a vintage amp. Reissue amps try to capture the best of both worlds: modern manufacturing methods and original circuit design, look, and feel.

Dialing in an Amp Sound

When you find an amp you want to try out, there are certain procedures you should follow to test it. Whether you're in a music store or in the privacy of your own home, you need to know how to test an amp for the first time (so you don't blow it out).

Amps have different controls and front-panel arrangements, but the following steps apply to any amp when you plug in for the first time to create your sound:

1. **Make sure the amp is plugged in to a live socket.**

   I know it sounds simple, but people sometimes forget this first step.

2. **Turn the amp's gain and master volume controls all the way down.**

   This step prevents you from blowing out your eardrums — and scaring the pants off those around you.

3. **Turn the guitar's volume and tone controls all the way up.**

   The guitar sounds the best when all its controls are opened all the way up. Be careful that you don't confuse the volume settings of the amp and guitar!

4. **Set the tone controls to their neutral, or flat, positions.**

   On most amps, this setting is the 12 o'clock position.

5. **Turn all the effects off or to their lowest position.**

   This position is usually fully counterclockwise.

6. **When you're ready to play, bring up the master volume first to establish your overall sound level.**

   • **For a clean sound,** turn the master up to a high number, such as six or seven. Turn the gain up slowly to only about two or three, or until it's loud enough to hear clearly but not too loud for comfort.

   • **For a distorted sound,** turn the master up to two or three. Slowly bring up the gain or channel volume control to at least the 12:00 position (maybe more). If the sound starts to become too loud at this point, turn down the master volume slightly and bring the gain up to achieve a working listening level — the idea is to get the gain nearly maxed out (in the fully clockwise position, or about 5:00) while still being at a reasonable listening level for you and those around you.

   If the amp you're working with has a boost switch, engage it when creating a distorted or lead sound, disengage it if you're setting up a clean or rhythm sound.

7. **Adjust the bass and treble controls first to get the right balance of boom and brightness.**

   Try *sweeping* the midrange control to see what effect that has on the sound. Sweeping is highlighting the different frequency (high and low) ranges of the tonal range.

8. **Introduce effects into your sound.**

   The previous steps set your dry tone — without any effects. This last step allows you to play around with the available selections such as reverb, vibrato, and delay.

Chronicling Classic Amps for Blues

Blues players love and respect their history — not only for the players and the recordings but also for the gear. And that doesn't just include vintage guitars. To whet your appetite for the blues amp, I show you in the next sections seven great blues amps and how they got to be classics. The amps that I've included are by no means an exhaustive representation, but I think most blues players agree that these are worthy members of the amp hall of fame.

Fender Bassman

The Fender Bassman amp was designed originally for a bass guitar. It had four 10-inch speakers (guitar amps more commonly use 12-inch), but the bottom end (bass end) thundered because it was designed for a bass, and the top end (the treble) sparkled. This thumping bass and sparkling treble is the classic Fender sound.

Many musicians have used this amp over the years. Stevie Ray Vaughan is one of the most famous in the blues genre. Check out the Fender Bassman amp in Figure 15-12.

Figure 15-12:
The Fender Bassman amp.

Fender Deluxe Reverb

The Fender Deluxe Reverb amp has only one speaker, and isn't as large or as powerful as the four-speaker Fender Bassman (see previous section) or the two-speaker Fender Twin (see the next section), but to most guitarists, the Fender Deluxe Reverb is the holy grail of blues tone, because it had sweetness as well as bite, and its distortion content was warm, natural, but not without edge when you really needed it.

Of particular desirability in this model is the mid-'60s *blackface* version, which refers to the grille cloth and faceplate under the controls. For a time, Fender made these amps in black instead of silver. If you find one, grab it; it will sound great and be worth some money!

Fender Twin Reverb

Larger and more powerful than the Deluxe Reverb (see the previous section), the Fender Twin Reverb is one of Fender's most popular amps and was everywhere on the live-performing circuit because of its sheer power and the ability to reach incredible volumes while still producing a relatively clean sound.

If you were a player looking for an amp with a prominent distorted sound, you'd have to look elsewhere or hook up a pedal or turn the volume up to ten and hope people didn't call the police!

Marshall JTM 45

The Marshall JTM 45 is made by an English amp company that originally modeled their products after early Fender amps. But because the same components weren't available, the company swapped out materials where they had to and came up with their own sound.

The JTM 45 (shown in Figure 15-13) was an early amp that diverged from the influence of Fender, and it's a highly sought-after amp. The front panel of the amp features a Plexiglas plate, and models with this feature often are referred to as *Plexis*.

Figure 15-13:
The
Marshall
JTM 45.

Marshall Plexi Super Lead 100

Built in the late '60s, the Marshall Plexi Super Lead 100 had changed from the 6L6 power tube (used in Fender amps) to the EL34, further distinguishing it from its American rival, and establishing the *Marshall crunch* sound versus the twangy Fender sound.

The Marshall crunch sound can be described as more distorted and clipped than Fender's distorted sound. The much-copied Marshall sound later became more generally known as the "British sound."

The Super Lead 100 wasn't only loud, it sounded great, especially for blues rockers looking for an edgy and distorted sound. Jimi Hendrix liked to rock out on the Super Lead, and so did Eddie Van Halen on the first two Van Halen albums.

Vox AC30

Another classic British amp maker is Vox, and their amps have a distinctive twangy sound favored by blues-based rockers and the British Invasion contingent. The Vox AC30 had a bright high end, different than the Fender sound, and, though it was British, further apart still from the Marshall sound.

The Rolling Stones (who were heavily influenced by American traditional blues) used the Vox AC30 in the early days. U2's The Edge uses them, as does Tom Petty and the Heartbreakers, and many other blues players who want bright, cutting sound. Oh, and a certain obscure rock band from Liverpool known as the Beatles also played through AC30s (and they *did* play the blues, especially in their younger days).

Check out the Vox AC30 in Figure 15-14.

Figure 15-14:
The Vox
AC30.

Mesa/Boogie Mark IIc+

Randall Smith started out as many amp makers do — hot rodding existing amps for selective clientele. His company, Mesa Engineering, originally based their amps on a Fender design. The Mesa/Boogie IIc+ amp soon came into its own as a great-sounding, powerful, and wonderfully built amp for blues and other types of music. The amps also included an onboard graphic equalizer and a power-regulator switch (that changed the way power was delivered to the amp instead of just relying on the volume), which was innovative at the time.

The name *Boogie* came from Carlos Santana, who, after playing through an early Mesa-designed amp, said, "This thing boogies!"

Figure 15-15 shows the mighty Mesa/Boogie.

Figure 15-15:
The Mesa/
Boogie
Mark IIc+.

Messing Around with Your Sound: Effects

In this section, I show you the world of effects and how they can enhance your sound. Some effects are already inside your amplifier — such as reverb — but introducing *outboard* (separate boxes that hook up between your guitar and amp through cords) effects offers a great range of flexibility. In the early days of blues, no one used effects (except what could be found on an amp), and some blues guitarists shun them. But many modern players, even when trying to emulate the effect-less masters, will use effects to create a more modern sound. And Eric, Jimi, and Stevie used them extensively, so what more justification do you need? In the following sections, I break down effects by category, describe what each one does, and then offer tips on how and when to use them.

Back in electric blues' formative years — the '40s and '50s — the basic sound was of a guitar going through an amp. That approach has remained intact through present-day blues, with only subtle enhancements to the sound, in the form of effects.

Unlike rock, blues tends *not* to be on the cutting edge of electronic technology but adopts aspects of it after the technology goes mainstream. So a modern blues player must be aware of new technology trends but respectful of the traditional sound they're responsible for upholding.

The following sections take you on a tour of guitar effects, according to what they do to your guitar sound. Effects that boost and distort your signal (the electronic impulses coming from your guitar before they become sound) are different than the ones that adjust the treble and bass, which are different from those that imbue your sound with ambient effects like reverberation and echo. This chapter helps you organize effects and make decisions on whether you can use them to play your particular brand of blues.

Juicing Up Your Sound

When you juice up your sound, you use gain-based effects. In electronic terms, *gain* refers to the signal strength or how much power is being pumped through your system. Typically, the higher the gain, the louder the sound you hear through your speakers, but you can influence the level with a master volume, which controls the overall loudness. High gain is a good thing, because a healthy signal keeps away noises that plague low-level signals or weak powered notes. But gain doesn't just make things louder. It also changes the bass and treble characteristics in certain ways that are considered pleasing in some musical situations.

When your sound is too hot to handle: Distortion

If you boost your guitar signal so that it's too powerful, or hot, for the amp to handle, distortion results, and the sound that comes through the speaker appears broken up compared to the incoming signal. Distortion is normally a bad thing in electronics, except in electric guitar tone. In this special case, distortion has a pleasing, useful, and musical effect. Distortion can be referred to by other names, like fuzz, overdrive, break-up, warmth, but it's all distortion, technically speaking.

Describing the tonal differences between the countless types of guitar distortion is tricky, but you can generally break gain-based distortion effects down into two categories:

- Those that seek to provide the realistic effect of driving an amp hard
- Those that go for over-the-top, buzz-saw, and synthetic-sounding effects — never mind the realism

Blues is primarily concerned with the last category, though some blues-rock players — notably Jimi Hendrix — certainly popularized more intense versions of guitar distortion, though he tended to save it for his rock rather than his blues tunes.

Distortion devices are by far the most numerous and varied, so simply selecting the right pedal for the job is half the battle. Pedals with names like "Metal Madness" shouldn't be used to imitate B.B. King, and usually the name of the effect or its description hints to its abilities.

Figure 15-16 shows a collection of some popular distortion effects used for the blues. From left to right in the figure, you see the Ibanez Tube Screamer, the Boss Blues Driver, and the Line 6 Pod XT.

Figure 15-16:
A collection of distortion devices.

a   b   c

The Ibanez Tube Screamer, as popularized by Stevie Ray Vaughan, is still considered by some to be the benchmark for stompbox distortion. Stevie used the TS-808 model, considered the smoothest and most natural sounding, followed in quality by the TS-9 and TS-10. Vintage TS-808 and TS-9 models sell for several hundred dollars, but the reissues are great and a lot cheaper.

Toying with Tone Quality

Effects that act on a guitar's quality, not its level, are called tone-based effects and are similar to the way an amp's controls work — but they're actually *outboard effects,* which connect between the guitar and amp, instead of being built into the amp. But a dedicated, outboard effect can provide more versatility and additional control over a guitar signal before it hits the amp.

EQ: The great tonal equalizer

Of all the effects a guitarist has in his arsenal, EQ is perhaps the most versatile. EQ effects can be placed in different parts of the chain depending on their function, and they can be used subtly or obviously. An EQ device can be used as an effect to make a single-coil pickup sound more like a humbucker, and vice-versa, or it can be used transparently to compensate for an imbalance in the bass and treble quality of the guitar's tone.

Wah-wah, the effect that is as it sounds

Wah-wah pedals work by sweeping a given range of frequencies (in accordance to your foot movements) and emphasizing them. In addition to providing a vocal-like quality to your notes, a wah-wah pedal is a performance device, because the physical movement of the treadle (the part of the pedal where you put your foot) can be synchronized to your playing. Besides Jimi Hendrix, Earl Hooker and Luther Allison were two of the few traditional blues players who experimented with the wah-wah pedal.

You can also use a wah-wah as a tonal device, by leaving the pedal in a fixed position. You can achieve a variety of tonal colors, from a hollow, boxy sound (like the sound coming out of a telephone) to a brittle and glassy one (like someone really cranked up the treble).

Modulation Effects, from Swooshy to Swirly

In traditional electric blues, you don't use much in the way of modulation effects, but any electric guitarist should be familiar with how they affect the sound of the guitar. Modulation includes effects that add rich, swirly textures to your sound, and they work by digitally recording the incoming signal and feeding the recorded sound back against the original, at some time-specified delay. The effect of the two signals interacting with each other is then further accentuated, or modulated in some way.

Check out the following sections for some popular modulation effects.

Stacking sounds for a fuller effect: Chorus

A *chorus* effect takes the original signal from your guitar, digitally records it, and plays it back against the original, but the sound is slightly delayed and out of tune. This concept is similar to what happens when humans — and instruments played by humans — try to sing or play in unison. It's not perfectly in time or in tune, but instead of the choir sounding bad or out of sync, they sound rich and full (like a chorus of sound should).

As a guitar effect, the application of even just a slight bit of chorus increases the perceived bigness of a sound and gives it a shimmering quality. Mild chorus sounds good with distortion for a slow, simple rhythm part, because it adds just a hint of vibrancy in the notes. For an even bigger sound, many guitarists run their chorus effects in stereo.

Swooshing, like a jet plane: Flangers and phase shifters

Flanging and phase shifting produce a *whooshing*, swirling sound that makes the guitar sound like it's under water or like a jet airplane taking off. Flanging and phase shifting sound best used over a clean or only mildly distorted signal.

You can adjust the rate, depth, and regeneration (also called feedback) to suit your tastes when you use these effects. The flanger and phaser usually come right before (closer to the guitar) the delay in your effects order, but you can put them after the delay for a slightly different effect. Usually, you use either chorus (covered in the previous section) or flanging or phase shifting, but not any two together; that just makes sonic mush.

Like a visit to the opera house: Vibrato and tremolo

Vibrato is the rapid fluctuation of pitch and the expressive quality that singers and string players apply to sustained notes to give the notes life. Amp vibrato is an effect not often built into amps despite models such as the popular Fender Vibrolux and Vibro-King that actually contain tremolo instead.

One of the few amps with true vibrato was the Magnatone from the early '60s favored by the great, but unsung, Lonnie Mack.

Tremolo is similar in effect to vibrato but is the rapid fluctuation of *volume*, not pitch. Both vibrato and tremolo feature depth and rate controls. *Depth* is the amplitude — or how pronounced the effect is — and *rate* is how fast the oscillating pitch or volume difference occurs. But players who want more versatility in their vibrato *and* tremolo (or who don't have them built into their amps) can use the outboard solution (as shown in Figure 15-17.)

Figure 15-17:
An outboard effect offers more variety and control.

A guitarist can achieve vibrato four ways:

1. Through left-hand bending and releasing of a fretted string
2. By jiggling the whammy bar if the guitar has a floating bridge
3. From the amp's effects section, if the amp has a vibrato control
4. From an outboard effect

Pretending (and Sounding Like) You're Somewhere You're Not

Ambient effects electronically simulate the sound of your guitar in a physical space, such as a room or concert hall, cathedral or canyon. Even a little bit of ambience gives your sound a sense of depth and keeps it from sounding too dry. Technically, all ambient sound is classified as reverberation, or reverb, for short, but guitarists can use two effects, delay and reverb, to simulate ambience.

Delaying sound in a cave-like way

A delay effect is sometimes called a digital delay or echo (unless the device is specifically analog, which is rare these days). The delay has four main features:

- **Time:** The amount of milliseconds between the straight signal and the delayed one
- **Feedback:** How many repeats of the effected signal are produced
- **Level:** How loud the delayed signal is compared to the original
- **Mode:** The specific range that the time control affects

The digital delay effect works by digitally recording the incoming signal from your guitar and outputting that copy along with the straight signal at a specified time interval after the original (the "delay"), measured in milliseconds (ms). A short setting (25 to 50 ms) creates a slight thickening effect. At longer settings (100 ms), you begin to hear the recorded signal as distinct from the original; it sounds like two guitars playing the same part. At delay times of 200 ms and longer, the effect sounds like the echo, or reverb (see the next section for more on reverb), in a cavern or mountainside.

Classic blues recordings from the '50s as produced by Chess Records in Chicago sometimes featured a degree of echo, but rockabilly players from the era were particularly fond of the effect. Scotty Moore, who played with Elvis Presley from 1954 to 1959, had a custom amp with built-in echo.

Adding reverb to make your sound slicker

Reverb is more complex than delay (delay is covered in the previous section) and is really what you hear when you listen to music in a large room or concert hall. A _reverb_ uses echo, or delay, but produces a more realistic surrounding effect than a digital delay can by applying additional processes. While a digital delay merely copies the original signal and plays it back, reverb combines repeats in various complex ways to simulate the way sound behaves in different spaces.

Most amps include one of several ways to attain the reverb effect:

- **A spring reverb unit:** This effect is a metal spring that the signal passes through. Users vary the intensity by a single control that feeds more or less signal into the spring. Use a little reverb to keep your sound from being too dry or sterile; use a lot for an exaggerated cavern effect.

✔ **Digital reverb sections:** This effect is a more complex electronic circuitry than a spring reverb and offers more control, such as time, feedback, and level. Use a digital reverb for more realistic ambient sounds than a spring reverb can provide or when you want more control over the individual reverb parameters.

✔ **Outboard units:** The guitarist interested in taking advantage of the best of digital modeling technology may want to go with an outboard unit (usually in the form of a pedal) and not the circuitry built into the amp.

Choosing an Effects Format

Effects are essential to creating a variety of sounds, but some guitarists rely more on them than others. If you use only an occasional one or two effects, you can get away with a couple of stomp boxes (the nickname for small pedals). But the more you employ effects into your sound and the more particular you get, the more you need to consider the different available formats, or physical setups, for incorporating effects into your arsenal.

A string of effects: Pedals on parade

The most popular format for individual effects is the pedal, or so-called stomp box. This often-inexpensive effect is usually a box the size of a deck of playing cards that you turn on and off with your foot (by "stomping" on it). Stomp boxes are usually single-function devices that connect together in daisy-chain fashion, with short patch cords. Figure 15-18 shows a collection of stomp boxes and the cables that connect them.

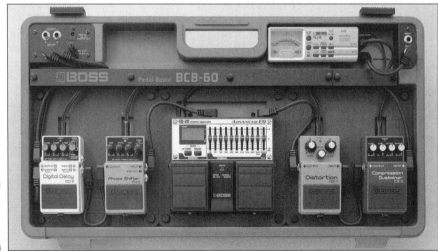

Figure 15-18:
The stomp
box solution.

Stomp boxes are inexpensive and easy to carry — you just throw them in your case or a bag, and you're off. For most players who only want one or two effects — and who like to keep their performing footprint small — stomp boxes are the way to go. Staying with stomp boxes allows you to mix and match pedals from different manufacturers, too.

A box to house them all at your feet

Floor effects or *floorboards* combine several single effects into one unit and are more compact than the same number of individual effects. Having all your effects in one box eliminates the need for cables to connect the various effects and having to power the effects individually (with multiple 9V batteries or AC adapters). Figure 15-19 shows the DigiTech GNX1 — a popular floor-mounted multi-effects processor.

Figure 15-19:
The Digi-Tech GNX1.

Floorboards are neat and convenient, because you don't have a lot of wires to contend with. They're not quite as modular as the stomp box approach because all the effects are provided by the same manufacturer, but you can always "patch in" your favorite effect, if necessary.

A box to house them all at hand level

For recording and non-gigging guitarists, who may not need to control everything with their feet, two other choices exist to house your effects: a table-top format and a rack-mount multi-effects unit.

Table-top format

A table-top format may be more user friendly for tone-tweaking purposes. It allows you to change the controls by hand and offers more knobs and switches than a floorboard unit does. Figure 15-20 shows a table-top format effect called the Line 6 Pod XT. It has many front-panel knobs and switches, which are more suited to tweaking by hand than your foot.

Many table-top units, including the Line 6 Pod XT, offer a floorboard add-on, so you can use this unit during performance and not just while you're in a rehearsal studio or your home studio recording your own music.

Rack-mount multi-effects unit

If you want the greatest power and flexibility with your effects choices and parameters within those effects, consider a rack-mount multi-effects unit. This format is *the* format of choice for manufacturers making the highest-quality components. You control these effects with an attached floorboard (which houses the switching mechanism), but the brains (the actual sound-effecting circuitry) are housed in a separate component in a rack unit at the back of the stage (or even offstage, run by a technician).

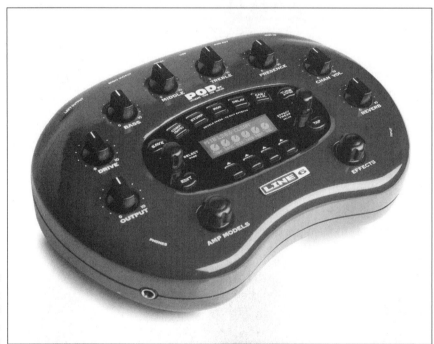

Figure 15-20:
The Line 6
Pod XT.

The company Line 6 makes their Pod Pro in a rack-mount configuration for pro-audio applications. The Line 6 Pod Pro is designed for high-end studio and stage work, and features a rack-mount unit and a floorboard controller. This model is shown in Figure 15-21.

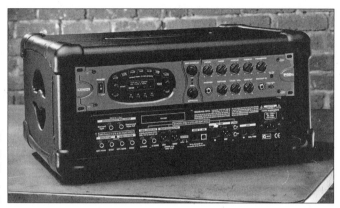

Figure 15-21:
The Line 6
Pod Pro.

Chapter 16

Changing Strings

. . . .

In This Chapter

▶ Knowing when and how to change your strings

▶ Shopping for the correct strings

▶ Changing out the old strings for the new

▶ Stocking your toolkit

. . . .

*P*laying the blues can be a sweaty, muscular, gritty activity — if you're doing it correctly, that is. And while your guitar can handle pretty much any abuse you deliver (within reason), your strings aren't so hardy. Through repeated contact with human hands and fingers, strings lose their tone and won't play in tune; they also wear out and eventually may break. Because of the repetitive use, you eventually have to change them. So do it regularly — just like changing the oil in your car, it's almost impossible to overdo it. And changing strings is less messy and a lot cheaper.

In this chapter, I break down the ins and outs of string-changing into the two most common types of guitars (electric and acoustic) you encounter when playing the blues.

Change Is Good, But When?

You may need to change the strings of your guitar in many different situations:

✔ A string breaks, providing a jolting reminder that all the strings may need changing

✔ The strings sound dull and lifeless; they may even look dull

✔ The strings no longer play in tune, exhibiting evidence they've lost their flexibility

If you break a string while playing, you need to replace at least one of the strings (the broken one, naturally) immediately. But you should also change all your strings (the entire set of six) every two to three months to keep the strings fresh — that is, in tune and able to produce a bright, lively tone.

No matter how gentle you are on the strings, the tone of your guitar isn't what it used to be after several months of constant playing, biochemical assaults from your fingers, and environmental changes. One sure-fire way to determine whether you need to change the strings? If you can't remember the last time you changed them — then it's *definitely* time!

Choosing the Right Strings

Chances are, when you purchased your guitar, it had the right type of strings attached. So hopefully, if you bought an electric guitar, it came with strings designed for an electric guitar in the appropriate gauge. But, just so you know what you're looking for when you want to replace your current strings (or if you want to experiment with different types of strings), consider the following list when making your string-changing decisions:

- ✔ The *gauge* of a string is its thickness and determines how easy the string is to fret and bend.

- ✔ *Fretting* involves pushing the string down onto the fretboard with your fingers.

- ✔ *Bending* is the act of pushing or pulling the strings sideways across the fretboard, which raises the pitch of the note.

- ✔ The *fretboard* is the top of the neck of the guitar — the part where the frets protrude and where your fingers press the strings when fretting.

Higher-numbered gauges (or *heavier* gauges, as guitarists call them) are stiffer and provide more resistance, but they also hold their tuning and tone better and wear out less quickly than lighter-gauge strings.

Striking a balance among playing comfort, string performance, and longevity is important. Here are a few tidbits to keep in mind when you're choosing your strings:

- ✔ Blues guitarists like their blues guitar set up with strings that *fight back*. This give and take allows the guitarist to really dig in to the strings. (Rock guitars, on the other hand, may have lighter-gauge strings, because the light ones facilitate super-fast playing and extreme string bending.)

- ✔ The more experienced you are as a player, the better you are at managing heavier gauges. But that doesn't mean you necessarily prefer them.

- ✔ Many blues guitarists go strictly for playability and comfort and put ultra-light-gauge strings on their guitars and then just get used to changing out the strings a lot.

In the end, the choice of string gauge is completely up to the player's individual preference.

Acoustic strings

If you're not sure what gauge strings you already have or what to replace them with, bring your guitar into the music store and have the salesperson or the store's guitar tech match a new set to the old. You can even use a tool called a *caliper* (a clamp-like device that yields measurements to the thousandth of an inch) to measure the diameter of the individual strings yourself. Table 16-1 shows you the most popular string gauges used for the acoustic guitar.

Table 16-1	Common Acoustic-Guitar String Sets by Gauge					
String Set Name	*1*	*2*	*3*	*4*	*5*	*6*
Extra light	.010	.014	.023	.030	.039	.047
Light	.012	.016	.024	.032	.042	.053
Medium	.013	.017	.026	.035	.045	.056

Considering the acoustic plain-third option

If you're an acoustic guitar player, your string sets include a wound third string (*wound* means a plain wire with a ridged winding around it, like all the lower three strings on a guitar).

If you're an electric guitar player, your strings come with a plain third because it's easier to bend, and blues players do a lot of third-string bending.

Though few electric guitarists (except for traditional jazz players) opt for a wound third, acoustic-blues players may want to consider an unwound, plain third-string for the following reasons:

✔ Having a plain third makes your acoustic guitar behave more like an electric, which means you can practice your electric string-bending licks on your acoustic. You can hear your electric-style playing acoustically without the aid of an amplifier.

✔ A plain third is lighter and more flexible than a wound third, making it easier on your left hand.

✔ Your electric and acoustic setups are more closely matched, making it easier to transition between the two guitars.

The disadvantages to a plain third on an acoustic include the following:

✔ The sound quality is thin.

✔ The strings feel loose under your fingers.

✔ The result is a strange sound and unusual feel because acoustics are set up for wound thirds. This may prevent you from playing other types of acoustic music convincingly.

If you don't perform a lot of third-string bending and you want the more-traditional acoustic-guitar sound, stay with a wound third. But if you do a lot of string bending — whether in your acoustic or in your electric playing — you may want to try stringing your acoustic with a plain third.

Acoustic guitars require more strength in the left hand to fret than do electrics because their necks are thicker and the string gauges are heavier. So acoustic-blues players often make string-gauge choices based solely on left-hand fretting and bending ability. Light gauge is far and away the most popular choice for acoustic blues players.

Electric strings

You'll do plenty of string-bending in electric-blues guitar but not to the extremes found in rock, for example. So you may want to run with a slightly heavier gauge for blues than rock, with all other things being equal. For instance, if you like a *nine* in rock, you might go with a *ten* in blues. Table 16-2 lists the common string sets for the electric guitar according to their gauges.

String sets are often referred to by their first-string measurement. So the set listed in Table 16-2 as *Super light* is called a *nine*.

Table 16-2	Common Electric-Guitar String Sets by Gauge					
String Set Name	*1*	*2*	*3*	*4*	*5*	*6*
Super light	.009	.011	.016	.024	.032	.042
Regular light	.010	.013	.017	.026	.036	.046
Medium	.011	.014	.018	.028	.038	.049
Heavy	.012	.016	.020	.032	.042	.054

Outfitting Your String-Changing Toolkit

You don't need any tools to change strings. But using a couple of simple items found in any hardware store (and shown in Figure 16-1) can at least speed up the job and are worth having. Saving time leaves you with more time to play the blues and may actually save your skin — like if you're on stage and you break a string in the first verse and have to replace it by the time your next guitar solo comes around — because you've been practicing that solo for weeks! Following is a list of three essential items that no time-conscious blues player should leave home without.

> ✔ **String winder:** These plastic cranks make quick work of the tedious job of turning your tuning keys. To bring a new, slack string up to pitch takes many, many revolutions of the tuning key. The string winder takes a fraction of the time. For acoustic players, a string winder has an added

benefit: a notch in the cup that allows for quick extraction of stubborn bridge pins. Just be careful not to catapult a pin into the abyss!

✔ **Needle-nose pliers/wire cutters:** Use these tools for getting the old string off more than for getting the new strings on. These tools come in handy when you need to dispatch the old string in a hurry and the tightly wound ends resist quick removal. You just snip the coils in one or two places, and the old string falls away.

✔ **Phillips and flathead screwdrivers (electric only):** Electric guitars are mechanical contraptions made of wood and wire and are put together with screws. Many of the adjustments you make to a guitar require tightening or loosening metal fasteners, so pack a couple of screwdrivers that fit the screw heads found on your particular instrument.

Figure 16-1:
Three tools that make string-changing and adjustments a cinch.

Removing Old Strings

You can take all the strings off at once, but a better way is to replace one string at a time. This way, the old strings keep tension on the neck, which makes tuning the new string easier. If you're changing strings on an electric guitar and you have a floating bridge (balanced with springs to allow movement by the vibrato bar), the instrument is even harder to tune with all the strings removed.

However, one reason to take all the strings off before putting on the new ones is if you're going to make any adjustments to the neck or bridge. It's sometimes easier to make adjustments with the strings off the guitar.

If you remove all the strings on a guitar with a floating bridge system, stick a shim (or wedge) between the bridge and the body to keep the bridge stationary while you restring.

To remove a string from your *acoustic* guitar

1. **Turn the tuning key in the direction that loosens the string or makes the sound go flat.**

2. **Turn the key for two or three complete revolutions (until the string is completely slack and the coils around the tuning post loosen).**

3. **Pull the coiled string off the post and remove the string end from the tuning post hole.**

4. **Remove the bridge pin, which holds the *ball* — a ring or hollow cylinder — end firmly in place (check out the information on bridge pins in the section "Stringing a Steel-String Acoustic" in this chapter).**

5. **Remove the string from the bridge to get the string completely off the guitar.**

To remove a string from your *electric* guitar

1. **Turn the tuning key in the direction that loosens the string or makes a note go flat.**

2. **Turn the key for two or three complete revolutions (until the string is completely slack and the coils around the tuning post loosen).**

3. **Pull the coiled string off the post and remove the string end from the tuning post hole.**

4. **Cut the string at its midpoint with wire cutters (if you don't plan to save the string for a spare), which allows easy removal through the hole (it takes time to snake the coiled end through the hole in the tailpiece or bridge).**

5. **Remove the string from the bridge to get the string completely off the guitar.**

Stringing a Steel-String Acoustic

One difference between acoustic- and electric-stringing is that an acoustic uses removable bridge pins to hold the strings in place at the bridge. Bridge pins require a little more fiddling to get them to secure correctly to the string in place at the bridge.

TIP

Take it slowly, look at the figures, and if you think you haven't executed a step correctly, simply undo what you've done and start over. Nothing you do in stringing a guitar is permanent, even when you crease or coil a string in the process!

The following steps outline the process for restringing your acoustic guitar:

1. **Drop the ball end of the new string in the bridge hole, and replace the pin.**

2. **Pull the new string until you feel the ball end come up against the bottom of the bridge pin.**

    Tug on the string to make sure that the pin doesn't pop out, but make sure not to crease the string as you grip it for tugging.

3. **Insert the string end through the appropriate tuning-post hole.**

    Make sure that the bridge and tuning-post holes correspond.

4. **Crease (or kink) the string toward the inside of the guitar (away from the tuning key).**

    For strings six, five, and four, kink the string to the right as you face the guitar; for strings three, two, and one, kink to the left. See Figure 16-2.

Figure 16-2:
Kinking the
string in the
proper
direction.

5. **Turn the tuning key so the string wraps around the post.**

   For strings six, five, and four, turn the keys so that the posts rotate counterclockwise; for strings three, two, and one, turn the tuning key so the posts rotate clockwise. Following this procedure ensures that the strings wrap from the middle of the neck over the top of the post and to the outside of the guitar (toward the tuning key). See Figure 16-3.

Figure 16-3:
Wrapping the strings in the proper direction.

6. **As you turn the key and wind the string around the post, make sure that the string coils from the top of the post downward toward the headstock surface. See Figure 16-4.**

   The string may want to flop around as you start to coil the string, so use your other hand (the one not turning the key) to control the string.

   If you have too much string, you'll run out of room on the post before the string is tightened up to pitch. If that happens, simply loosen the string, pull a little more string through the post hole, re-kink the string, and begin the winding process again.

7. **Keep turning the tuning key.**

   As you do this, the coils around the post tighten, the slack in the string disappears, and the string begins to produce a recognizable musical pitch. Be sure that the string is inside the appropriate nut slot before the string becomes too taut to manipulate it further.

8. **Bring the string up to the proper pitch by turning the tuning key slowly.**

   You can determine the correct pitch by the adjacent string, using the tuning methods described in Chapter 3.

9. **Clip away the excess string sticking out of the tuning post, as shown in Figure 16-5.**

   Cut the wire as close to the tuning post as your wire cutters will reach so the point doesn't jab you in the finger!

Figure 16-4:
Coiling the
string on
the post.

TIP

If you don't have wire cutters available, loop the excess string into a
circle or break the string by repeatedly bending the string back and
forth across the crease.

Figure 16-5:
Clipping the
string end
close to
the post.

REMEMBER

New strings will continue to stretch (causing them to go flat) even after you
tune them up to pitch. To help get the stretchiness out of the string

1. **Pull on the string, gently but firmly with your fingers, bringing it directly above the fingerboard, as shown in Figure 16-6.**

2. **Tune the string up to pitch by turning the key.**

   After each pull, the string will be flat (under pitch), so repeat the process of pulling the string with your fingers and tuning up with the tuning key until the string no longer goes flat after you pull on it. You may have to do this three or four times, but the whole procedure shouldn't take more than a couple of minutes.

Figure 16-6: Pulling on the string to stretch it out after it's tuned up.

Stringing an Electric Guitar

An electric guitar uses lighter-gauge strings (than an acoustic guitar), which makes the strings easier to control when stringing. But these types of strings are stretchier, so tuning takes a little longer. Lighter, skinnier strings also provide more wraps around the post, so allow more string length for wrapping around the post. Also, electric guitars don't use bridge pins like acoustics do, so restringing electric guitars focuses mostly on the tuning-post end of the guitar.

The steps for changing the strings on an electric guitar can be a little different.

You may have a guitar with a system that's different from the one described in this section, so you may have to adjust the directions slightly. But the principles of good string-changing apply no matter what type of system you use.

The following steps outline the process for restringing your electric guitar:

1. **Thread the plain end of the string through the hole.**

   The ball end prevents the string from completely passing through the hole.

2. **Pull the string all the way through the tailpiece or bridge until the ball stops the string.**

3. **Insert the string through the appropriate tuning-post hole.**

   Make sure that the tailpiece hole, bridge slot (or saddle), and tuning post all correspond. For example, if you're changing the first string, make sure that you're threading the string through the outside, right-most hole as you face the guitar.

4. **Crease (or kink) the string toward the inside of the guitar (away from the tuning key).**

   On guitars with *inline* tuners (all six tuners on the same side of the head-stock), like the one shown in Figure 16-7, the kink goes to the right as you face the guitar. For a *split-tuner* configuration (three on each side), the three lower strings (six, five, and four) kink to the right, the three upper strings (three, two, and one) kink to the left.

Figure 16-7:
Kinking the string in the proper direction for inline and split tuners.

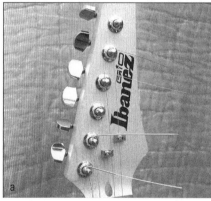

5. **Turn the tuning key so the string wraps around the post.**

   For inline tuners, turn the keys so that all six posts rotate counterclockwise. For split tuners, turn the three lower-string (six, five, and four) tuning posts counterclockwise, and the three upper-string (three, two, and one) tuning posts clockwise. Following this procedure ensures that the strings wrap from the middle of the neck over the top of the post and to the outside, as shown in Figure 16-8.

Figure 16-8: Wrapping the strings in the proper direction.

6. **As you turn the key and wind the string around the post, make sure that it coils from the top of the post downward toward the headstock surface, as shown in Figure 16-9.**

   Use your other hand (the one not turning the key) to create tight, gapless winds on the post.

   If you have too much string, you'll run out of room on the post before the string is tightened up to pitch. If that happens, simply loosen the string, pull a little more string through the post hole, re-kink the string, and begin the winding process again.

7. **Keep turning the tuning key.**

   As you turn the key, the coils around the post tighten, the slack in the string disappears, and the string begins to produce a recognizable musical pitch. Be sure that the string is inside the appropriate nut slot before the string becomes too taught to manipulate it further.

8. **Slowly bring the string up to the proper pitch by turning the tuning key slowly.**

   You can determine the correct pitch by the adjacent string, using the tuning methods described in Chapter 3.

Figure 16-9:
Coiling the string on the post.

9. **Stretch out the string.**

   New strings will continue to stretch (causing them to go flat), even after you tune them up to pitch. To help get the stretchiness out of the string, pull on the string gently but firmly with your fingers, bringing it directly above the fingerboard, as shown in Figure 16-10. After each pull, the string will be flat (under pitch), so tune it up to pitch by turning the key. Repeat the process of pulling the string with your fingers and tuning up with the tuning key until the string no longer goes flat after you pull on it. You may have to do this four or five times — generally a few times more than you would for acoustic strings — but the whole procedure shouldn't take more than a couple of minutes.

Locking systems, floating bridges

Locking bridge systems, such as the Floyd Rose, require a different stringing approach. The strings don't pass through a tailpiece from the back or top. Instead, they get clamped right at the bridge using a screw mechanism. (Some systems require you to clip off the ball before installing.) Then the string passes through a *locking nut*, which uses another clamp system, after the string is brought up to tune with the tuning keys. After the nut is locked off, any further tuning adjustments must be made at the bridge using microtuners. Locking systems are widely used in rock playing because they offer high tuning-stability when used with extreme whammy bar moves. Locking systems aren't as common in guitars used for blues playing, but they do offer an extra level of tuning security in any guitar where you desire a floating bridge.

10. Clip away the excess string sticking out of the tuning post.

Cut the wire as close to the tuning post as your wire cutters can reach so the point doesn't jab you in the finger!

If you don't have wire cutters available, loop the excess string into a circle or break the string by repeatedly bending the string back and forth across the crease.

Part VI
The Part of Tens

The 5th Wave   By Rich Tennant

SUBURBAN BLUES LEGENDS AND THEIR HIT RECORDS

"Muddy Driveway"

Muddy Driveway
GOT MY VOLVO WORKING

"Howlin' Leafblower"

HOWLIN LEAFBLOWER
"Oh No-It's Fall Again"

"B.B. Que"

B.B. QUE
The Blues Are Done!

"Lightnin' Fireplace"

SEND THE BLUES UP THE FLUE

Lightnin' Fireplace and the Andirons

In this part . . .

The Part of Tens chapters read like a top-ten list from late-night TV talk shows. The three chapters in this part reduce complex and deep issues into short spurts of information. For example, Chapter 19 presents ten blues-guitar giants who've made a contribution to the blues and have earned a place in the company of the greats. And some of those great guitartists played the guitar models in Chapter 20. Chapter 21 contains a list of ten recordings to take to a desert island — or an abandoned shack in the Delta — if you really wanted to hunker down and study the essence of the blues.

Chapter 17

Ten Blues Guitar Giants

*T*o narrow a list of all the blues greats to ten was a hard choice, but I think you'd be hard pressed to dispute the ones I've come up with. Each guitarist occupies a permanent and revered place in the history of the blues.

Robert Johnson (1911–38)

Robert Johnson was one of the last blues players on the Delta scene, but for many blues enthusiasts, he's the most important. Johnson died at the young age of 27 and only recorded 29 songs, but he's immortalized for his haunting acoustic-guitar picking and singing, as well as for the songs he wrote. He rightly wears the mantle of "king of the Delta blues." Some of his songs include

- ✔ "Hell Hound on My Trail"
- ✔ "Cross Road Blues" (covered by Cream with Eric Clapton)
- ✔ "Love in Vain Blues" (covered by the Rolling Stones)
- ✔ "Come on in My Kitchen"
- ✔ "I Believe I'll Dust My Broom"
- ✔ "Sweet Home Chicago"
- ✔ "Me and the Devil Blues" (helped start the "devil" legend)

Johnson was a mythic figure, who allegedly sold his soul to the devil in exchange for his talent, and who may have been poisoned by a jealous husband in a juke joint. But one thing is certain: His genius with the guitar is evident in the small body of recorded work.

Flip back to Chapter 11 for the nitty-gritty on Johnson and his blues style.

Elmore James (1918–63)

Elmore James was an inspired slide player who started the transition from the acoustic blues of Robert Johnson to the emerging electrified sound that was to be known as the Chicago blues. He was known as "king of the slide guitar," and his cover of Johnson's "Dust My Broom" contains the classic slide lick that every blues guitarist must know. James influenced guitarists Jimi Hendrix and Duane Allman, who both cited him as a major influence.

T-Bone Walker (1910–75)

Born in Texas, Aaron Thibeaux Walker ("T-Bone" was a corruption of his middle name) is universally recognized as not only the father of the electric blues but also one of its greatest practitioners. When recordings of Walker's all-melody-based electric guitar reached the mainstream, he defined the concept of electric lead guitarist, and influenced all who immediately followed, including B.B. King and Duane Allman of the Allman Brothers Band ("Stormy Monday" is one of their most famous songs). As if that weren't enough, Walker was an accomplished showman, performing splits, behind-the-back playing, and other stage antics that were adopted a quarter century later by another devotee, Jimi Hendrix.

Muddy Waters (1915–83)

Waters's influence is all over the history of rock and the development of blues: He helped Chuck Berry get his first record contract; the Rolling Stones named their band after a lyric in Waters's "Mannish Boy"; and Led Zeppelin covered his "You Shook Me," as well as basing their hit "Whole Lotta Love" on his "You Need Love." Waters played with virtually every other blues musician of note: Little Walter, Big Walter Horton, James Cotton, Junior Wells, Willie Dixon, Otis Spann, Pinetop Perkins, Buddy Guy, and Jimmie Rogers.

His classics include "Got My Mojo Working," "Hoochie Coochie Man," "I Just Want to Make Love to You" (covered by the Rolling Stones and Foghat), and "Rolling and Tumbling." See Chapter 12 for more info on Waters.

Albert King (1923–92)

Albert King was a big man and an original and fiery player, who, along with B.B. King, followed the path carved by T-Bone Walker for playing lead electric guitar. But Albert's style was distinctive and unique, because he played a right-handed guitar upside down (see Chapter 12 for details). As well, he played in unusual tunings, and he bent strings by pulling them downward, toward the floor, instead of upward like other guitarists, which made it even harder to pin down his style.

B.B. King (b. 1925)

Because of his unmatched technique, long career, and brilliant artistry, B.B. King is the most enduring and important blues guitarist of all time. King uses his voice, performance persona, and lyrical, soulful soloing to the envy of every blues player who came after him. His early records were produced by Elvis discoverer Sam Phillips, and of particular note, King's vibrato is considered the most evolved of any blues guitarist. Chapter 12 contains more info on B.B.

Albert Collins (1932–93)

Albert Collins was the consummate blues performer and showman. He hailed from Texas and his highly distinctive style is characterized by explosive, stinging, and abrupt punctuated phrases delivered by a twangy, alternative-tuned Telecaster, which he fingerpicked and often capoed high on the neck. Collins influenced such modern blues players as Debbie Davies, Stevie Ray Vaughan, Jonny Lang, Kenny Wayne Shepherd, and John Mayer, and had a profound influence on Robert Cray. Flip back to Chapter 12 for more on Collins.

Otis Rush (b. 1934)

Otis Rush was the leader in the West Side blues scene, which included Buddy Guy and Magic Sam. His expressive technique and lyrical string-bending became hallmarks of the style. Rush influenced an astonishing number of guitarists: Jimmy Page, Peter Green, Michael Bloomfield, Eric Clapton, and Stevie Ray Vaughan. Check out Chapter 12 for more info on Rush.

Eric Clapton (b. 1945)

Eric Clapton is perhaps the most successful and influential blues player in history. He was a student of traditional American blues in his native England and distinguished himself on the local music scene with his deep knowledge and assimilation of the blues. He's been a part of several bands over the years: The Yardbirds, John Mayall & the Bluesbreakers, and Cream.

Clapton continued his success in many different formats, including a friendship with George Harrison and the Beatles (that's Clapton on lead guitar in Harrison's "While My Guitar Gently Weeps"), the band Derek and the Dominos (with Duane Allman), and an identity as a solo artist. Through controversy and comeback, in acoustic and electric settings, and as a guitarist and singer/songwriter, Clapton always eventually lands on top, and continues to play as brilliantly as ever. Flip to Chapter 13 for more details on Clapton.

Stevie Ray Vaughan (1954–90)

Stevie Ray Vaughan could play it all. He had firm roots in his heavy influence from Albert King, Buddy Guy, and Lonnie Mack, but he delivered with the virtuosity and abandon of Jimi Hendrix (who was also a big influence) and the soul of Eric Clapton (covered in the previous section). Vaughan developed a unique playing style — an integration of lead and rhythm that was similar to the way Hendrix often played. Chapter 13 has more info on Vaughan.

Chapter 18

Ten Great Blues Guitars

In This Chapter

▶ Discovering great acoustic and electric guitars

▶ Studying the best guitars through history

*B*efore the blues and folk revival in the 1960s and the blues renaissance of
the '80s, led by Stevie Ray Vaughan and Robert Cray, guitar makers didn't
focus on creating blues guitars specifically. They were more concerned with
other popular genres, such as country, jazz, and rock 'n' roll. Only recently, in
artist models — such as Fender's Stevie Ray Vaughan and Gibson's B.B. King —
have guitars been created specifically to pay homage to the blues. In this chapter, I give you ten guitars that blues performers have adopted as their own and
that have played an important role in helping define the sound of blues guitar.

Gibson L-1 Flattop

Gibson's "L" line of small-bodied flattop acoustic guitars — the ones with
round soundholes in the middle as opposed to the jazzier F-hole models —
later fell out of favor for the larger-bodied Jumbo series, which was introduced
in 1935. But the L series was the guitar of choice for solo blues players because
of its manageability and incredible tonal balance. In one of the only known
photos of Robert Johnson, he's pictured holding a Gibson L-1. Robert Jr.
Lockwood (Robert Johnson's "stepson"), played the L-0, which was the L-1's
predecessor.

Gibson ES-175 Archtop

An archtop is so named because the top is curved, or arched, instead of
being table-top flat as it is on a flattop. (You can see the arch better if you
hold the guitar sideways, parallel to the floor, and raise it to eye level.) This
guitar also has F-holes (like a violin) instead of the round soundhole of a
flattop. Archtops were first acoustic and then became electrified and are

often referred to as "hollowbody," to distinguish them from models that had a similar silhouette but were "semi-solidbody" or "semi-hollowbody." Gibson made many archtop models. Kenny Burrell — whose blues-inflected jazz was inspired by Lightnin' Hopkins, T-Bone Walker, and Muddy Waters — played the ES-175.

National Steel

In the mid-1920s, John Dopyera (who later created the Dobro company) and George Beauchamp formed the National Stringed Instrument Co. to produce their patented invention: an all-metal-body guitar with a mechanical-amplification system of aluminum cones or resonators. This design met the need for louder guitars, but these men didn't anticipate that the guitar's tonal qualities would be what attracted early acoustic blues artists to their instrument. Though the company's innovation was eclipsed by the development of the electric guitar in the late '30s, the National Steel is still a popular acoustic blues guitar today. Its unique, metallic sound continues to live on through the efforts of Bob Brozman and other modern blues performers.

Gibson J-200

Gibson released the Jumbo, or J, series of guitars in 1935 to respond to the "dreadnought" model from rival C.F. Martin & Co. But Martins never caught on with the blues players the way the big Gibsons did. The J-200 represents the "Cadillac" of the J line, but it has some illustrious brethren. Reverend Robert Wilkins, the composer of "Prodigal Son" that the Rolling Stones famously covered, played a J-45, perhaps Gibson's most popular Jumbo. Skip James played an SJ-185 (introduced in 1951, as a smaller and more affordable choice to the J-200) in the mid-'60s. A big guitar, the J-200 has been the favorite choice for blues players who could afford it and were looking for an acoustic with a little meat on its bones. Reverend Gary Davis, Mance Lipscomb, and Big Bill Broonzy are well-known J-200 players, and Muddy Waters played a square-shouldered Southern Jumbo.

Fender Telecaster

The electric solidbody Telecaster was introduced in 1950 (under the name "Broadcaster," which was soon dropped for legal reasons), and was greeted with skepticism by musicians and industry insiders alike, who thought it was ugly. They called this ugly model a *canoe paddle* and *the plank guitar*.

As the first commercially available electric solidbody, it is now the longest surviving electric guitar of its kind, pre-dating the Les Paul by two years and the Stratocaster by four years. It features two widely spaced single-coil pick-ups versus the Strat's three. The Telecaster is known for being "twangier" than the Strat, and many blues players use this edge to good advantage, notably Muddy Waters, Albert Collins, and blues-rock idol Keith Richards.

Gibson Les Paul

Right behind the Stratocaster and the Gibson ES-335, 345, and 355 semi-hollow guitars in popularity for electric blues players is the solidbody Gibson Les Paul. Many legendary blues-rock artists have played Les Pauls, including Keith Richards, Eric Clapton, Duane Allman, Led Zeppelin's Jimmy Page, and Aerosmith's Joe Perry. The more traditional players who at one time or another donned a Les Paul include Muddy Waters, Hubert Sumlin and Jody Williams from Howlin' Wolf's band, Freddie King, and Buddy Guy (who switched to the Strat after his Les Paul was stolen from a club). Guitar Slim is pictured in a famous publicity shot holding a gold-top Les Paul.

Fender Stratocaster

Deemed the most popular guitar in history, the Fender Stratocaster is revered by players of all genres, including electric blues — both traditional and modern. Buddy Guy plays one. Jimi Hendrix's famous white Strat (a right-handed version, but restrung, so it played normally) is the single guitar that's most associated with his style. Clapton had his famous "Blackie," made of various cannibalized parts, and Stevie Ray Vaughan played one with ungodly heavy strings (a .013 on the high E) — see Chapter 16 for more information on strings. Fender created the Stevie Ray Vaughan artist model based on Vaughan's favorite axe (guitar), which features a rosewood fingerboard, inverted left-handed vibrato system, sunburst finish, and etched "SRV" initials on the pickguard.

Gibson ES-335

The ES-335 was created in 1958 as an attempt to combine the resonant properties of a hollowbody with the sustain of a solidbody. The body was made thin so that it wouldn't feed back, and a stop tailpiece (where the bridge affixes to studs midway down the body, instead of attaching to a trapeze, which hangs off the edge) was anchored into a solid maple block that ran down the center of the body.

The ES-335 was, from the start, and still is, a hit with blues guitarists and launched the whole category of semi-hollowbodies, including the ES-355 (in the next section) and ES-345, as well as countless imitators from other manufacturers. B.B. King played an ES-335 before going to the ES-355, and Eric Clapton played an ES-335 for Cream's last tour in 1968.

Gibson ES-355

The ES-355 is a semi-hollowbody electric with F-holes in the top and a solid block running down the center of the body. The 355 had more ornate appointments and was wired in stereo like the ES-345, but had the same appeal. Chuck Berry, Freddie King, Otis Rush, and B.B. King all played a 355.

B.B. King played an ES-355 but wanted some personal touches added to his guitar, so Gibson and King joined forces in 1982 to build the artist model now known as the B.B. King Lucille. King's modifications included doing away with the F-holes to help eliminate feedback and adding a fine-tuning tailpiece.

Gibson SG

A solidbody with two humbucker pickups, the SG was designed in part to compete with the more trebly-sounding Fenders and address complaints that the Les Paul was too heavy and didn't have a double cutaway. The SG, with its design improvements, overthrew the king of Gibson's solidbody line in the '60s as Gibson ceased production until Eric Clapton and Mike Bloomfield discovered the rich tone and incredible sustain of the late-'50s sunburst models, and Gibson was forced to start building them again in 1968. However, the SG did become a player in electric blues guitar history. The 6/12 double-neck model was immortalized by Jimmy Page, and Earl Hooker before him, while Jimi Hendrix played a white three-pickup SG Custom. Eric Clapton played a psychedelically colored, custom-painted SG Standard in Cream. Duane Allman played slide on a '60s SG Standard when he was with Derek and the Dominos and on the band's megahit "Layla."

Chapter 19

Ten (Plus One) Must-Have Blues Guitar Albums

*T*o acquire the original versions of classic blues records requires thousands of dollars and to play them requires a little thing called the turntable. But thanks to modern technology, blues recordings get recycled and reissued more than reruns of *Seinfeld,* so you can pretty much find any recording on a CD if you look hard enough — including the earliest records from the 1920s. You can collect original records as collectors' items, if you like and if you have the money, but if you don't want to break the bank and you're interested in *hearing* important blues recordings, stick with me for the top ten recordings, which include a mix of artist-specific and genre recordings that can enrich your listening life with the sound of the blues.

Robert Johnson: The Complete Recordings

Columbia/Legacy, 1990. *Robert Johnson: The Complete Recordings* is *the* source for Robert Johnson's music. The sound is completely foreign and worlds away from the blues of, say, Eric Clapton or Robert Cray, but the blues doesn't get any more real than this. Robert Johnson *is* the blues of the Mississippi Delta in the 1920s and '30s, and all the blues that followed came from here. For more info on Johnson himself, check out Chapter 11.

Blues Masters: The Very Best of Lightnin' Hopkins

Rhino, 2000. Lightnin' Hopkins (1912–82) was one of the originators of Texas blues, which had a more swinging, jazzier feel than the harder-edged Chicago style. This compilation highlights the best of his work, recorded early in his career, and Rhino chose well in assembling 16 tracks that show Hopkins in his prime, from 1947 to 1961. Hopkins's long career spanned six decades, beginning in the '20s when he served as the legendary Blind Lemon Jefferson's guide and continuing until his death in 1982.

T-Bone Walker: Complete Capitol Black & White Recordings

Capitol, 1995. *Complete Capitol Black & White Recordings* is a three-CD boxed set that contains 75 tracks of vintage T-Bone Walker music, all recorded in the '40s. This set includes Walker's original version of "Call It Stormy Monday" (covered by the Allman Brothers on their most well-known album, *At Fillmore East*). For more info on Walker, flip back to Chapter 12.

T-Bone Walker: Complete Imperial Recordings

EMI America, 1991. Walker is so important that he merits two selections. His Imperial recordings from the '50s are perhaps even more spectacular as the material, arrangements, and backing bands perfectly complement his mature style. "Cold, Cold Feeling," "I Got the Blues," and the sensational swinging shuffles in "Strollin' with Bone," "The Hustle Is On," "You Don't Love Me," and "Party Girl" are definitive postwar electric blues.

The Best of Muddy Waters

Chess, 1975. Muddy Waters defined the Chicago sound by bringing his Delta-influenced music north from the Delta in the early 1940s. This compilation is

12 of Waters's best songs, including his R&B chart successes "I'm Your Hoochie Coochie Man," "Long Distance Call," "I'm Ready," "Honey Bee," "I Just Wanna Make Love to You," "Still a Fool," and "Rollin' Stone" — the song which inspired publisher Jann Wenner to name his music magazine. Chapter 12 contains more info on Waters.

B.B. King: Live at the Regal

MCA, 1965. *Live at the Regal* is one of the best live blues albums of all time, and it showcases B.B. King's spectacular guitar work, piercing voice, and talent for working a live theater audience. The gems found in this treasure chest include "Every Day I Have the Blues," "Sweet Little Angel," "How Blue Can You Get," "Worry, Worry," and "You Upset Me Baby." If you ever forget that the blues is best served up as a live listening experience, go back to this album and to King as he tears the joint up. Check out Chapter 12 for more information on King.

The Very Best of Buddy Guy

Rhino, 1992. Buddy Guy's long career is captured well on this Rhino compilation, which includes songs from Guy's multi-label associations — Chess and Vanguard in the '60s and Atlantic in the '70s. The music shows off the varied selection of the different styles that Buddy trafficked in (funk, R&B), and this disc highlights Guy's incredible range in the early and middle part of his career. Along with Otis Rush and Muddy Waters, Buddy Guy was one of the architects of the Chicago sound (and, along with Rush and Magic Sam, known as a leader of the "West Side" school of blues).

Robert Cray: Bad Influence

Mercury, 1986. Robert Cray's versatility really shines on this album, especially in the canny way he pays homage to his influences Johnnie "Guitar" Watson, Albert Collins, and Buddy Guy. Cray proved here, and in subsequent releases, to be a triple threat in songwriting, singing, and playing, and he's in a class by himself for finding the right formula to bring the traditional blues into the modern era.

Masters of the Delta Blues: Friends of Charlie Patton

Yazoo, 1991. This album is named for Charlie Patton — one of the earliest and most influential acoustic country blues figures, known as "The Father of Delta Blues." Featured performers on this album include Bukka White, House, and Tommy Johnson. Especially interesting are the six cuts of House from 1930. It was these very recordings that Alan Lomax heard, and that inspired the archivist to seek out and record the powerhouse for the Library of Congress in the early 1940s.

Mean Old World: The Blues from 1940 to 1994

Smithsonian, 1996. This four-CD, 80-song boxed set covers more than 50 years of the blues and is a great introduction to the major blues guitar figures, especially in the period between 1940 and 1970. *Mean Old World* is a good single-source reference for the many styles and personalities that make up guitar-based blues.

Chicago: The Blues Today

Vanguard, 1999. This anthology has been remastered with improved fidelity. A great encapsulation of the vibrant mid-'60s blues scene as it was in Chicago, this set is noteworthy because it isn't a mere compilation of unrelated tracks but a series of closely spaced sessions produced by blues scholar and producer Samuel Charters.

Part VII
Appendixes

The 5th Wave   By Rich Tennant

"You told me to write the B flat section a whole step lower than the C section you're writing."

In this part . . .

The Appendixes provide extra information to help you master the art of playing blues guitar. You don't need to read music to play the guitar, but if you can already read music — even just a little bit — you can use Appendix A to answer most of your questions about what all those fancy dots and squiggles mean in the figures of this book. Appendix A also includes a diagram of all the available notes on the guitar, presented one string at a time. Appendix B lists every track on the CD identified by the figure number and with a description. And if you've never used a CD-ROM before, Appendix B also walks you through the process, so you can enjoy the multimedia benefits of this CD-ROM. You can also use the CD in a regular old CD player just for the music portions.

Appendix A

How to Read Music

*R*eading music can seem intimidating at first, but it's not difficult at all. Even little children can do it. This appendix explains the concepts of reading music in the context of a familiar song (and if this isn't familiar to you, ask someone older than you are!). After reading this, you can practice your music reading by working on the songs throughout this book using the standard notation instead of the tab. (If you have trouble getting the durations, you can check them against the CD-ROM. And if you have trouble with the pitches, you can refer to the tab.)

The important thing to understand about written music is that it tells you three kinds of information all at the same time: *pitch* (the note's name), *duration* (how long to hold the note), and *expression and articulation* (how you play the note). If you think about how it all fits together, you recognize that our written music system is really pretty ingenious — three kinds of information all at the same time and in such a way that any musician can look at it and play just what the composer intended! Take a closer look at these three kinds of information that written music conveys simultaneously:

- ✔ **Pitch:** This element tells you which notes (or pitches) to play (A, B, C, E♭, and so on) by the location of *noteheads* (the oval-shaped symbols) on a five-line *staff*. The notes take their names from the first seven letters of the alphabet (A–G), with the pitches getting higher as the letters proceed from A. After G, the next higher note is A again. (If you ask someone to play an "H," you're sure to get some funny looks.)

- ✔ **Duration:** This element of music tells you how long to hold each note *relative to the pulse* or *beat*. You may, for example, hold a note for one beat or two beats or only half a beat. The symbols that music scores use for duration are whole notes (o), half notes (♩), quarter notes (♩), eighth notes (♪), 16th notes (♪), and so on.

- ✔ **Expression and articulation:** These elements tell you *how* to play the notes — loudly or softly, smoothly or detached, with great emotion or with no emotion (that one's rare, especially for the blues). These instructions can consist of either little marks written above or below the noteheads or little verbal messages written into the music. Often, the words are in Italian (*piano, mezzo-forte, staccato*) because when composers started adding expression and articulation to their scores, the Italians had the most influence in the music scene. Besides, Italian sounds so much more romantic than English or German.

The Elements of Music Notation

Figure A-1 shows the music for the song "Shine On Harvest Moon" with the various notational elements numbered.

Review the notational elements in order, referring to the explanations that follow for each number. Numbers 1 to 6 explain the mechanics of reading pitches; 7 to 19 explain the mechanics of reading durations; and 20 to 26 explain expression and articulation markings.

Reading pitch

Table A-1 explains what the various symbols dealing with pitch mean in music notation. Refer to Figure A-1 and this table for the meanings of the symbols. Table A-1 refers to the symbols numbered from 1 to 6 in Figure A-1.

Table A-1		Pitch Symbols and Their Meanings
Number in Figure A-1	*What It's Called*	*What It Means*
1	Staff	Composers write music on a five-line system called a *staff*. In talking about the individual lines of the staff, refer to the bottom line as the *first line*. Between the five lines are four spaces. Refer to the bottom space as the *first space*. You can place *noteheads* on lines or in spaces. As the noteheads get higher on the staff, they get correspondingly higher in pitch. The distance from one line to the next higher space (or from one space to the next higher line) is one letter of the alphabet (for example, A to B).
2	Clef	The staff alone doesn't tell you the pitches (letter names) of the various lines and spaces. But a symbol called a *clef*, at the left edge of each staff, identifies a particular note on the staff. From that note, you can determine all the other notes by moving alphabetically up and down the staff (line to space to line, and so on). The clef that you use in guitar music is called the *treble clef* (or G clef — see **G note** following).
3	G note	The **clef** that you use in guitar music is the *treble clef* (sometimes called the *G clef*), which vaguely resembles an old-fashioned letter G. It curls around the second line of the **staff** and indicates that this line is G, and any note on that line is a G note. Some people memorize the letter names of all the lines (E, G, B, D, F, bottom to top) by the mnemonic "Every Good Boy Does Fine." For the spaces (F, A, C, E, bottom to top), they think of the word *face*.

(continued)

Table A-1 *(continued)*

Number in Figure A-1	What It's Called	What It Means
4	Ledger lines	If you want to write notes higher or lower than the **staff**, you can "extend" the staff, above or below, by adding very short additional staff lines called *ledger lines*. The notes (letter names) move up and down alphabetically on the ledger lines just as they do on the normal staff lines.
5	Accidentals (sharps, flats, and naturals)	The seven notes that correspond to the first seven letters of the alphabet (sometimes called *natural* notes) aren't the only notes in our musical system. Five other notes occur in between certain of the natural notes. Picture a piano keyboard. The white keys correspond to the seven natural notes, and the black keys are the five extra notes. Because these "black-key" notes don't have names of their own, musicians refer to them by their "white-key" names, along with special suffixes or symbols. To refer to the black key to the *right* of a white key (a half step higher), use the term *sharp*. The musical symbol for a sharp is ♯. So the black key to the right of C, for example, is C-sharp (or C♯). On the guitar, you play a C♯ one fret higher than you play a C. Conversely, to indicate the black key to the *left* of a white key (a half step lower), you use the term *flat*. The musical symbol for a flat is ♭. So the black key to the left of B, for example, is B-flat (or B♭). On the guitar, you play a B♭ one fret lower than B. If you sharp or flat a note, you can undo it (that is, restore it to its natural, "white-key" state) by canceling the sharp or flat with a symbol known as a *natural* sign (♮). The last note of the first staff of Figure A-1, A-natural, shows this kind of cancellation.
6	Key signature	Sometimes you play a particular pitch (or pitches) as a sharp or flat (see the preceding explanation of **accidentals**) consistently throughout a song. Rather than indicate a flat every time a B occurs, for example, you may see a single flat on the B line just after the **clef**. That indicates that you play *every* B in the song as B♭. Sharps or flats appearing that way are known as a *key signature*. A key signature tells you which notes to sharp or flat throughout a song. If you need to restore one of the affected notes to its natural state, a natural sign (♮) in front of the note indicates that you play the natural note (as in the seventh note of figure A-1, where the natural sign restores B-flat to B-natural).

Reading duration

A note's shape helps tell how long you need to hold it. Notes can have a hollow notehead (as in the case of the whole note and half note) or a solid notehead (quarter notes, eighth notes, and sixteenth notes), and the solid noteheads can even have vertical lines (called *stems*) with *flags* (curly lines) dangling off them. If you join together two or more notes, *beams* (horizontal lines between the stems) replace the flags. Table A-2 refers to the symbols numbered from 7 to 19 in Figure A-1.

Table A-2		Duration Symbols and Their Meanings
Number in Figure A-1	*What It's Called*	*What It Means*
7	Whole note	The longest note is the *whole note*, which has a hollow oval head with no stem.
8	Half note	The *half note* has a hollow oval head with a stem. It lasts half as long as the **whole note**.
9	Quarter note	The *quarter note* has a solid oval head with a stem. It lasts half as long as the **half note**.
10	Eighth note	The *eighth note* has a solid oval head with a stem and a flag or beam. It lasts half as long as a **quarter note**.
11	Sixteenth note	The *sixteenth note* has a solid oval head with a stem and either two flags or two beams. It lasts half as long as the **eighth note**.
12	Rest	Music consists not only of notes, but of silences, too. What makes music interesting is how the notes and silences interact. Silences in music are indicated by *rests*. The rest in Figure A-1 is a quarter rest, equal in duration to a **quarter note**. Other rests, also equal in duration to their corresponding notes, are the *whole rest* (¯), *half rest* (¯), *eighth rest* (⁊) and *sixteenth rest* (⁊).
13	Tempo heading	The *tempo heading* tells you how fast or slow the song's beat, or pulse, is. As you listen to music, you (usually) hear an immediately recognizable beat. The beat is what you tap your foot or snap your fingers to.

(continued)

Table A-2 *(continued)*

Number in Figure A-1	What It's Called	What It Means
14	Time signature	Most songs group their beats in twos, threes, or fours. A song's beats may, for example, sound out as "One-two-three-four, one-two-three-four, one-two-three-four" and not as "One-two-three-four-five-six-seven-eight-nine-ten-eleven-twelve." The time signature looks like a fraction (but actually is two numbers sitting one above the other, but with no dividing line), and it tells you two things: First, the top number tells you how many beats make up one grouping. In "Shine On Harvest Moon," for example, the top number, 4, tells you that each grouping contains four beats. Second, the bottom number tells you which type of note (quarter note, half note, and so on) gets one beat. In this case, the bottom number, 4, tells you that the quarter note gets one beat. Assigning the quarter note one beat is very common and so is having four beats per grouping. In fact, 4/4 time is sometimes called simply *common time,* and you sometimes indicate it by using the letter *C* instead of the numbers 4/4.
15	Bar line	A *bar line* is a vertical line drawn through the staff after each grouping that the **time signature** indicates. In "Shine On Harvest Moon," a bar line appears after each four beats.
16	Double bar line	A *double bar line* indicates the end of a song.
17	Measure (bar)	The space between two consecutive **bar lines** is known as a *measure,* or *bar.* Each measure consists of the number of beats that the **time signature** indicates (in the case of Figure A-1, four). Those four beats can comprise any combination of note values that add up to four beats. You may have four **quarter notes,** or two **half notes,** or one **whole note,** or one half note and one quarter and two **eighth notes** — or any other combination. You can even use **rests** (silences) as long as everything adds up to four. Check out each measure of "Shine On Harvest Moon" to see various combinations.

Number in Figure A-1	What It's Called	What It Means
18	Tie	A short curved line that connects two notes of the same pitch is known as a tie. A *tie* tells you to not strike the second of the two notes, but to leave the first note sustaining for the combined time value of both notes.
19	Augmentation dot (also called a dot)	A *dot* appearing after a note increases that note's time value by half. If a **half note** is equal to two beats, for example, a dotted half note is equal to three — two plus half of two, or two plus one, or three.

Expression, articulation, and miscellaneous terms and symbols

Expression and *articulation* deal with how you play the music. Table A-3, in conjunction with Figure A-1, tells you about the symbols and terms that deal with these issues. Table A-3 deals with the symbols numbered 20 to 26 in Figure A-1.

Table A-3	Expression, Articulation, and Miscellaneous Symbols	
Number in Figure A-1	**What It's Called**	**What It Means**
20	Dynamic marking	A *dynamic marking* tells you how loud or soft to play. These markings are usually abbreviations of Italian words. Some of the common markings, from soft to loud, are *pp* (*pianissimo*), very soft; *p* (*piano*), soft; *mp* (*mezzo-piano*), moderately soft; *mf* (*mezzo-forte*), moderately loud; *f* (*forte*), loud; and *ff* (*fortissimo*), very loud.

(continued)

Table A-3 *(continued)*

Number in Figure A-1	What It's Called	What It Means
21	Crescendo and Ritardando	The wedge-shaped symbol is known as a *crescendo* and indicates that the music gets gradually louder. If the wedge-shaped symbol goes from open to closed, it indicates a *decrescendo*, or a gradual softening. Often, instead of wedges (or, as some musicians call them, "hairpins"), the abbreviation *cresc.* or *decresc.* appears instead. Another term you can use to indicate a softening of volume is *diminuendo*, abbreviated *dim.* The abbreviation *rit.* (sometimes abbreviated *ritard.*) stands for *ritardando* and indicates a gradual slowing of the tempo. *Rallentando* (abbreviated *rall.*) means the same thing. A gradual increase in tempo you can indicate by using *accel.*, which stands for *accelerando*.
22	Slur	A *slur* is a curved line that connects two notes of different pitch. A slur tells you to connect the notes smoothly, with no break in the sound.
23	Staccato dot	*Staccato dots* above or below notes tell you to play the notes short and detached.
24	Accent	An *accent mark* above or below a note tells you to stress it, or play it louder than normal.
25	Repeat sign	The *repeat sign* tells you to repeat certain measures. The symbol ‖: brackets the repeated section at the beginning (in this case, measure 1), and :‖ brackets it at the end (refer to measure 8 of "Shine On Harvest Moon").
26	Ending brackets	Sometimes a repeated section starts the same both times but ends differently. These different endings you indicate by using numbered *ending brackets*. Play the measures under the first ending bracket the first time, but substitute the measures under the second ending bracket the second time. Taking "Shine On Harvest Moon" as an example, you first play measures 1–8; you then play measures 1–5 again, and then 9–11.

Appendix B

How to Use the CD

*E*very music example in *Blues Guitar For Dummies* is performed on the CD that comes with this book — over 120 examples! This makes *Blues Guitar For Dummies* a true multimedia experience. You have text explaining the techniques used, visual graphics of the music in two forms — guitar tablature and standard music notation — and audio performances of the music (playable on your CD or MP3 player), and the appropriate accompaniment settings.

One fun way to experience *Blues Guitar For Dummies* is to just scan the text by music examples, looking at the printed music in the book and listening to the corresponding performances on the CD. When you hear something you like, read the text that goes into detail about that particular piece of music. Or go to a particular chapter that interests you (say, Chapter 11 on acoustic blues), skip to the appropriate tracks on the CD, and see if you can hack it. A little above your head at this point? Better go back to Chapter 4 on barre chords!

Relating the Text to the CD

Whenever you see written music in the text and you want to hear what it sounds like on the CD, refer to the box in the upper-right-hand corner, which tells you the track number and start time (in minutes and seconds).

Use the *track skip* control on your CD or MP3 player's front panel or remote to go to the desired track number and then use the cue button of the *cue/review* function (also known as the "fast forward/rewind" control) to go to the specific time, indicated in minutes and seconds, within that track. When you get on or near the start time, release the cue button and the example plays.

If you want to play along with the CD, "cue up" to a spot a few seconds before the start time. Giving yourself a few seconds head start allows you to put down the remote and place your hands in a ready position on the guitar.

Count-offs

Many of the music examples are preceded by a *count-off,* which is a metronome clicking in rhythm before the music begins. This tells you what the tempo is, or the speed at which the music is played. It's like having your own conductor going, "A-one, and a-two . . ." so that you can hit the *downbeat* (first note of music) in time with the CD.

Stereo separation

I recorded some of the examples in what's known as a *stereo split.* In certain pieces, the backing, or accompanying, music appears on the left channel of your stereo, while the featured guitar appears on the right. If you leave your stereo's *balance control* in its normal position (straight up, or 12:00), you'll hear both the rhythm tracks and the featured guitar equally — one from each speaker. By selectively adjusting the balance control (turning the knob to the left or right) you can gradually or drastically reduce the volume of one or the other.

Why would you want to do this? If you have practiced the lead part to a certain example and feel you've got it down good enough to where you want to try it "along with the band," take the balance knob and turn it all the way to the left. Now only the sound from the left speaker comes out, which is the backing tracks. The count-off clicks are in *both* channels, so you'll always receive your cue to play in time with the music. You can reverse the process and listen to just the lead part, too, which means you play the chords against the recorded lead part. Good, well-rounded blues guitarists work on both their rhythm *and* their lead playing.

Always keep the CD with the book, rather than mixed in with your rack of CDs. The plastic envelope helps protect the CD's surface from scuffs and scratches, and whenever you want to refer to *Blues Guitar For Dummies* (the book), the CD will always be right where you expect it. Try to get in the habit of following along with the printed music whenever you listen to the CD, even if your sight-reading skills aren't quite up to snuff. You absorb more than you expect just by moving your eyes across the page in time to the music, associating sound and sight. So store the CD and book together as constant companions and use them together as well for a rich visual and aural experience.

System Requirements

Audio CD players

The CD included with this book will work just fine in any standard CD player. Just put it into your home stereo system, and check out "CD audio tracks," later in the chapter, for the track descriptions.

Computer CD-ROM drives

If you have a computer, you can pop the accompanying CD into your CD-ROM drive to access the MP3 files that I've included. Make sure that your computer meets the minimum system requirements shown here.

- ✔ A computer running Microsoft Windows or Mac OS
- ✔ Software capable of playing MP3s and CD Audio
- ✔ A CD-ROM drive
- ✔ A sound card for PCs (Mac OS computers have built-in sound support)

Using the CD with Microsoft Windows

To install the items from the CD to your hard drive, follow these steps:

1. **Insert the CD into your computer's CD-ROM drive.**

2. **The CD-ROM interface will appear.**

   The interface provides a simple point-and-click way to explore the contents of the CD.

If you don't have autorun enabled, or if the CD-ROM interface doesn't appear, follow these steps to access the CD:

1. **Click Start⇨Run.**

2. **In the dialog box that appears, type *d*:\setup.exe, where *d* is the letter of your CD-ROM drive.**

   This brings up the autorun window described in the preceding set of steps.

Using the CD with Mac OS

To install the items from the CD to your hard drive, follow these steps:

1. **Insert the CD into your computer's CD-ROM drive.**

   In a moment, two icons representing the CD you just inserted appear on your Mac desktop. Chances are good that both icons look like a CD-ROM. In addition, the Audio portion of the CD may automatically begin playing, depending on how you have your Mac set up.

2. **Double-click the CD icon labeled "Blues Guitar FD" to show the CD-ROM's extra content.**

   If you want to use your Mac's CD player to merely play the audio on the CD, you can either let it play automatically, or you can double-click on the icon labeled "Audio CD" to view the individual tracks. Double-click on a track to play it.

3. **Double-click the License Agreement icon, then double-click the Read Me First icon.**

   This is the license that you agree to by using the CD. You can close this window once you've looked over the agreement. The Read Me First text file contains information about the CD's programs and any last-minute instructions you may need in order to correctly install them.

4. **To install files from the CD onto your computer, just drag each file from the CD window and drop it on your hard drive icon.**

What You'll Find on the CD

CD audio tracks

Here is a list of the tracks on the CD along with the figure numbers that they correspond to in the book. Use this as a quick cross-reference to finding more about interesting-sounding tracks on the CD. The first number equates to the chapter that explains how to play the track. Then just flip through the captions and songs in order until you find the track you're interested in playing. To ease matters a bit, the exercises also contain the track numbers (and times, if appropriate) to help you find just the track you need.

Track	(Time)	Figure Number	Song Title/Description
1		n/a	Tuning Reference
2		4-3	Five common major barre chords in the blues
3		4-6	Progression using E-based forms
4		4-9	Progression using A-based forms
5	(0:00)	4-10	Progression using mixed qualities of A-based chords
	(0:21)	4-11	Progression using mixed E and A forms
6	(0:00)	5-1	Strumming E chord in quarter notes
	(0:12)	5-2	Playing eighth-note and quarter-note strums in downstrokes
	(0:25)	5-3	Strumming in quarter and eighth notes, using downstrokes and upstrokes
7		5-4	Bass-and-chord pick-strum pattern for country blues
8		5-5	Two-beat, or cut shuffle, feel alternates bass notes with the chords
9		5-6	Pick-strum pattern in a slow 12/8 feel
10	(0:00)	5-8	Straight-eighth progression in A that uses common syncopation figures
	(0:16)	5-9	Shuffle in A that uses common syncopation figures
	(0:32)	5-10	Strumming pattern that employs left-hand muting to simulate syncopation
11		5-11	Rhythm figure with palm mutes and accents
12		5-12	Fingerstyle blues with a quarter-note bass
13		5-13	Shuffle feel is the most common groove in the blues
14		5-14	Straight-four feel is used for a more-driving, rock-based sound
15		5-15	12/8 feel is used for slow-tempo blues
16		5-16	Two-beat feel is for jump-style blues
17		5-17	16 feel for funky-sounding blues grooves
18	(0:00)	6-2	12-bar blues in E
	(0:37)	6-3	Quick-four change in E blues

(continued)

Track	(Time)	Figure Number	Song Title/Description
19		6-4	V chord substituting for I in the last bar
20		6-5	Slow blues in 12/8 with added chords
21		6-6	8-bar blues that uses various chords
22		6-7	Straight-four progression with a variation
23		6-8	Jimmy Reed move in E
24		6-9	Jimmy Reed move in G
25		6-10	Jimmy Reed move in A.
26		6-11	A minor blues progression that uses minor-seventh chords
27	(0:00)	6-12	Simple two-bar intro
	(0:08)	6-13	Four-bar intro
	(0:22)	6-14	Two-bar turnaround
28	(0:00)	6-15	Two-bar turnaround with chord changes every two beats
	(0:10)	6-16	Two-bar turnaround with chromatic movement
29	(0:00)	6-17	Typical ending for a slow blues
	(0:13)	6-18	Two-bar turnaround in a shuffle feel
30		6-22	High moves in a 12-bar blues in E
31	(0:00)	7-1	Boogie bassline in quarter notes
	(0:16)	7-2	Boogie bassline with double-struck eighth notes
	(0:32)	7-3	Stop-time riff in eighth notes
32	(0:00)	7-4	Eighth-note riff in the style of Freddie King's "Hide Away."
	(0:21)	7-5	16th-note riff, using alternate picking
	(0:32)	7-6	Eighth-note riff featuring common syncopation figures
33	(0:00)	7-7	Expanded version of the classic 5-6 move in straight eighths
	(0:13)	7-8	Variation of the 5-6 move in swing eighths
	(0:28)	7-9	Expanded version of the classic 5-6 move
34		7-10	Progression fusing chords, single-notes, and double-stops

Track	(Time)	Figure Number	Song Title/Description
35		7-11	Quick-four move over open-position E and A chords
36	(0:00)	7-12	Triplet-based intro riff in E
	(0:11)	7-13	Double-stop intro riff in E
	(0:21)	7-14	Melodic intro riff based in all triplet eighth-notes
	(0:30)	7-15	Descending double-stop turnaround riff in A in the style of Robert Johnson
37	(0:00)	7-16	Turnaround riff in E featuring contrary motion
	(0:12)	7-17	Turnaround riff in C with gospel flavor
	(0:22)	7-18	Triplet-based ending riff
	(0:33)	7-19	A low-note ending riff in E, using double-stops in a three-note grouping
38		7-20	Country-blues ending, or tag
39		7-21	Rhythm groove over a 12-bar blues in E
40		8-1	Alternate picking on high-E string in straight eighth-notes
41		8-2	Alternate picking on the second string in swing eighths
42		8-3	Alternate picking on the third string with left-hand fretting
43		8-4	Alternate picking with fretted notes on all six strings
44		8-6	Ascending E minor pentatonic scale
45		8-7	12-bar blues with an E minor pentatonic lead over it
46		8-9	E blues scale soloing over 12-bar blues
47		8-10	Major third added to blues scale
48		8-11	Major sixth sweet note added to blues scale
49	(0:00)	9-3	Passage that uses the descending fifth-position A minor pentatonic scale
	(0:12)	9-4	Passage in fifth-position A blues
50	(0:00)	9-5	Five notes in the eighth position A minor pentatonic
	(0:12)	9-6	Lick in eighth position using the high blue note on the 11th fret

(continued)

Track	(Time)	Figure Number	Song Title/Description
51	(0:00)	9-7	Four notes in third-position A minor pentatonic
	(0:08)	9-8	Shifting from fifth to eighth position and from third to fifth position
52		9-9	Slide that facilitates a shift from fifth to eighth position
53		9-13	Passage with shifts that take you in and out of multiple positions
54		9-14	Sweet-note pattern with a familiar fingering pattern
55		10-1	Call-and-response exchange can benefit from a contrast in dynamics
56	(0:00)	10-2	Accented notes are struck harder than the surrounding notes
	(0:15)	10-3	Muted notes interrupted by occasional accented notes
57	(0:00)	10-4	Slides into and out of individual notes
	(0:13)	10-5	Passage with rhythmic slides between notes
58	(0:00)	10-6	Three types of hammer-ons
	(0:11)	10-7	A passage using various hammer-ons
59	(0:00)	10-8	Three types of pull-offs
	(0:14)	10-9	Pull-off licks with hammer-ons
60		10-10	Whole note with vibrato
61	(0:00)	10-11	Three types of bends on the third string
	(0:17)	10-12	Bending in rhythm
	(0:31)	10-13	A bend and release
62		10-14	Two pre-bend and release phrases
63		10-15	"Express Yourself Blues" uses a variety of expressive techniques
64		11-1	12-bar blues in the Delta blues style
65		11-2	12-bar blues in E with variations
66		11-3	Lick in the key of A in the style of Robert Johnson
67		11-4	Progression in the style of Robert Johnson
68		11-5	Bouncy Piedmont passage

Track	(Time)	Figure Number	Song Title/Description
69		11-6	Ragtime chord progression with bass runs
70		11-7	Country blues with a melody on top of an alternating bass
71		11-8	Single-note ragtime tag in C
72		11-9	Deluxe ragtime tag that uses chords, an arpeggio, and single notes
73		11-10	A rockabilly progression with a hard-driving alternating bass
74		11-11	Slide lick in standard tuning
75		11-12	Standard-tuning slide lick in the style of "Dust My Broom"
76		11-13	Slide lick in open E
77		11-14	Slide lick in open G
78		12-1	Slow blues in the style of T-Bone Walker
79		12-2	Passage in the style of Muddy Waters
80		12-3	Lick in the style of Elmore James's "Dust My Broom"
81		12-4	Single-note lick in the style of Otis Rush
82		12-5	Passage in the style of guitar great Buddy Guy
83		12-6	Classic Texas shuffle
84		12-7	String-bending passage in the style of Albert King
85		12-8	Blues lead style and hallmark vibrato of B.B. King
86		12-9	Lick in the infectious, melodic style of Freddie King
87		12-10	Robert Cray's tasteful and economical lead approach
88		12-11	Open-A slide solo in the style of Bonnie Raitt
89		13-1	Lead break in the Chuck Berry style
90		13-2	Fiery string bends and flawless technique are hallmarks of Eric Clapton's style
91		13-3	Hendrix's brand of "psychedelic blues"
92		13-4	Blues scale in overdrive in the style of Jimmy Page

(continued)

Track	(Time)	Figure Number	Song Title/Description
93		13-5	Slide riff in the style of the great Duane Allman
94		13-6	Line similar to one played in Johnny Winter's aggressive style
95		13-7	Smoldering riffs and edge-of-the-pick harmonics in a classic Gibbons tribute
96		13-8	Stevie Ray Vaughan-style chord vamp and leadDigital music

Digital music

All the audio tracks from the CD have also been stored on the CD-ROM in MP3 format. To use them, just fire up your favorite MP3-capable media player. You can even put them on a portable player! You'll find these bonus MP3s by browsing the CD-ROM on your computer.

Troubleshooting

If you have trouble with the CD ROM, please call the Wiley Product Technical Support phone number: 800-762-2974. Outside the United States, call 1-317-572-3994. You can also contact Wiley Product Technical Support at www.wiley.com/techsupport. Wiley Publishing provides technical support only for installation and other general quality control items.

Index

• C •

Wiley Publishing, Inc.
End-User License Agreement

READ THIS. You should carefully read these terms and conditions before opening the software packet(s) included with this book "Book". This is a license agreement "Agreement" between you and Wiley Publishing, Inc. "WPI". By opening the accompanying software packet(s), you acknowledge that you have read and accept the following terms and conditions. If you do not agree and do not want to be bound by such terms and conditions, promptly return the Book and the unopened software packet(s) to the place you obtained them for a full refund.

1. **License Grant.** WPI grants to you (either an individual or entity) a nonexclusive license to use one copy of the enclosed software program(s) (collectively, the "Software") solely for your own personal or business purposes on a single computer (whether a standard computer or a workstation component of a multi-user network). The Software is in use on a computer when it is loaded into temporary memory (RAM) or installed into permanent memory (hard disk, CD-ROM, or other storage device). WPI reserves all rights not expressly granted herein.

2. **Ownership.** WPI is the owner of all right, title, and interest, including copyright, in and to the compilation of the Software recorded on the physical packet included with this Book "Software Media". Copyright to the individual programs recorded on the Software Media is owned by the author or other authorized copyright owner of each program. Ownership of the Software and all proprietary rights relating thereto remain with WPI and its licensers.

3. **Restrictions on Use and Transfer.**

   (a) You may only (i) make one copy of the Software for backup or archival purposes, or (ii) transfer the Software to a single hard disk, provided that you keep the original for backup or archival purposes. You may not (i) rent or lease the Software, (ii) copy or reproduce the Software through a LAN or other network system or through any computer subscriber system or bulletin-board system, or (iii) modify, adapt, or create derivative works based on the Software.

   (b) You may not reverse engineer, decompile, or disassemble the Software. You may transfer the Software and user documentation on a permanent basis, provided that the transferee agrees to accept the terms and conditions of this Agreement and you retain no copies. If the Software is an update or has been updated, any transfer must include the most recent update and all prior versions.

4. **Restrictions on Use of Individual Programs.** You must follow the individual requirements and restrictions detailed for each individual program in the "About the CD" appendix of this Book or on the Software Media. These limitations are also contained in the individual license agreements recorded on the Software Media. These limitations may include a requirement that after using the program for a specified period of time, the user must pay a registration fee or discontinue use. By opening the Software packet(s), you agree to abide by the licenses and restrictions for these individual programs that are detailed in the "How to Use the CD" appendix and/or on the Software Media. None of the material on this Software Media or listed in this Book may ever be redistributed, in original or modified form, for commercial purposes.

5. **Limited Warranty.**

   (a) WPI warrants that the Software and Software Media are free from defects in materials and workmanship under normal use for a period of sixty (60) days from the date of purchase of this Book. If WPI receives notification within the warranty period of defects in materials or workmanship, WPI will replace the defective Software Media.

   (b) WPI AND THE AUTHOR(S) OF THE BOOK DISCLAIM ALL OTHER WARRANTIES, EXPRESS OR IMPLIED, INCLUDING WITHOUT LIMITATION IMPLIED WARRANTIES OF MERCHANTABILITY AND FITNESS FOR A PARTICULAR PURPOSE, WITH RESPECT TO THE SOFTWARE, THE PROGRAMS, THE SOURCE CODE CONTAINED THEREIN, AND/OR THE TECHNIQUES DESCRIBED IN THIS BOOK. WPI DOES NOT WARRANT THAT THE FUNCTIONS CONTAINED IN THE SOFTWARE WILL MEET YOUR REQUIREMENTS OR THAT THE OPERATION OF THE SOFTWARE WILL BE ERROR FREE.

   (c) This limited warranty gives you specific legal rights, and you may have other rights that vary from jurisdiction to jurisdiction.

6. **Remedies.**

   (a) WPI's entire liability and your exclusive remedy for defects in materials and workmanship shall be limited to replacement of the Software Media, which may be returned to WPI with a copy of your receipt at the following address: Software Media Fulfillment Department, Attn.: *Blues Guitar For Dummies*, Wiley Publishing, Inc., 10475 Crosspoint Blvd., Indianapolis, IN 46256, or call 1-800-762-2974. Please allow four to six weeks for delivery. This Limited Warranty is void if failure of the Software Media has resulted from accident, abuse, or misapplication. Any replacement Software Media will be warranted for the remainder of the original warranty period or thirty (30) days, whichever is longer.

   (b) In no event shall WPI or the author be liable for any damages whatsoever (including without limitation damages for loss of business profits, business interruption, loss of business information, or any other pecuniary loss) arising from the use of or inability to use the Book or the Software, even if WPI has been advised of the possibility of such damages.

   (c) Because some jurisdictions do not allow the exclusion or limitation of liability for consequential or incidental damages, the above limitation or exclusion may not apply to you.

7. **U.S. Government Restricted Rights.** Use, duplication, or disclosure of the Software for or on behalf of the United States of America, its agencies and/or instrumentalities "U.S. Government" is subject to restrictions as stated in paragraph (c)(1)(ii) of the Rights in Technical Data and Computer Software clause of DFARS 252.227-7013, or subparagraphs (c)(1) and (2) of the Commercial Computer Software - Restricted Rights clause at FAR 52.227-19, and in similar clauses in the NASA FAR supplement, as applicable.

8. **General.** This Agreement constitutes the entire understanding of the parties and revokes and supersedes all prior agreements, oral or written, between them and may not be modified or amended except in a writing signed by both parties hereto that specifically refers to this Agreement. This Agreement shall take precedence over any other documents that may be in conflict herewith. If any one or more provisions contained in this Agreement are held by any court or tribunal to be invalid, illegal, or otherwise unenforceable, each and every other provision shall remain in full force and effect.

BUSINESS, CAREERS & PERSONAL FINANCE

Grant Writing FOR DUMMIES

A Reference for the Rest of Us!

0-7645-5307-0

Home Buying FOR DUMMIES 2nd Edition

A Reference for the Rest of Us!

0-7645-5331-3 *†

Also available:

- Accounting For Dummies †
  0-7645-5314-3
- Business Plans Kit For Dummies †
  0-7645-5365-8
- Cover Letters For Dummies
  0-7645-5224-4
- Frugal Living For Dummies
  0-7645-5403-4
- Leadership For Dummies
  0-7645-5176-0
- Managing For Dummies
  0-7645-1771-6

- Marketing For Dummies
  0-7645-5600-2
- Personal Finance For Dummies *
  0-7645-2590-5
- Project Management For Dummies
  0-7645-5283-X
- Resumes For Dummies †
  0-7645-5471-9
- Selling For Dummies
  0-7645-5363-1
- Small Business Kit For Dummies *†
  0-7645-5093-4

HOME & BUSINESS COMPUTER BASICS

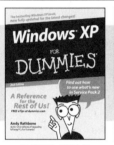

Windows XP FOR DUMMIES 2nd Edition

A Reference for the Rest of Us!

Andy Rathbone

0-7645-4074-2

Microsoft Office Excel 2003 ALL-IN-ONE DESK REFERENCE FOR DUMMIES

9 BOOKS IN 1

Greg Harvey

0-7645-3758-X

Also available:

- ACT! 6 For Dummies
  0-7645-2645-6
- iLife '04 All-in-One Desk Reference
  For Dummies
  0-7645-7347-0
- iPAQ For Dummies
  0-7645-6769-1
- Mac OS X Panther Timesaving
  Techniques For Dummies
  0-7645-5812-9
- Macs For Dummies
  0-7645-5656-8

- Microsoft Money 2004 For Dummies
  0-7645-4195-1
- Office 2003 All-in-One Desk Reference
  For Dummies
  0-7645-3883-7
- Outlook 2003 For Dummies
  0-7645-3759-8
- PCs For Dummies
  0-7645-4074-2
- TiVo For Dummies
  0-7645-6923-6
- Upgrading and Fixing PCs For Dummies
  0-7645-1665-5
- Windows XP Timesaving Techniques
  For Dummies
  0-7645-3748-2

FOOD, HOME, GARDEN, HOBBIES, MUSIC & PETS

Feng Shui FOR DUMMIES

A Reference for the Rest of Us!

0-7645-5295-3

Poker FOR DUMMIES

A Reference for the Rest of Us!

0-7645-5232-5

Also available:

- Bass Guitar For Dummies
  0-7645-2487-9
- Diabetes Cookbook For Dummies
  0-7645-5230-9
- Gardening For Dummies *
  0-7645-5130-2
- Guitar For Dummies
  0-7645-5106-X
- Holiday Decorating For Dummies
  0-7645-2570-0
- Home Improvement All-in-One
  For Dummies
  0-7645-5680-0

- Knitting For Dummies
  0-7645-5395-X
- Piano For Dummies
  0-7645-5105-1
- Puppies For Dummies
  0-7645-5255-4
- Scrapbooking For Dummies
  0-7645-7208-3
- Senior Dogs For Dummies
  0-7645-5818-8
- Singing For Dummies
  0-7645-2475-5
- 30-Minute Meals For Dummies
  0-7645-2589-1

INTERNET & DIGITAL MEDIA

Digital Photography FOR DUMMIES

Photoshop Elements and other tryouts on CD-ROM

A Reference for the Rest of Us!

Julie Adair King

0-7645-1664-7

Starting an eBay Business FOR DUMMIES 2nd Edition

Packed with tips on eBay retailing and marketing strategies!

A Reference for the Rest of Us!

Marsha Collier

0-7645-6924-4

Also available:

- 2005 Online Shopping Directory
  For Dummies
  0-7645-7495-7
- CD & DVD Recording For Dummies
  0-7645-5956-7
- eBay For Dummies
  0-7645-5654-1
- Fighting Spam For Dummies
  0-7645-5965-6
- Genealogy Online For Dummies
  0-7645-5964-8
- Google For Dummies
  0-7645-4420-9

- Home Recording For Musicians
  For Dummies
  0-7645-1634-5
- The Internet For Dummies
  0-7645-4173-0
- iPod & iTunes For Dummies
  0-7645-7772-7
- Preventing Identity Theft For Dummies
  0-7645-7336-5
- Pro Tools All-in-One Desk Reference
  For Dummies
  0-7645-5714-9
- Roxio Easy Media Creator For Dummies
  0-7645-7131-1

* Separate Canadian edition also available

† Separate U.K. edition also available

Available wherever books are sold. For more information or to order direct: U.S. customers visit www.dummies.com or call 1-877-762-2974.
U.K. customers visit www.wileyeurope.com or call 0800 243407. Canadian customers visit www.wiley.ca or call 1-800-567-4797.

WILEY

SPORTS, FITNESS, PARENTING, RELIGION & SPIRITUALITY

0-7645-5146-9

0-7645-5418-2

Also available:

- Adoption For Dummies
  0-7645-5488-3
- Basketball For Dummies
  0-7645-5248-1
- The Bible For Dummies
  0-7645-5296-1
- Buddhism For Dummies
  0-7645-5359-3
- Catholicism For Dummies
  0-7645-5391-7
- Hockey For Dummies
  0-7645-5228-7

- Judaism For Dummies
  0-7645-5299-6
- Martial Arts For Dummies
  0-7645-5358-5
- Pilates For Dummies
  0-7645-5397-6
- Religion For Dummies
  0-7645-5264-3
- Teaching Kids to Read For Dummies
  0-7645-4043-2
- Weight Training For Dummies
  0-7645-5168-X
- Yoga For Dummies
  0-7645-5117-5

TRAVEL

0-7645-5438-7

0-7645-5453-0

Also available:

- Alaska For Dummies
  0-7645-1761-9
- Arizona For Dummies
  0-7645-6938-4
- Cancún and the Yucatán For Dummies
  0-7645-2437-2
- Cruise Vacations For Dummies
  0-7645-6941-4
- Europe For Dummies
  0-7645-5456-5
- Ireland For Dummies
  0-7645-5455-7

- Las Vegas For Dummies
  0-7645-5448-4
- London For Dummies
  0-7645-4277-X
- New York City For Dummies
  0-7645-6945-7
- Paris For Dummies
  0-7645-5494-8
- RV Vacations For Dummies
  0-7645-5443-3
- Walt Disney World & Orlando For Dummies
  0-7645-6943-0

GRAPHICS, DESIGN & WEB DEVELOPMENT

0-7645-4345-8

0-7645-5589-8

Also available:

- Adobe Acrobat 6 PDF For Dummies
  0-7645-3760-1
- Building a Web Site For Dummies
  0-7645-7144-3
- Dreamweaver MX 2004 For Dummies
  0-7645-4342-3
- FrontPage 2003 For Dummies
  0-7645-3882-9
- HTML 4 For Dummies
  0-7645-1995-6
- Illustrator CS For Dummies
  0-7645-4084-X

- Macromedia Flash MX 2004 For Dummies
  0-7645-4358-X
- Photoshop 7 All-in-One Desk Reference For Dummies
  0-7645-1667-1
- Photoshop CS Timesaving Techniques For Dummies
  0-7645-6782-9
- PHP 5 For Dummies
  0-7645-4166-8
- PowerPoint 2003 For Dummies
  0-7645-3908-6
- QuarkXPress 6 For Dummies
  0-7645-2593-X

NETWORKING, SECURITY, PROGRAMMING & DATABASES

0-7645-6852-3

0-7645-5784-X

Also available:

- A+ Certification For Dummies
  0-7645-4187-0
- Access 2003 All-in-One Desk Reference For Dummies
  0-7645-3988-4
- Beginning Programming For Dummies
  0-7645-4997-9
- C For Dummies
  0-7645-7068-4
- Firewalls For Dummies
  0-7645-4048-3
- Home Networking For Dummies
  0-7645-42796

- Network Security For Dummies
  0-7645-1679-5
- Networking For Dummies
  0-7645-1677-9
- TCP/IP For Dummies
  0-7645-1760-0
- VBA For Dummies
  0-7645-3989-2
- Wireless All-in-One Desk Reference For Dummies
  0-7645-7496-5
- Wireless Home Networking For Dummies
  0-7645-3910-8